C000109081

PROFESSOR LONGHAIR
– A SCRAPBOOK –

"In Fess's music you could see the Mardi Gras Indians comin' down the Street". Allen Toussaint, a "Professor Longhair disciple". Photograph, taken in 1935. Courtesy, the Henrl Schindler Collection, Hogan Jazz Archive, Tulane University.

PROFESSOR LONGHAIR
– A SCRAPBOOK –

Per Oldaeus

With a contribution by Jonas Bernholm

PELICAN PUBLISHING
NEW ORLEANS 2020

For Tilda and Karina, with love.

Copyright © 2019
By Per Oldaeus
All rights reserved

First edition, 2014
First Pelican edition, 2019

----

*The word "Pelican" and the depiction of a pelican are
trademarks of Arcadia Publishing Company Inc. and are
registered in the U.S. Patent and Trademark Office.*

ISBN 9781455624591
Ebook ISBN 9781455624607

Front-cover photo by **Erik Lindahl**: Fess in Gothenburg, Sweden, April 1,
1979. Used by permission. With sincere thanks to Erik. Book design by Per
Oldaeus and Niels Pettersson Sandmark, with thanks to Karina Engman.

Printed in the United States of America
Published by Pelican Publishing
New Orleans, LA
www.pelicanpub.com

ACKNOWLEDGMENTS

This book could not have come into existence without the direct cooperation, friendship and helpfulness of many guys. If I have omitted any deserving individuals, I can only apologize!

Sweden: Nils-Gunnar Anderby, Hans Andréasson, Laila Baumgartner, Robert Carter, Christer "Cacka" Ekhé, Björn Englund, Lars Falk, Nina Falk Aronsen, Sven Gustafsson, Eva & Håkan Håkansson, Hans Ivarsson, Jens Lindgren, Eva Lagergren, Hans Lychou, Bo Lindström, Per "Stockholm Slim" Notini, Jan Oldaeus, Claes Ringqvist, Håkan Rosenqvist, Bo Sandell, Niels Pettersson Sandmark Bo Scherman, Hans Schweitz, Lars "Sumpen" Sundbom, Sven Stålberg, Tom Nässbjer, Rolf Wahl, Jan Ytterberg; and the guys at The Swedish Centre for Folk Music Research and Swedish Jazz History.

Finland: Pete Hoppula.

Germany: Gerhard Wieben, Klaus Kilian, Rudiger Marx, Wolfgang Lorenz, & Karl Gert zur Heide.

UK: Alan Balfour, Mick Burns, Dave Clarke, Mike Dine, Fred Eatherton, Robert Greenwood, Paul Harris, Raymond Lee, Gwyn Lewis, Trevor Richards, Tom Stagg, Clive Wilson, & Brian Wood.

Belgium: Jempi de Donder, Katy Joly, & Marcel Joly.

US: David Barard; John Broven; Henry "Hank" Drevich; Lars Edegran; George French; Jeff Hannusch; Kelly McGregor Fournier; Bruce Raeburn, Lynn Abbott, & Alaina W. Hébert, Hogan Jazz Archive, Amistad Research Center, Tulane University, New Orleans; Lon Price; Ned Torney (Keyboard Magazine), & Clive Wilson.

Australia: Peter Haby, & Tony Standish.

Switzerland: James Suber

Books, periodicals, magazines, pamphlets, and newspapers consulted:

Sweden: Olle Helander, Jazzens väg; Per Oldaeus, Professor Longhair: A Selected Discography (unpublished); Bunk Johnson Information; Hans Andréasson & Hans Schweitz, Sam Charters (2016); Estrad; Tradjazznytt; Jefferson; Orkester Journalen; Arbetet; Sydsvenska Dagbladet.

Finland: Blues News Magazine.

US: Jason Berry, John Foose & Tad Jones, Up From The Cradle Of Jazz; Tom Bethell, George Lewis: A Jazzman from New Orleans; John Broven, Rhythm and Blues in New Orleans (2nd edition); Mick Burns, The Great Olympia Band; Jan Clifford, Leslie Blackshear Smith, The New Orleans Jazz and Heritage Festival; The Incomplete, Year-By-Year, Selectively Quirky, Prime Facts Edition of the History New Orleans Jazz and Heritage Festival; Program Books; Galen Gart, "First Pressings: The History of R&B; Peter Guralnick,

A Listener's Guide To The Blues; Jeff Hannusch, I Hear You Knockin': The Sound of New Orleans R&B, & The Soul of New Orleans: a legacy of the rhythm and blues; Al Kennedy, Chord Changes on the Chalkboard; Sam Leandro's New Orleans & Louisiana Calendar; Earl Palmer & Tony Sherman, Backbeat: Earl Palmer's Story; Herlin Riley, John Vidacovich & Dan Thress, New Orleans Jazz and Second Line Drumming; Mac Rebennack, & Jack Rummel, Under The Hoodoo Moon: The Life of Dr. John the Night Tripper; Michael Smith & Allison Miner, Jazz Fest Memories; Pete Welding, Toby Byron, Robert Palmer (Professor Longhair chapter), Bluesland: Portraits of Twelve Major American Blues Masters; John Wirt, Huey "Piano" Smith and the Rocking Pneumonia Blues; The American 45 and 78 RPM Record Dating Guide 1940–1959"; Wavelength; Offbeat; The Jazz Archivist: The Newsletter for The Hogan Jazz Archive; Modern Drummer; Living Blues; Blues Revue; Whiskey, Women and...; Goldmine; Downbeat; Rolling Stone; Figaro; Blue Flame; The New Yorker; Spin; FI - The Magazine of Music and Sound; Talking Blues; Blues Access; The Advocate; Louisiana Weekly; The New Orleans Times-Picayune.

UK: John Broven, Walking to New Orleans; Mike Leadbitter & Neil Slaven, Blues Records 1943 to 1970, Volume One and Volume Two; Tom Stagg & Charlie Crump, "New Orleans, The Revival": A Tape and Discography of Negro Jazz Recorded in New Orleans or by New Orleans Bands 1937-1972, Bashall Eaves Publication, UK, 1973; Blues Unlimited; Storyville; Shout; Mojo; Juke Blues; Footnote magazine; Blues & Rhythm; Pickin' The Blues; Melody Maker; Soul Music Monthly; Jazz News; New Orleans Music magazine; John Crosby, Professor Longhair: a bio & discography, Tony Russell, The Blues Collection No. 64; Ray Topping, New Orleans Rhythm & Blues Record Label Listings.

The Netherlands: Eddy Determeyer, Big Easy Big Bands: Dawn and Rise of the Jazz Orchestra.

Germany: Blues Forum. France: Soul Bag. Australia: Crazy Music.

ROY BYRD

PROFESSOR LONGHAIR &
THE ORIGINAL 4 HAIRS COMBO

1522 S. RAMPART
N.O., LA.

BOOKINGS:
947-3215

CONTENTS

"In New Orleans, everything – food, music, religion, even the way people talk and act – has deep, deep roots; and, like the tangled veins of cypress roots that meander this way and that in the swamp, everything in New Orleans is interrelated, wrapped around itself in ways that aren't always obvious". Malcolm "Mac" Rebennack

1. FESSOLOGY – Part One

Henry Roland "Fess" Byrd, was the son of Ella Mae Rhodes, "a housekeeper", and James Lucius Byrd, "a clothes cleaner and presser". Fess was born in the Washington Parish of Bogalusa, La., December 19, 1918. His grandfather was Americus Byrd. In the *Living Blues* interview (No. 26, March-April, 1976.), Fess declared that his father was a musician. His mother was born in Brookhaven, Mississippi. James and Ella Mae met in McComb, Mississippi. They split when Fess was around two months old. He once stated that his mother: "played a lot of ragtime music".

Fess 1949. Courtesy: Rick Coleman.

William T. "Champion Jack" Dupree (1909?-1992), piano and vocal:
Excerpt from an interview, 1991.

Allison Miner: You had a very active life here in New Orleans before you left, and studied under such people as […] a gentleman named Willie Hall, "Drive 'Em Down".

Dupree: "Well, he was one of the greatest barrel house piano players in New Orleans. And then, for me, I worked together with Professor Longhair, we worked together in Atlantic Boudoir [S. Rampart St.] and he learned a lot from me. I don't class myself as a piano player because I don't know one note from the other, but I know what I play." [1]

Isidore "Tuts" Washington (1907–1984), piano:
"I taught a lot of these fellows. When I was playing at the Kotton Club [sic. The Cotton Club, S. Rampart, between Calliope and Clio

Streets], Fess used to come in and watch me at the piano [in the mid-1930s]. He'd rub smut on his lip so it would look like a mustache and he could look older and fool the owners. I tried to show him some of these strides that I play, but he couldn't make it. He had to make a fist and roll his left hand to cover what I could cover." [2]

Fess and Tuts, September 1973, (Footnote magazine, UK). Photograph and courtesy: Gorm Valentin. Used by permission.

Robert Parker (born 1930), saxophone and vocal:

"Professor Longhair gave me my big break. He played at a little club across the river called the Pepper Pot [Gretna, La.]. That's where I met him at. I got together with him and I played with him about a year and a half. We knew of each other because I was at the Tijuana [Club Tijuana, 1207 Saratoga St., "Hungry" Williams was the drummer] and he played at the Caldonia Inn. I used to go by his gigs and talk with him [mid 1940s]. The next thing I knew I was across the river one Saturday night, just going around, and he needed a saxophone player. I just happened to have my horn in the trunk and I started working with him that night—just sitting in. He was playing 'Mardi Gras In New Orleans' then, but nobody knew about it.

Professor Longhair was very musically inclined and all he wanted to do was just create. I'd never met a fellow like him on piano—he'd kick that piano with his foot. Every piano that he play on [sic], you could tell it was him because you could see the knocked-off paint on the bottom of it. That's the way he would get his groove. His left hand would be doing one thing, his right hand would be doing something else. That's the way he would play. He had different kinds of rhythm patterns he would use—he had some great things. He didn't record all the things he had in his head. He just recorded the things that people told him to do.

We'd rehearse every Tuesday across the river at the Pepper Pot. Anyway, we got together at Cosimo's studio when it was down on [North] Rampart St., went in there about 12 o'clock one day. The record company was in town listening to Fess. He said, 'Well, we're going to do "Mardi Gras in New Orleans." 'I said, 'Whatcha' going to do—change the back-

ROBERT PARKER

Courtesy: Inside New Orleans, April 9, 1966.

ground'? And he said 'We 're going to keep the same background.' We just played what he wanted to play and it come out to be alright.

Of course, he recorded it over with another group, later on in the year [...] But we were the first ones that did it – me and a trumpet player named Al Miller, a drummer named Louis Joseph and Fess. There was a bass player but I can't recall his name right now.

There was one microphone. He had the microphone, we didn't have any. We just had to blow loud. Professor Longhair didn't need no microphone in the piano. His hands were just heavy like that—a stone piano player all the way. Fess and Fats Domino [1928-2017] were the only two piano players I knew back then in those days raising sand." [3]

Alice Walton Byrd (1921-1989):
"When I first met him was back in those jitterbug days. He was playin' the piano, wearin' the piano out. He had so many glasses lined up on the piano he couldn't hardly play it, from his friends settin'

him up with Dr. Nut and Muscat wine. You know how the ladies is about musicianers. They wild over them all. He was really kinda' shy 'bout bringin' me on gigs with him, 'cause he knew my motto: Long as you don't do me nothin', I ain't got nothin' to do you. But some of 'em is so brazen and all I wanted to do is be left alone. Do what you want - kiss him, hug him, choke him, do what you want. Mess with him, just leave me alone. 'Cause when the gig is over, I knew where he's goin'. He gonna bring me home. And maybe bring some of that money home with him too." [4]

Alice W. Byrd, at the Old Absinthe House, Bourbon St., circa 1986. Photograph and courtesy: Lynn Abbott. Alice and Fess met in 1958, and married in August 19, 1978. Used by permission.

Harold "Duke" Dejan (1909-2002), reeds & bandleader:
"I played two jobs with Professor Longhair's band. He used to play at the Gypsy Tea Room [No 2., later the Caldonia Club/Inn] on St. Philip and St. Claude. Mike Tessitore [1899-1972], the owner of the place, gave him that name. He had hair on his head so he used to call him "Longhair." He called

the drummer "Short Hair" [Clarence Fritz] and the bass player "No Hair", yeah. They were nicknames. Well, it was the place we used to come to after we came from the steamer [S.S.] Dixie. If we got in on Wednesday, we'd always have a job there when we came in, for dance. There was always a contest with another band they called the Alleycats and the place would be packed, lineup all the way to [North] Rampart and St. Philip, to get in to the place. I had a drummer by the name of Judge Riley playing with me, he's a good drummer. I had Wendell Eugene's brother, Homer, playing guitar. [Lester] "Blackie" Santiago was playing piano for a while and then I got Alton Purnell. We had a nice little outfit." [5]

Edward "Ed" Blackwell (1929–1992), drums:
"Now the rhythms they [the Mardi Gras Indian tribes] played with their tambourines, that was something else. Most of the Indians were congregated down below Canal [Street], and down in that section is where Professor Longhair lived. And they were very heavy on that rhythmic thing. In fact, we used to go down to their practices where they would have their rehearsals." [6]

Edgar "Dooky" Chase Jr. (1928-2016), trumpet, bandleader & restaurant proprietor:
"Dooky" Chase Jr. did Artists and Repertoire work for Mercury Records in 1949.

"Professor Longhair made his first recording [in 1949]. He was playing at the Caldonia Inn, on St. Philip and Liberty Streets. I set that up for him. My band [the Dooky Chase Orchestra] was happening at the time. I didn't have time for that kind of work. Just contacted Professor and put him in contact with whoever. I was doing my own little things at that time." [7]

Thomas "Tommy" Ridgley (1925-1999), vocal & piano:
Interviewed by Tad Jones.

"I can relate with Fess in 1950, 51, 52, when he had the Hungarian Trio […], when I was with Dave Bartholomew. We used to play at the San Jacinto on Dumaine Street. And that's where I really got to know Fess.

So, I say, we go way, way back there. We'd sit down talk about old times, you know. I'd like to listen Fess talk, he had a funny way, you know [chuckle]. And I'd like to look at him play piano […]

When Professor Longhair had that Hungarian Trio, Jessie Hill was playing drums, Fess was on piano, "Papoose" [Nelson] was on guitar, and I don't think I can remember a bass player. 'Cause it was the Hungarian Trio. And boy, they used to make good money, and everybody *would love* to listen to Fess. But he had this thing with a piano, and everybody, especially us in the music business, we want to get close to see him kick that piano. Fess was like I said my buddy, we made a lot of jobs together. And I remember one night we played at, Fess was on the show, we played at the San Jacinto […] We had a 49-cent dance, 49-cents to get in at the place […] And I remember another dance, Percy Mayfield [1920-1984, the Louisiana born singer & composer.], we played a show with Percy Mayfield there. This is how a met Percy Mayfield, and Fess was on the show too. I remember Percy Mayfield before he had a wreck, you know Percy Mayfield had a hole in his head [after a 1952 car accident]. I don't know exactly where from a wreck. The hole in his head, they never did close it up. He's dead now […] but boy, he could sing, he had his own style. That's when I really remember the Hungarian Trio […] And another thing I remember was how the people used to fight and empty the place up. Every time you played there [at the San Jacinto Club] they had a crowd there, you bet it was a hall-emptied-fight. I always stood close to the bandstand, and in all fights, the people never bothered me.

Jones: We talked about having an influence on Professor Longhairs' comeback and who was involved in his comeback.

Ridgley: OK, one morning, I can't remember what day it was. But anyway, Gary Edwards [producer, and owner of the *Sound of New Orleans* label, etc.] was at Allied, I forgot his partner's name, Gary had' a partner over there. But, on my way in town I stopped by Professor Longhair's house because I heard that he had been sick and you know he was my buddy, and sure enough. He tell me he just had a stroke and how bad things were going. We talked about an hour and I said 'I'll call him [Gary] and I'll see if I can do some things for you'. And I left and went to Allied [a music store]. And […] Gary and I got to talking. And he say, 'I sure want to see old Professor Longhair'. I said 'what a coincident I just left Fess', he said 'oh really, I'd like to see him.' And I said 'I can go get him'. So I got in my car, went back to Fess' house up on [1811 South] Rampart Street. I got Fess and brought Fess back to Gary. And Gary and Fess talked. Gary gave Fess a piano that day. Fess did some recordings for Gary too in his garage. See, Gary has tapes. And he said, he was always reluctant, he really didn't know what to do with them [...]

Jones: What year was this that you brought him to Gary Edwards?

Ridgley: [...] This has to be around '75, this was in the 70s. I can't pinpoint it.

Jones: I was thinking, maybe, if this is before Quint Davis it was probably around 1969/70.

Ridgley: This was before Quint Davis [...] Let me tell you a little a story to that. Gary and Fess stayed together about a year or so and then Quint Davis came in [around 1972]. Gary was really the one that brought back Fess into public in New Orleans, and then Davis came in. [...] And Mr. Winstein just picked up being his manager for *no fee, no nothing* all he did was just took it. [David Winstein (1909-1997), a former reed player. President of the Local 496, 1948-1994]. You'd be surprised of the money he got over the sea, you wouldn't believe it. All those trips Fess made to England, Germany [plus France and Scandinavia etc.].

Courtesy: Louisiana Weekly, early January 1959.

All those albums he made over there, you'd be surprised [roughly six LPs & CDs] [...] I know some more things I won't dare say [...]!

Jones: Yeah, for the record we can leave that.

Ridgley: [chuckle] When I was at the studio, Allen Toussaint came and say, Ridgley, play some Professor Longhair, I could never do… And he went into this 'Big Chief' thing. He's Professor Longhair ate up [laughter]." [8]

Charles Connor (born 1935), drums and vocal:
"My first professional job was at the Hi Hat with Fess [during the Mardi Gras] in 1950 [or 1951?]. When I was playing behind Fess, Fess used to smoke pot a lot. I'd look at Fess and he'd wink at me. And if he'd wink at you that'd mean that you're doing something he'd liked. He kept winking and I said, 'Well, this cat's winking and I know he's not gay'. Fess picked me up one Saturday evening. And he was talking to my mother. 'Okay, Mrs. Connor, I'm gonna take care of your boy and everything. I'm not gonna let him smoke no "mootees" (marijuana). I'll just let him drink one beer.' And my mother said, 'Okay Professor'– he used to like to be called 'Professor.' And we'd get in the car and Fess said, 'You be a good boy and I'll let you drink two'. You had to be a special kind of drummer to play behind Fess, because Fess was so tricky you'd lose the tempo. You had to do all those little fills and stuff." [9]

"He was only a piano player, but he had different style from anyone, and it was a known thing around New Orleans that if you could play with Fess you was considered as being a professional drummer. He had the rhumba and the conga and all that stuff, and a little bit of blues. He wasn't a dancer, not that I know – he would play his piano. A couple of friends of mine was playin' with Fess at this time, called Milton Batiste – he was the trumpet player — and another guy by the name of Edwin Meyer, they called him 'Guitar Red' [Edwin "Guitar Red" Maire, born 1928]. And then he had another friend of mine Nathaniel Perillat [Perrilliat] – he used to be with Fats Domino: He died on the road of an overdose with Fats, but at that time I didn't know him to take narcotics or nothin' like that. [...]

Well Professor, he'd just play around town, wouldn't move, he was makin' enough money round town, and the thing about it was he didn't want to travel on the road, but I wanted to go to other places. I quit high school at 17 to go traveling on the road, and that's how I got hooked up with Shirley & Lee. (Champion) Jack Dupree and also Smiley Lewis [sic]." [10]

"I was real excited. [Connor commented his first Fess gig]. My whole family came–my mother, sister and brother and also kids I went to school with we had a huge crowd people. There were one or two policemen for crowd control, but none of the security guards we have now. It felt real good to play with Longhair. It felt real. After you play

with someone like Fess, you're considered a recognized musician.
I was nervous playin' with […] Fess. I had heard that if Longhair didn't like how you played, especially the drummers, he would give you a dirty look–a cold look. You had to be fast and quick, had to stay behind the beat just a hair and keep up with his improvisations on the fly.

Publicity photo, for the movie, Don't Knock the Rock, 1956.
Charles Connor with Little Richard's Upsetters.

I can't remember the name of our first number, but I remember when it ended, I looked at Longhair and he stared me dead in the eyes. I almost dropped my drumsticks I was so nervous, but he didn't look angry or cold. He wasn't certain of me – he was sizin' me up. He turned around and started in on the second number and it was a fast thing. I knew I had been given a second chance and I made sure to not think, just play. That's when you do the best playin', when you shut your brain off and just feel. It's a sweet spot. Many times, when you are in that zone, you realize you are in it and you fall out of it. The key is to stay lucid.

The second number wrapped up and Longhair turned back to look at me. Wouldn't you know it, the man was smilin' this big shinin' smile, on account of his gold-capped front teeth. That's when I really stared to believe in myself. After the set was over, hey man, I mean, Fess gave me a big hug.

I saw my family out in the crowd, too. My mother was just beamin' with pride. My father was yellin', 'Play, Poppa' (He used to call me that when I'd play) He sounded so crazy to everyone in the audience, but whenever someone would look at him he'd say, 'That's my son up there! That's my boy!'

I had always had confidence—you have to if you're gonna make it music. But, seeing my daddy yellin' for me and Longhair gave me something else: a certainty and a sense of validation. This man had played with other great drummers who had started with him. Guys like Earl Palmer and Jessie Hill. It wasn't all in my head; I was actually a drummer – a left handed – drummer.

After that Frank Robinson started booking us on a lot of gigs with Longhair. We played many shows out town, like Sunrise, LA. We played in Baton Rouge, Morgan City – a lot of places. We even played some gigs in Mississippi, like Biloxi. It was nice to play outside of New Orleans. In some of those other states we were actually able to walk in through the front doors. In New Orleans, we always had to enter through the back doors and leave that way when we were done.

"Hungry" Williams (circa 1955), one of the greatest New Orleans drummers. He's funky and swinging drumming was captured on countless of recordings. Williams left New Orleans for New York around 1960. He died there after a long battle with Paget's disease (a type of bone cancer). Photograph by Alvin "Red" Tyler, via Tad Jones & the Wavelength mag.

I stopped going to school and devoted my whole life to music. I was in the 11th grade. Since I didn't go to school anymore, my father expected me to bring my money. There was a little comin' in from the Longhair gigs. But, since they were largely in and around Louisiana and mostly on weekends, I still had time to pick up a day job!" [11]

Charles "Hungry" Williams (1935-1986), drums & vocal:

"There was a place called the Pepper Pot in Gretna, and that's how I met Fess. I used to go up there to dance and things, and Fess was playing up there. I'd worry Fess to death to sit in with him. At the time, he had a guy named Milton Stevens on drums. He was one of the best brush men to ever come out of New Orleans. And right after that, after Milton left, I think he got Honeyboy (Charles Otis), plus he had Papoose (Walter Nelson Jr.). That's all – he only had three pieces. I finally convinced him to let me sit in. My timing and things was bad, but I did the best I could do." [12]

Huey "Piano" Smith (born 1934), piano, composer & bandleader:
"Let Fess have his glory. They say, 'Yeah, we heard you was the father of this music around here.' I say, 'What music?' What we're playing.' I say, 'Well, that would be impossible because when I was a kid I listen at Professor Longhair [...] I put a bass player in my band with my left hand. So I had to do that with an octave. And I amplified it. And it was no specific plan, not that that's the way I would normally play. In fact, it limited me because I didn't play too much with it. And Professor Longhair also was playing a bass line, all the time". [13]

Lloyd Price (born 1933), singer and songwriter:
"The club scene around New Orleans [circa 1950] as I know it, I was quite a young kid, really was not able to go in most of them but as a musician we had a little bit more privileges than most of the kids [...] When, it was a black dance it was a black dance. I can't really speak on whether or not it was black and white 'cause I never saw that. You know there's a lot of mulatto, a lot of Creole, a lot of different colors of people in New Orleans, by just going in for the sake of going in you saw a lot of different colors, but I can't say whether or not they were black, all black and all white because the law was that they would, should be all black. I would imagine during that time, during the time in the early Fifties when I played for whites, it was whites. And when I played for blacks it was for blacks. If I had to play for blacks and whites it would be the blacks would either be the spectators or the whites would be the spectators. Some would be upstairs, if it was black the white would be upstairs and if it was white, the black would be upstairs. There would be spectators, that was in the early Fifties. It never was no real mingling together [...] in New Orleans. Professor Longhair of course was really a favorite, for, in the French Quarters, now he played for a lot of whites in the French Quarters but it was for only whites. And of course, if

he came Up Town to the Dew Drop or the Syngen Center [sic], one of those places for blacks where he played. [Fess never played at the Dew Drop] And I would suspect there was some white in there but you couldn't really tell because of the, again, the Creole in the color line". [14]

Cosimo "Cos" Matassa (1926-2014), recording producer and studio owner:
"[Fess], is real gentle, so he would never demand anything. He almost had to understand that he was having a problem and do something about it. 'Cause he wouldn't say what bothers me and I like you to do something about it. He probably wouldn't say that.

That was also his problems through life, because he didn't get to record as much as he might have if he'd been more aggressive. He didn't get paid like he should have if he'd been more aggressive. He probably lost many, many opportunities because of that." [15]

"Without wanting to sound like I thought ill of him he had two problems. One was he really he didn't work real hard at it. The other was that he was unable to take care of business. 'Tipitina,' which incidentally I helped him put together in its final form for record and 'Mardi Gras In New Orleans,' if it hadn't been for me he never would have had writing contracts on them.

He was an absolutely, totally natural talent. I always thought of his playing as a series of single notes, almost like trumpet playing, you know, the sense of the part, that staccato succession. He was unique; there will never be another one like him." [16]

"There were a lot of fine uptown folks that always referred to my studio as the "nigger" studio, which it wasn't. I did a lot of white guys. But some people focused on that in their lives.
But I never let them bother me, and my relatives and friends never did, and all my black friends obviously didn't. In fact, in really early days, my studio was one of the few places that a black musician could meet his white girlfriend and not worry about the police coming in. But nobody said anything about that, it just happened." [17]

Matassa, and music writer Rick Coleman, in front of the entrance to Matassa's former recording studio at 525 Governor Nicholls St., October 2007. Photograph and courtesy: Lars Cederberg. Used by permission.

Jerry Wexler (1917–2008), record producer etc.:

"New Orleans produced a powerful school of R&B laureates. But if the Nobel committee ever decides to give a price in funk, as well it should, I pray they have the wisdom to first elect Professor Longhair, the illustrious Henry Roeland "Roy" Byrd. He belongs in that rare company with Louis Armstrong, Sidney Bechet and Jelly Roll Morton, other Crescent City innovators whose contributions to our musical culture are immeasurable. His immortality is ensured not only by the records he made but by the few men who mastered his style, the apostles who carried the pianistic gospel according to Fess to the world: James Booker, Fats Domino, Huey Smith, Allen Toussaint, Art Neville, and Mac Rebennack. Longhair is the Picasso of keyboard funk.

When Ahmet and I recorded him in New Orleans in 1953 – his second session for the ["Atlantic"] label – I was surprised that beyond his standard stock of ten or twelve tunes, he had no material."

Later Mac Rebennack would explain: 'During gigs he'd take a calyp-so, combine it with some cornball tune like 'A-Tisket A-Tasket,' add some boogie-woogie, mash it all together, and come out with some-thing weird but funky as the devil. That was Fess's way of writing.' Right then and there, Ahmet [Ertegun] and I pitched in by suggesting that he make some along the lines of "Tra La La" or Smiley Lewis's current hit, "Tee Nah Nah". The non-sense titles were supposed to refer to reefer; we thought that something along those lines would do for a Fess song. We went to work, searching for secret and allur-ing code words, pasting together a phonetic concoction that became "Tipitina," a group of yodeling honky-tonk sounds strung together: "Tipitina oo-la-malla-walla-dalla try-my-tra-la-la"–"try-my-tra-la-la" being an invitation to smoke? Perhaps. The music was eight-bar blues, the forms so favored in New Orleans, with roots going back to "Stagger-Lee." The song wasn't a hit but has lived on in the liturgy.

The other tunes from that session –"In the Night", "Ball the Wall", "Who's Been Fooling You"– were hatched in the same way: on-the-spot improvisations. "Ball the Wall, "for example, was how Fess inter-preted our suggestion to put something together 'off the wall.'"[...] [18]

"Longhair to me, is significant because he trained many piano play-ers. His most gifted students were Doctor John, Alan Toussaint [sic], Huey Smith, Fats Domino, and a pianist named James Booker, not that well-known, who is sometimes considered to be the best of Long-hair's pupils." [19]

Earl Palmer (1924–2008), drums & arrangements etc.:
"Professor Longhair? I never thought of him as anything special. Peo-ple got caught up in the excitement and never heard all the bad notes. A totally unschooled piano player and not a very intelligent person, didn't even know he was funny. He played at Caldonia's on Liberty [sic] and St. Philip, just a guy that played for nothing, for fun, wine." [20]

"My first meeting with Fess was at a place called the Caldonia Inn that was torn down and replaced by the Louis Armstrong Park. It was not your nicest place, but the Professor used to hang around there and just play the piano for the fun of it. When Fats Domino [and Dave Bartholomew's band] went on his first tour after having his first hit record, "Detroit City" and "Fat Man Blues" [sic] on the other side, there was this girl in New Orleans named Jewel King who had a bigger record out than Fats, called "Three Times Seven" [3 x 7 = 21].

She refused to go on the tour because her husband's band [Jack Scott] wasn't going. That was a mistake because you haven't heard from her since. In place of Jewel King on that tour was Professor Longhair. The tour was a flop, but anyhow, the Professor was a hit everywhere we went. He was a bigger hit than Fats.

The Professor had just had a record out which we did, 'Stagger Lee'. [21] We went to Kansas City, Las Vegas and Los Angeles, but that's all I remember because they were the highlights of the tour, since it did so badly." [22]

"[Fats Domino's] material was something that you heard once and you could sing it right away, not maybe remember the lyrics, but you hummed the melody with... just stuck right with you because it was so simple. You could relate to it immediately even non-musicians could relate right away because it was that simple and uncomplicated and it was also, his sound if you will... as we were talking about it, his sound ah that he did was very [...] reminiscent of what you later heard [...] Professor Longhair doing [...], and that all went way back to guys who... piano players [...] in the neighborhood bars like Bernell [Burnell] Santiago and [...] what's the old guy that was on this documentary with Alan [Allen Toussaint] and [Tuts] Toots Washington [...] was the guy that actually Professor Longhair used to listen to all the time and copy playing in the Caledonia and ah it was Toots Washington that really was the forerunner as far back as I can remember and Bernell [Burnell] Santiago [1915-1943] who played those very [...] basic New Orleans feel like [...] just plum caught a few notes on the piano and became [a] fantastic pianist from doing just that." [23]

Clarence "Frogman" Henry (born 1937), piano & vocal etc.:
"You may not have heard of Longhair but he sure can sing and has given me a lot of musical inspiration [...] Prof. Longhair? Yeah, me

and him are good friends from way back, He was born in Norlands (phonetic sp.) La. [New Orleans]. He must be about 50-52 years old nowadays [in 1976] I see him quite often, No he ain't bald, He's semi bald-and tall. We meet up regular in small clubs in N. O. There's the "Sands", yeah and the "Pepperpot". I was still at school when he was having hit discs. My record "Tore Up" that was a big hit six months back. Didn't make any charts but it sure made a noise. Longhair and Fats [Domino] been my greatest influences all along. His act? No, he don't move around just sits there and plays piano. He'd drop in when I was singing and I'd drop in when he was singing. Huey Smith, Irma Thomas, Lee Dorsey, yeah, they're all circulatin'. Songs? Oh well, he'd sing the real old stuff, "Baldhead" and "Mardi Gras In New Orleans". Yeah, does "Big Chief" too. I guess he was influenced by Fats Pichon [Walter "Fats" Pichon: 1905-1967], yeah, that's French. Lot of French people in Louisiana. What you'd call Creole musicians. Longhair married? Yeah, gotta wife and a lotta kids. Real nice friendly people […]."

"Professor Longhair: Well, he's playing what we call 'feeling' music. But he never did get off the ground—always was a local guy. Roy Byrd—that's right. He stopped playing for a while, but he's back now. He recorded some new stuff lately. "Big Chief" was one, along with Earl King. He's a good songwriter, and he had a lot of local hits, but nothing really national. " [24]

Alvin "Red" Tyler (1925–1998), saxophones:
"Now the thing about Professor Longhair is that his piano playing is unorthodox. You know, usually with a trained musician we have a certain pattern we are going to follow... He would throw them all out the window... The things he did were so unorthodox until when he'd do some of these things it would just amuse you. You understood what he was doing, but it was really unorthodox, and it was a gas." [25]

"What was it like working with Professor Longhair with his unorthodox playing and impeccable rhythm?

From being around New Orleans, it wasn't strange to us as it might be to other people. He used to play uprights in the clubs and we had a baby grand in the studio. He used to bang on the side of the upright with his foot to keep the beat. He couldn't do that in the studio, so we got a wooden Coca-Cola case and set it up so he could keep his rhythm. It was phenomenal the way he played, even by himself. It was sort of a Latin, Cuban flavor. "[...]

Alvin "Red" Tyler, circa 1984. Photo and courtesy Lynn Abbott. Used by permission.

Usually, when an artist would come in, it was up to us to come up with the arrangements on the spot. We'd just hum things to each other and keep it in our heads. We'd try things until we got something that worked.

How would you compare Tut's style with Professor Longhair's?

Two completely different styles. I don't think they were really comparable at all. A documentary was done in New Orleans on piano players that very seldom play together. I saw a scene when Allen Toussaint, Tuts [Washington], and Professor Longhair were trying to play together. It was really hard for them to get together.

How divesting was it to the New Orleans music scene to have Professor Longhair banned by the union from playing all those years? Were the other musicians pulling for him?

You have to realize that it was segregated in the clubs, so many whites didn't know about him. As he got older, then whites started picking up on what he was doing, so he started to make a little money before he died. There wasn't much money to be made in the clubs. Everybody loved to play with him because he was self-taught, and the things he did—he didn't know he wasn't supposed to do them. If you don't know you're not supposed to do something, you do it." [26] (New Orleans, June, 1996.)

Tad Jones: "Wasn't Charlie ["Hungry" Williams] *different from Earl?*

Tyler: Yeah, very much so. The thing is, Earl Palmer had an uncanny sense of time and keeping the tempo steady and playing what was needed to make the arrangement happen. Whereas "Hungry", Charles Williams, came along and he did things not knowing that a drummer wasn't supposed to do that. So, he did it anyhow and it put another kick in it. You know a trained drummer would say, well okay, I'm gonna' do this here. Charlie Williams didn't know that a drummer wouldn't ordinarily do something because it was very difficult to do, but he did it. Not knowing he wasn't supposed to be able to do that, and it worked.

Jones: So, you guys where probably doing double takes?

Tyler: Yeah, and you know it was humor in his playing. A lot of guys that have all techniques, and all knowledge, in the world, but, no, humor. Professor Longhair had humor in his playing.

Jones: Well, his on my list here. Do you remember that session you played? ["Atlantic" Records 1953].

Tyler: Oh, yeah [laughter]. The thing is, we'd seen Fess play like for instance with Dave [Bartholomew], we'd ran across him at intermissions at different places like the original Caldonia. He would play intermissions. I would play with [trumpeter] Frank Mitchell. And Johnny Fernandez Sr. [real name Albert Walters 1905-1980, piano & trumpet] had a band over at the original Caldonia. And when we'd take a break, Professor Longhair would bring his trio up. We often laughed at Professor Longhair playing upright pianos. He's way of keeping the tempo was the side of his foot, to kick the leg of the upright piano [...] And when he came to the [J&M] studio they didn't have that post on the grand except for the back so he didn't have anything to kick. The ideal was to come up with something for him to kick and they had the wooden Coca Cola cases. They propped one of those up and that's what he kicked at. We thought that was so funny.

Jones: You said he had a trio, do you know who was in his trio?

Tyler: No, I don't recall. It was a drum, a saxophone...

Jones: And you were in a band with Frank Mitchell in?

Tyler: Frank Mitchell was in the band. Frank had called me but it was Johnny Fernandez Sr.'s band [with him on piano]. I don't remember who else was in the band. But we would do the Caldonia, take a break and Fess would come in with his trio ["Caldonia", by Fleecie Moore, once Louis Jordan's wife, waxed in 1945].

Jones: Wasn't that Fess' name place, the Caldonia?

Tyler: Yeah, he came up in that area that's where he played. The original Caledonia was something else, it was dimly lit, and all kind of characters. And you had to know you way around to be accepted in there.

Back when I first started playing [circa 1946, when he begun at the Grunewald School of Music] everybody wasn't hip so you considered who was hip, the waitresses, the pimps, whoever was hanging out late at night were the in crowd. And they got to know each other. The everyday person would come in, go out for certain entertainment at night, and then go home, and the rest of us, musicians and so forth, would hang out. So, that was the in crown.

Jones: Was Fess with the in crowd?

Tyler: Oh, yeah, he was part of all of that. And each bar and club had

27

its followers and their regulars [the Dew Drop and Club Tijuana were mentioned]. But the Caldonia had another clientele, raunchy.

Jones: So, when you were in the studio, recording with him, was he good at directing musicians? [...]

Tyler: We would usually adept to whatever he wanted. Sometimes he would say: 'I want the horns do something, make a spew'. I said what's a spew? 'You know, spew' [tries to mimic Fess' 'spew', laughter]." [27]

Milton "Half A Head" Batiste (1934-2001), trumpet & vocal:
"So people begun to hire us [Milton Batiste and the House Rockers, his first band, around 1952] and, in the meantime, my aunt was very good friends with Mr. William Houston, who was the president of the American Federations of Musicians, the black local. At that time, it cost you $8 to join. The secretary, the man who collected the money, was Mr. Sidney Cates Jnr., who played the guitar. So he sent me to work, in the Sixth Ward, the next area or section of the City community from where I lived. They had plenty of nightclubs there: The High Hat, The Caldonia and other dance halls. It was close to the red light district, where Louis [Armstrong] and all those famous names lived and played. It was adjacent to the red light district, Storyville, near what's known today as the French Quarter. That's where the colored people congregated and lived and socialized. This was the very epitome of where blues and jazz actually was born.

So, he sent me this guy who had a band. This wasn't a big band, but it had a drummer called "Short Hair" [Clarence Fritz] and a bass player called "No Hair" and a piano player called "Long Hair". And there I was, I was the youngster with a band. There wasn't any horns at this time except me, although on other jobs they had a saxophone player called 'Batman.' His name was Leroy Rankins and they gave him the job on account of he walked the bar and laid on the floor and honked this horn, and all that kind of stuff. This was my first professional job.

Now you must know that the light skinned people, who we called Creoles, were high society people, high dicty people who had the better jobs, as school teachers and mail carriers and other different jobs, that paid something like $14 to $15 a week ["dicty", is black American slang for someone who pretentiously imitates whites, sometimes utilized by Louis Armstrong.] Most people who made their living at $5, $6 or $7 a week—well, Professor Longhair was like an outcast musician—downgraded because he played this obnoxious blues music, you understand. He played in joints where there were the hookers and gamblers worked. This is the downgrade, this is like. 'Ooh I'm not gonna be caught in such a place or with that type of music'. But I was a very young boy and I didn't know or care about that. I just knew I was gonna play professionally. I didn't know then that one day I was going to play with a band that played in a barroom. It was unheard of to play in a barroom at that age. I was about 17 then. That would be about 1950 or '51 and I was still in the high school band. When I got the Longhair job I had to learn what they're playing. Those guys didn't play with any music. I remember Professor Longhair had a theme song: it was Pin up the baby's diaper. The name of the place was the High Hat Club [28] and the proprietor was named Freeman [Riles] and he called Longhair, 'Prof.' He was a little chunky fellow, real dark skin, big lips and he smoked a cigar. Very nice person, too. He'd say to Professor Longhair, 'See you got you a little young boy gonna' play with you, but listen, quit kicking my piano.' Fess did have a thing about playing, he'd take his right foot and instead of using the pedals as piano players did in those days, you could tell if Professor Longhair played a piano. It was all worn, where the foot would sorta go in the motion of a clock, like tick tock tick tock, from the heel he'd hit with the toe, boom, boom, boom, boom. That's how you started playing, the drummer would start playing and he would be kicking on the thing.

Well, he opened up with this boogie-woogie and started singing: 'Pin up the baby's diaper, pin up the baby's diaper, pin up the baby's diaper before the chocolate go to the floor.' That was my introduction to the blues. He used to say 'Come on man, play that thing, okay, it's your turn to blow now.' I was the only horn at the time on the gig. You played somewhere, you got paid 75 cents, it wasn't much, but it was pretty regular, on the weekends: Saturday, Sunday in the daytime, maybe Friday night, it all depended. Now here's what it was like: in that section of the City lived the people who worked on the riverfront, because it was close by. The riverfront workers were known as banana handlers, longshoremen, yeah, stevedores. Well, the stevedores were white, they were the people who told you what to do. But the longshoremen, the freight handlers, banana handlers, rubber truckers, they were colored. In the section where I played with Professor Longhair, lived the people who hustled them, the pimps, the whores, the good-time charlies, the gamblers. That's the area I came into as a young man, learning how to play the music, and I met many who later became famous musicians in that area. I was with Longhair, on and off, up to 1961.

Milton Batiste, with Dejan's Olympia Brass Band, New Orleans, September 3, 1965. A funeral parade for drummer "Big" George Williams. Batiste played his first parade with Williams' brass band. Photograph and courtesy: Rolf Wahl. Used by permission.

During Mardi Gras 1958, I remember my mother and father and my little brother coming to hear me play at the High Hat Club. *Sepia* was an early black magazine and there was a picture of me in that magazine [around 1952] playing at The High Hat Club. Longhair was a nice guy to work with, oh man, he was something boy, he was fun. You know the way people describe him, glorifying him now, he would have been so happy. His popularity and his making of money commenced after he died. People gouged him; he played for nothing. He recorded for nothing. Right now people are stealing his music, his popularity, the things that he paid for with his life, they're stealing him blind. There are some people in New Orleans right now who drew on the later years in his life, when he worked at The One Stop Record Shop as a porter and a cleanup man. He was used, I mean used and as of today they're still using him. Now I don't care if you print that. Yeah, it needs to be known. To this day, the family of Longhair are going to court. I believe his lawyers are trying to get royalties and stuff that's due to Professor Longhair. He's not only been cheated but his family's been cheated. His wife is dead, he's dead and his woman of those days who kept him at her house and fed him, she's gone. Her name was Willa Mae and he even did a song for her. It was called 'Willa Mae I want you for my own, Willa Mae'. He talked about her and sang about her ["Willie Mae", "Atlantic", Oct. 1949]. He's a glorified hero now of the "ism." He called it his "ism"; this Latinism and blackism put together. Now you know what the name of the group was? Professor Longhair and the Shuffling Hungarians. I was one of the original Hungarians.

Keeping a sequence with the Longhair gigs, we would play at different places like The Club Desire and The New Pelican and different places around the city, but Longhair didn't get to play what we call society gigs. Places such as Frank Painia's Dew Drop [Inn] were considered the high society places. Well naturally, I would go where all the other musicians were going. Blues musicians hang out at The Dew Drop in the late '50s and early '60s. Ray Charles came and Big Joe Turner, they lived there and Guitar Slim. Little Richard came into town to do recordings and different things, he used a band.

That was the time when Dave Bartholomew was recording for Imperial with people like Lee Allen, Earl Palmer and the guitar player Ernest McLean, and the alto player Meyer Kennedy and the Knox brothers [sic]—one played tenor and the other played baritone [Duncan and Edward Knott]. All these recorded with Dave Bartholomew, who were good musicians. But Professor Longhair's music was known as "dirty music." In other words, because they didn't read music, they played the joints where there was a lot of drinking and gambling and where hustling women worked. But it was fun, because I learned life. I learned how life really goes and the blues and standards. Because in bands in those days, we played the standards, Longhair played the blues, he didn't read music. No Longhair never read music. No, Longhair didn't know what a piece of music was. He made up all his stuff. It was in his head, it was a God given talent. He never played anything the same way twice. That's the beautiful part of his music, that's the beautiful part of music today and millions of bands and musicians now never play the same thing twice. So if you ever hear live music, you can appreciate the fact that you are hearing something played for the first time, even if it's three notes.

So I'm now playing with Longhair and I'm also trying to organize my own group. I'm also round at the Dew Drop getting gigs with other people and I'm ready to finish high school. Now, man, I wanna go on the road" [...] [29] (Batiste, interviews by Burns, Switzerland, UK, and New Orleans, between 1991 & 2000)

When interviewed by Tad Jones, February 5, 1997, Batiste stated:

"I joined the [Musicians] Union through my first professional band to play with, Professor Longhair in 1951, and we played at the Hi Hat [musical bar, grille and hotel]. It didn't cost but $8, but $8 was a lot of money then. And they had such shows as female impersonator shows, people dancing with snakes and fire. Mattie Campbell was the snake dancer. "Frim Fram" was the fire dancer, he put fire and shut it out his mouth. Lloyd Ignicious was dancing. It was a big show there. People would come from all of the city to this club. It was a black night club in the sixth ward ["North Villere at St. Ann", Treme]. That was some of my first jobs". During Batiste's years with Fess's Shuffling Hungarians, the members were, off and on: "Batman" Rankins, Nat Perrilliat, saxophones; Bill Sinigal, bass and tenor sax; Edwin 'Guitar Red' Maire, guitar; and Sam Noel, drums. Jessie Hill sang with the group sometimes. "Tippolite" sang with

Big Splash Opening!

CLUB HIGH HAT

TONIGHT

THURSDAY

Featuring

SPORTY JOHNSON

His Show and His Band

Wining   Souvenirs
Dining   Fun For All
Dancing   9 'Til Late

North Villere at St. Ann
(Formerly Old Gypsy Tea Room)

Courtesy: Louisiana Weekly, September 3, 1949.

Fess, he was a blues singer. His last name was Johnson because he was 'Smokey' Johnson's uncle.

Tad Jones: When you joined [Fess's] band was that like top gig at the time?

Batiste: OH YEAH, because Professor Longhair played the Pepper Pot, he played in the Graystone [Ballroom], we went out to Backbash? […], Brasserie?, we went to Baton Rouge. All those little places along the river had little nightclubs and Professor Longhair was popular about playing these places, mostly on weekends it was. His main spot was, like I said, the High Hat. He played the High Hat all the time, or down at Charlie Armsted's Club Desire [2604 Desire St.]. They put a pillow at bottom of the upright piano, they had a panel down there. And Professor Longhair, when he played he wiggled his right foot, he called that the "ism" [laughter].If you didn't have that "ism" you couldn't be in Professor Longhair's band [laughter].

Jones: Did you have the "ism"?

Batiste: I hope I did [laughter]? I learned a lot from Fess, man. I learned a lot of music that people are trying to play today. His feeling of music had African, Jamaican rhythms to it, and in those days Reggae wasn't even recognized in the culture of music, but it's *there*. The last place I played [with Fess] was the San Jacinto". [30]

"C. P." Love (Carleton Pierre Love, born 1945), vocal:
"I came in and sang some Bobby Mitchell tunes and Fess backed me [at Jessie's El Grande Lounge in Marrero, La., where Love shared the bill with Fess, in the early 1960s]. The band consisted of just Fess and a drummer. I think that his name was Lionel and he was from Algiers. All he had was a snare, bass drum and one cymbal. But when he played he sounded like two drummers. We were in the middle of the set when a guy came in the club with a shovel and hit two guys over the head with it. They were fighting over a woman and all hell broke loose. Me and Fess grabbed his [electric] piano and carried it outside. He was driving an old limousine with the seats pulled out of the back. We just slide the piano inside and sat in the front seat. Jessie [the owner] came outside after the fight was over and asked us to start

playing again. Fess said, 'No we're going home.' He was a quiet guy who didn't go for any humbug." [31]

Malcolm "Mac" Rebennack (born 1940), piano, guitar & vocal, songwriter:
"I studied with Fess' guitar player at the time, Papoose (Walter Nelson [Jr.]) who later on went with Fats Domino. My first real big break was to work on Fess' session of "Mardi Gras In New Orleans" ["Go to the Mardi Gras", "RON", 1959], which is the big standard record that's played everywhere in New Orleans for the Mardi Gras. After we did that record, that more or less tied the whole thing up, where from then on I was accepted by the clique." [32]

"Tell me about Professor Longhair: He was totally self-taught, wasn't he?

He started off as a dancer, which a lot of the great drummers start off as, but not many piano players. But Professor Longhair's piano playing was akin to drumming. It was melodic, too, but he had a real powerful vibe. When we first recorded him [in 1959], we used to have to put a muffled board between his foot and the piano because he worked a lot of gigs without a band and he'd use the piano as a bass drum.

Did he beat on the piano with his foot?

He was used to playin' uprights and usin' the sideboard as a bass drum. We had to protect the grand piano in the studio or he would break it.

Did you learn by watching him?

I played guitar for him. I was playing a gig at the Lincoln Beach, which was a black beach. I was playing in Roy Brown's band, and in front of Roy he says, 'Look I have a job, do you think any of you all could make it?' Well, we all just said 'Yeah, Fess,' and quit. That's how much we thought of him. It's a shame we didn't respect Roy Brown because we just up and left him without a band to make just one job. And the kick of it was that all we ever did with Fess was rehearse. He only had one job – and I don't mean one night a week – I mean one job. He'd been busted for reefer and couldn't work in the state.

I started to hang out with him. To be honest, I had eyes for his daughter. He had one beautiful daughter... I shouldn't be gettin' into this, but anyway, I would hang around his pad. My teacher, Papoose, was Longhair's guitar player and I was takin' his place and I would just hang with him. I was a real nuisance. I would sit behind him and he would tell me what to do on the guitar.

Was he doing a lot of strange fingerings?

Yes. He would do what he called overs-and-unders and he'd double note crossovers flyin' up and down the piano. He didn't even know the right keys. He'd call E flat, for instance, E minus, which sounds like E minor. You'd have to pay real close attention. Everything he had was his own thing. It was close to musician language but he always had his own words. Once he said, 'There's too much confusement,' meaning we were playing too many notes. Or he'd look at me and say, 'Ya got too much extortion on your amplifier'.

Is that where you got your love of wordplay?

Yeah. He became a father figure to me. My father had passed away. He was always giving me good advice about life. He used to say: 'Why do you want to shoot that dope? If you just smoke this weed you'll be better off than that.'

I would go to any extreme to help him, but he gave me way more than I ever did for him. If I knew he needed to get to a gig, I would drive him – even if it would make me late for my gig. But he would do stuff on the ride that would be ten times worth more than I was gonna' make on the gig. There's no way I can put price on what he taught me about life. He taught us how to – like he used to say – frolic. And when he said frolic he meant he wanted the band to lift you up a notch. If he said we still ain't frolickin', he'd want us to lift it few more notches. It was something about playing like that and loosenin' it up . . . but to keep the groove, and not move the tempo. When you're young you've got a tendency to play on top of the rhythm. You got a tendency to push the music. It makes it almost impossible for the drummer to keep the time; the drummer will creep up. But he was so locked into time, he knew when the drummer was creepin' up, and why – that it was the cats playin' on top of the groove. He forced us to be able to play relaxed, keep the groove, and not move the tempo. Not move the time at all, and yet liftin' it up all the time.

Getting intensity without speeding up?

It's hard to do it and stay relaxed, and it's hard to do it without playing on the top of the groove. He had the ability because his time was so perfect. When he got sick in the seventies, and he had been to hell and back physically, he bought a metronome. What he did was run it at the extremes.

I bet he hated it.

No! He used it, but he used it like it was never meant to be used. He used it like some old percussion guy. He never played with the tempo that the metronome was playing, like 1-2-3-4. He's usin' it like eighth notes against the quarter notes. He'd set it really fast, like dugga-dugga-dugga, and he'd play a groove with that. He started callin' the tempos by the names on the metronome. He'd say play presto, but what he meant was play the groove he played to presto, which might be real abstract to whatever presto was on the metronome, 'cause he played two or three rhythms inside of each other all the time.

One of the things that used to fascinate me was to watch Professor Longhair play for a dance. He could play some song like "Tipitina"and you'd see some people dancing slow to it, you'd see some people dancing to a straight meter to it, and you'd see some people dancing to a double time meter to it 'cause you could feel all three rhythms all the time. It made some real magic happen. But that was part of what the second line was, people danced to music different ways because they're used to that rhythm. See, because he was connected to all different kinds of rhythm-not just the Jamaican and calypso stuff, but also the African and Cuban stuff – he mixed all of it. All these guys from all these different places played in his band, and he changed them. He changed guys for life, because he had a feel for all of it and he just mixed it all up into a second line kind of thing." [33]

"He could sing a song like "Bald Head (She Ain't Got No Hair)," and there would be some chicks in the joint that would whip off their wigs just to let him know there was some baldheads in there.

Sylvester A. St. Cyr. 1960. The author's collection. Courtesy: Jet Magazine.

There was a time I used to see Fess wasn't playin' music. He had gotten busted by this narc called the Beatnik [Sylvester Armand St. Cyr, an undercover police agent,] on Mardi Gras day [in 1960] for sellin' reefer.

It wasn't like he was a dealer or somethin', back then it was just a local little thing for the friends. But because of this bust, he wasn't able to play. And he was workin', he'd hustle card games at night, then in the day he'd go and work at like the One-Stop record shop sweepin' the place up. Doin' real demeaning type stuff. But even through that time, he never let nothin' get next to him. He'd get on a break and go in the back room and sit down at the piano and start playin' for us. And we'd be like white on rice watching his shit.

He'd take these gigs in those days between New Orleans and somewhere in Mississippi, like Gulfport or Biloxi, and I mean he'd play sometime in maybe like a grocery store. He would take these gigs in places where they would literally move the groceries out of the way to make room for people to dance.

He wasn't the kind of guy to go promote his music or even to leave New Orleans, basically. To him back then, goin' on the road was to go to Mississippi. That was about as far as it went and as far he'd go. He would go in this little weather-whipped-ass car. I remember them coming back from a gig on the rims. He didn't have no spares and he drove all the way on the rims. And as he was gettin' back to New Orleans, he had to go over an overpass and the car just wouldn't make it. It was like in its death throes. And as the car went up the overpass and wasn't goin' any further, I remember them jumpin' out of the car and abandonin' it. 'Go on home from here, fellas.' And they just left the damn thing there. I thought, 'These guys are out of their goddamn minds!' But that wasn't an important thing to him at all.

The guys in his bands used to do all those old vaudeville routines but in a rhythm & blues kind of way. The guy would walk the bar with the sax, go in the ladies' room, come out with these big women's underwear on the horn, playin' till he'd pass out. Then they'd do this bit where while the guy's playin' like he's passed out, they would pour a big bottle of whiskey down the guy and it wouldn't faze him, he'd still be passed out. And then they'd blow some smoke in the guy's face, and that wouldn't faze him. And then they'd take the big women's drawers off the saxophone and wave in his face and that guy'd come up playin' his ass off. " [34]

"*Allen* [Toussaint] *told me how much you and he loved Fess.*

Well, you know, in between takes, on those dates we always did something that Fess was doing at the time. That was like the code between us all. There was something about Fess that connected everybody. All the cats coming up, we knew that what Fess was doing was leading toward something. Even drummers like Earl Palmer and Zigaboo [Joseph Modeliste] was connected to Fess' stuff [sic].

What made Professor Longhair unique, from a piano player's perspective?

There was something real magic about his concept. For one thing, Fess didn't even think of the piano like it was a piano. He looked at it like he was playing all the Caribbean stuff in one thing. When he would sit down and play medleys of Caribbean music, it was amazing. I got him to record one of them once. But there was stuff I remember him to doing when he used to work at the One Stop record shop. That was a side of him a lot of people didn't ever hear. All the way to the end I was trying to get him to remember some of that stuff, but he had forgot. When he got sick and his health wasn't that good no more, he hung with what he could remember. It was like people saw a piece of Fess but really didn't know what he was all about.

I loved Fess. When my father passed away, Fess became like a father figure to me. He was a lot of things. He was a good man. He taught me about how to make a band frolic. When he said, 'Let's frolic, boys!' he wanted us to get behind the soloist and kick ass, keeping the groove right there but kicking. And man! That's what Allen did for his first album, The Wild Sound Of Toussaint [The Wild Sound of New Orleans by Tousan, "RCA", 1958]. All the piano players around New Orleans knew Fess' stuff to some degree. He inspired all of us. I used to love to hear Huey Smith do Fess: it was Fess' notes but in Huey's lazy vibe. And I used to hear Allen do the way Huey would do Fess. That's a magical thing. He had that vibe you could feel. And different people feel it totally different. [James] Booker would do Fess' stuff much more precise like. Allen had a looseness with it.

When Allen talked about seeing Fess for the first time, he sounded like a lot of alto players talking about Bird [Charlie Parker].

When I first heard Fess, I wasn't ten years old – maybe younger, I don't know. What I do know, he left an impression on me. I used to see posters of him and I heard records, but on gigs I remember just him and a guy who didn't even have a set of drums. The guy had something he played with his one foot and something else – maybe a chair. Fess kept kicking the piano like a bass drum. They had a trumpet, and that was it. And I thought, 'What the hell is that?!'

At the time, I was really into Pete Johnson [1904-1967]. When I was a kid I used to love Big Joe Turner [1911-1985] records because I liked the way Pete Johnson played. But when I heard Fess on that gig, it was like when guys tell me when they heard Art Tatum [1910-1956], like they're looking at God. That thing was so different. Everybody who heard him at the time was blown away—had no idea what the hell he was doing. Paul Gayten [1920-1991] for example, was never a great piano player. He was a record producer. But he told me, 'See, what Fess is to you, he doesn't mean the same thing to guys in my generation. But we love him because he's changing things that y'all don't even see.'

And I later saw how it changed the music – the way people felt grooves, the way they moved to the changes. I used to ask Fess,

'Where did your thing come from?' and he'd tell me that he'd learned stuff from Tuts Washington, Little Brother Montgomery, and guys I never heard of, like Kid Stormy Weather [Edmond Joseph] and Piano Blue. But he was a dancer – he did tell me that.

Mac Rebennack and Allen Toussaint, Montreux, Switzerland, June 30, 1973. Photo and courtesy Jan Ytterberg. Used by permission.

So you consider Fess a revolutionary?

Oh yeah! He'd just mix all that Caribbean music up with that New Orleans parade thing and made it one kind of new music. Then he'd mix up Mardi Gras Indian music with Caribbean music that set a trend for the Indians without them even knowing that. It was a big thrill that the guy would even let me hang out with him. And Fess encouraged me a lot. He was always saying, 'Don't just talk about it, do it.'" [35]

"He used that piano like a drum or marimba or like all kind of things that wasn't a piano, but he developed ways of playing real syncopated compound rhythms. Now 'a-days people call that funk but in his days it was no exact thing of what people considered funky music, back in the '40s and '50s. When he did it, he was way ahead of his time in what he created with rhythms.

He had ways that made his grooves lay differently. He was conscious of how certain little patterns would help his songs but they'd be like takeoff patterns. He'd expect you to take that and cook it more and leave it out behind the solos but still have the basic essence of that. It was a total different learning procedure than I ever had before on how to comp with somebody.

Fess'd play a straight-up 12-bar blues and sometimes that same blues would come out to 16 bars or 14 bars. It was real definite why he was doing something – he'd put some extra bars in to build up in a section or something that made his music special, unlike other music that had different amount of bars in a 12-bar blues." [36]

"Fess danced for a while but he always wanted to sing. He had this yodeling thing he used to do. He told me he always liked to sing the hillbilly sound á la Ivory Joe Hunter [1914-1974, a black singer/pianist & songwriter], but he liked to sing it with a 'groove' so he could 'frolic' with the hillbillies. (Fess had a thing about getting high on reefer when he played. When he was high as a pine and feeling fine, he was ready to 'frolic.')" [37]

"No, I can't tell you his exact age either. I've seen so many conflicting birth-dates for him that it's hard to say. I mean there are ten years difference in some of the dates suggested. He may have seemed older than he was because he'd been in a lot of pain over the years from a number of physical problems." [38]

John Boudreaux (1936-2017), drums and saxophone:
"The first time I played with Professor Longhair was about 1952. I was never his regular drummer – I just played a few gigs with him. He would never call me to play with him, but he'd have someone else call me. I guess he had other drummers ahead of me. The first place we played was in a little park by the Lafitte Projects. There was me, Fess and Harold Battiste [1931-2015] on saxophone." [39]

"Basically he would play two or three, maybe four rhythms just by himself. He would kick the piano with one foot, play a bass line sort of in halftime, play his right hand in a double-time motion, and sometimes a triple or quadruple motion. It was sort of like a very hip rumba. That's the only way I can explain it.

He made everybody start thinking rhythmically a little different. He was the closest thing to rock'n' roll because of the rhythms that he played. Of course, he was considered a rhythm & blues player but he did something different from all regular rhythm & blues players.

Professor Longhair changed the course of rock 'n' roll and the blues because he started playing the straight eight notes. That's where it came from, but the drummers wasn't playing a backbeat with him. They was playing something else. It just worked its way into that straight-eight thing with a backbeat. Earl Palmer probably had something to do with that, you know?" [sic] [40]

"Jessie Hill used to be a funky drummer, too, before he started singing. He used to play with Fess. In fact he showed me the beat I had to play with Fess. […] Honey-boy [Charles Otis] was one of his main drummers, and Jessie, and Louis Joseph.

The cymbals resonates all over the music. I mean, in jazz, that's the thing. That's what they want. But this funky music, you can't really play that tight if you're playing it on the cymbal, you know? You play that funk real tight. Most New Orleans drummers had a knack of playing on the snare drum because it came from the parade thing, the second line. It just had a funkier sound." [41]

John Boudreaux, 1960. Courtesy Jeff Hannusch.

Vernon "Dr. Daddy-O" Winslow (1911-1993), radio disc jockey:
"My favorite Mardi Gras songs are what 'Fess does. I didn't realize that my Mardi Gras music comes from what Fess did, maybe because

I was close to him. It just is his whistling and his gruffly gruff way of rhyming things. And that odd kind of beat that he always found.

I would just see him at his recording sessions down at Cosimo's and get pretty much of the person he was from the music that he would do even in rehearsal. I used to kid him about his long shoes and he would just laugh and say. 'Like 'em?' And he just had a tremendous friendliness about him, but when he sat down at the piano and took that typical position with his feet he was ready for business.

Professor Longhair's beat was a calypso. How he just picked that up amazes me. I think it was his feeling of what the Indian presence meant. He really interpreted the calypso quality of Mardi Gras. We used to look at the piano regretfully after every session where 'Fess had kicked it, but he was just a person, a musician, who was an individual. And we just thought, 'Gol-lee, wow, that cat goes on with some power.' Fats [Domino] was different. Fats was listening for his brass, listening for his drums. He was more of an interpretation of Dave Bartholomew. But 'Fess was not. 'Fess was somewhere way out in another country. And how he could whistle so beautifully!

Vernon Winslow. From a 1974 advertisement for the local: WYLD: Radio 94.

He knew that he knew something that other musicians didn't know. And he was an authority on it. But he never made you feel small for suggesting something that you thought ought to be put into the song. He'd put it in." [42]

Alex "Duke" Burrell (1920-1993), piano:
"Man, couldn't nobody in the world play like him. I don't know where Fess got that style from, but man, he had a heck of a style of his own ... It'd make your feet pat." [43]

Ronnie Barron (Ronald R. Barosse: 1943-1997), piano & vocal:
"My first influence was Professor Longhair. I heard him and I was gone! He was the main ingredient of the New Orleans sound and probably the founder of rock and roll.

Hey Now Baby ["Hey Now Honey Child", "AIM" 1038., is] my homage to Professor Longhair. We both used to work on the West Side [Bank?] at the Orchid Lounge where he taught me to play this song". [44]

Walter Kimble (Walter Kimball, 1938-1988), saxophones:
"We were down at the One Stop Record Shop, me Wardell (Quezergue), Earl King, [trumpeter Warren "Porgy"] Jones and Fess. We always used to fool around there. And they had an old raggedy piano back there. Earl King said, 'Look, Fess, let's write a Mardi Gras tune'. Fess said, 'Man I don't know nothin' about writin' no tunes.' The man who owned One-Stop Record Shop, we called him "Big Chief". Earl said, 'Let's write a tune about Big Chief.' So everybody thinks that it was written about the Indians, but it was written about a white boy, an Italian. His name was Joe Assunto [Joseph F. Assunto 1914-1981]. And a lot of people don't know on the record it's not Fess singing, it's Earl King. We just threw it together, man, and the next thing you know, every carnival if you don't play "Big Chief", there ain't nothin' happenin'". [45]

Wardell Quezergue (1930-2011), composer, arr., trumpet & piano:
"The one I did is the big band "Big Chief". Smokey Johnson was playing the drums and he was playing the drums so hard that between his thumb and forefinger, he got blisters and started bleeding he was playing so hard. That was all live. I remember that quite well. We did it at Cosimo's, I think when it was on [748] Camp Street. He had another place, I think it was on Governor Nicholls." [46]

"The best-kept secret about "Big Chief" is that we had to tie Fess's right hand to his back because he was interfering with what the band was doing. He played the whole thing with his left hand. Still we couldn't get the sound we wanted so we sent "Big Chief" to Atlanta for overdubbing and then remixed it in New Orleans." [47]

Onward Brassband, left to right. Louis Barbarin, Louis Nelson, Albert "Fernandez" Walters Sr., Avery "Kid" Howard, Jerry Green, Paul Babarin, Wardell Quezergue, Ernest Cagnolatti, Louis Cottrell, Jack Willis, Mike Casimir, & Dick Allen, Tulane University. Photo by Jack Hurley, November 3, 1962. Courtesy Hogan Jazz Archive, Tulane University, with thanks to Alaina Hébert. Used by permission.

Earl King (Earl Silas Johnson, 1934–2003), guitar, piano, vocal & songwriter:

"I always thought that Huey [Smith] was an incredible you know he was going to some things. Huey really inspired me in some ways to do a lot of things, writing. Especially at the outset of things, because Huey sometimes, when I'd be weary, he said: 'I know man, you can do that!' And you do it. You know! Huey, he was always pianos and speaking about Huey and Allen and all of them was listening at Fess, you know, other than Fess, Huey was listening to Little Willie Littlefield and of course Charles Brown and Ray Charles [...]." [48]

Tad Jones [1952-2007]: *"In the early days, piano players seemed to be the dominant influence on people.*

King: Piano players mainly in New Orleans, because in small units

45

here you didn't have a bass guitar. Everything relied on a pulsation in the rhythm section on the piano. Usually the piano players had to be extremely good with their left hand, like Byrd, [Huey] Smith. Because you really look for that support. Actually the boogie-woogie era, Huey would be like "Fess"(Longhair). He would be a left-hand boogie-woogie player. Huey had just about the heaviest hand in town, heavier than Byrd [...]

King: You gonna hear Huey even without a mike. He had a good, fantastic left hand. So when you playing in those groups with no bass, you need someone like Byrd and them who have a heavy left hand to help you along.

Earl King, & Leo Noncentelli, TV Show, Oct. 30, 1974, Chicago. The acts included were: Fess; Dr. John; and the Meters, Photo & courtesy Hans Andréasson. Used by permission.

Jones: How much influence did Longhair have on local musicians?

King: A lot of 'em wasn't really listening at Professor back there. They heard him but they didn't hear him. You know what I mean. They might say that's cool, it's just some funky music.

Jones: Did you listen to him at an early age?

King: Yeah, very, very early. One of his first songs that I ever learned how to play was "Hey Now Baby" ["Hey Now Baby, Hey Now Honey Child"] on guitar. [Cut by Fess in 1949 & 1959.]

Jones: Where did you hear it?

King: I used to hear it on the radio, jukeboxes, stuff like that. I used to get frustrated with what I heard behind "Fess" back there. I always used to be hummin' bass parts that I thought should be behind whatever he was singin'. I used get furious when I hear somebody do something behind Byrd that don't give any thought to the bass structure of what's going on in it. That's why I always said that if I got a chance to do something with Professor Longhair, I'd do it on a big scale. That's the first time I tried to use 15 (pieces) behind the "Big Chief" ["Watch", 1964]. That's the way I heard Byrd and I thought that's the way you should implement everything that he's doing on that level. He sounds good with a funky little group, but I think to highlight some of the things he's doing, make it a real signatory...give it some thought.

As far as influence, I think Byrd started a rhythmic thing. I think that people just fell in the line with that rhythmic thing. Everything was a mood or a little groove.

Jones: It seemed to me that Longhair wasn't copied per se. He never had the commercial success. As Domino was copied per se, everybody sounded like Domino exactly. "Fess" wasn't copied, but he was used. They would take what he had done and built off of it. In that sense, he's more important than Domino.

King: They would take the vital parts that they would hear...

Jones: They would use the rhythm. I think that Allen (Toussaint) used the rhythm. Now parts he copied per se and Huey copied. So in that sense he was very important. If you listen to Allen's early stuff you can hear Professor Longhair all through what he was doing.

King: Yeah, well, he (Allen) [Toussaint] will tell you that. Longhair has always been a favorite of Allen's, he's crazy about him. Loves him to the bone. He thinks he's the end of piano players, that's Allen's version of Longhair. He told me something about a week ago, he was sayin' that he had heard Longhair recently and says that everything that they say about Longhair is true. He's amazing, one of the greatest he had heard. And most people, I guess, if they listen at Longhair, I don't think you should listen at him to hear melodies, tonations [sic] and stuff like that, 'cause I think listening at Longhair the rhythms that he play is phenomenal. It's almost ridiculous. [...]

He was like a source, a lifeline for people to draw upon. You right, you very right about that. It really came from Byrd but it was magnified through another source [sic].

Jones: Then Huey transposed it. Then Allen took pieces and transposed it into what he was doing. Art Neville, the Meters have taken bits and pieces and added it to their act.

King: Byrd made me become drum conscious about certain things back there. Although you didn't hear it on Byrd's pieces, but some of the drummers that really had listened at Byrd, he gave them other ideas on how to organize their plan [...].

The Dew Drop Inn, the Tijuana, and they had other smaller clubs, like the Club Rocket...and [South] Rampart Street had a buncha' little clubs that were bookin' little groups: The Dixie Bell, The Big Apple and all those dives.

Jones: Those are the places Fess (Professor Longhair) used to play.

King: Yeah, "Fess" knew all about that area there. Monjura's and the Pelican [301 South Rampart St.], which was a popular place in later years. The Big 225, the Astoria [235-37 S. Rampart], that was like a strip. They catered to small groups, freedos and stuff like that. They didn't have no cover charge. The Tijuana and the Dew Drop were the only places that really put a cover charge on you. And the Dew Drop with high drinks; like what you would pay now.

Jones: "What about the record you did for Professor Longhair?

King: Well, "Big Chief", I wrote that for Professor Longhair. And on "Big Chief" nobody saw my name, not even as a writer on there. You look there and see a pseudonym I used to use: my mother's name, E. Gaines. I used that after my mother remarried, or her maiden name, Hampton [...] I wrote it for him to do and I always wanted to write something for Professor Longhair and play guitar with him. I had been wanting to do this since I was real young. And I got a chance at that point to write something for him [sic].

The Astoria, S. Rampart Street, 1942 (demolished in 1972). Photo: Bill Russell. Courtesy: Hogan Jazz Archive, Special Collections, Howard-Tilton Memorial Library. Tulane University. Used by permission.

Jones: What problems did you have in the studio on "Big Chief"?

King: I wrote that song for "Fess" to do and we were runnin' behind in the studio, and "Fess" is very hard to catch on to lyrics and things— it takes a while. Joe Assunto and Henry Hildebrand was employin' us with the Watch label. Joe was in a hurry, so he told me, 'Don't make no problems out of it – just go in the studio and sing the record, and we'll put your name and 'Fess name on the record.' We cut and everything came out OK. So we had a meetin' about two days later and they said, 'How's your contract with Motown?' I said, 'It's at my lawyer's office and I really haven't had a chance to go through it.' So I went through it and checked it out, it looked cool. So I don't know which one, Henry or Joe said they thought it wouldn't be too cool to put my name on the record 'cause they might have had some clause in the contract. So we just leave it Professor Longhair, and we just split the artist royalties. I don't think 'Fess' got any artist royalties, 'cause I know I didn't. I didn't get any writer's royalties until I really went through some changes.

People would say, 'I heard the Professor Longhair recording and I knew that was you singin' on that.' Then I say, 'Well, Fess told me to go on do it.' Because at that point I think he had something in his

49

mind. He still thinks like that right now. He was tryin' to get a group together and he thought we could work up some kind of team. That's what he was really up to at the time.

Tad Jones: Did you have trouble with the beat in the studio?

King: Well, there were a whole lotta' complications, but especially at the introduction. The melodics that the Professor is playin' on the piano is so syncopated, till Smokey Johnson, the drummer, couldn't count how to come in and start playin'. We did about 15 takes messin' up on the intro before the drummer could get in on that count. Smokey got furious because he couldn't never come in on time after Professor play that little funny thing and he was out there in left field somewhere.

But the gas of the whole session was, Fess didn't know that we were going to use all those pieces on that session.

He thought we were going to use about four pieces; just him and a bass, a drummer and maybe a horn. Unconcerned as he is, he came and looked around and he was wonderin' why all these people was in there. He thought they were going to be on somebody else's session. And we weren't overdubbin' nothin'. We were just puttin' everything on at once.

So when the music started, "Fess" started playin' with the rhythm section. We had 11 horns on that, and when "Fess" heard all that stuff go off in there behind him, he stopped playin' the piano. He was just shocked. Listenin' at the record you can't hear too much, because the few mikes we were usin' with all them pieces up in there. If you coulda been in the studio and heard it, it was something to hear. Everybody in there was fascinated with it. So we had to take an intermission so "Fess" could compose himself awhile, get himself together mentally.

Tad Jones: Who decided on that arrangement? It was very heavy with the brass.

King: The roots of it, the rhythm section I arranged myself. And most times I prefer not to put my name on the recording as co-arranger or nothin' like that. I don't think it's necessary really, I'm just bein' impressed with the product that's comin' out well. Whoever does the rest of the arrangement, they can get credit.

The "President, is expected to attend" (sic), the Albuquerque Journal, NM, US. February 1, 1956.

Wardell Quezergue did the orchestration on it. The Big Chief thing is the way I really wanted to hear Professor musically behind him. On the record as you'll notice Wardell Quezergue's name on there. But like everything that I've ever done that Wardell is on it as an arranger, it's always dictations of my own ideas that I project. I always handle my own rhythm, I don't let nobody tamper with that. If there's anything I want, horns or you name it, I'll dictate it to him. Wardell can write fast as you can write a letter, with music. He's real fast […].

But I think Wardell and I used to work pretty good, we used to come up with pretty good things... like when I brought him the "Big Chief" thing and he heard it, I said, "How many pieces you think are on here?" I said, 'I hear about 15.' He said, 'Cool, I hear it, too,' as simple as that.

The "Big Chief" thing, we really were going to do a series of things. I really wanted to do some creative things (on "Fess") and that was the first one I had a chance to do. We were tryin' to create another kinda sound up under Professor Longhair. I guess it was different from most of the stuff that he cut. He's the type of person that likes inspiration, and certain people can project him. Like today they record Professor, like thing he has done before and that's about all. He's done a new version of "Big Chief", he's cut a new one and it sounds good. I think you can get some new things outta him if you rile him up enough. Get him fired up and inspired to sit up and do a few songs." [49]

"Smokey" Johnson (New Orleans, Oct. 23, 2014), at the premier screening of the documentary: the BIG BEAT, on Fats Domino & Dave Bartholomew. In Aug. 1949, the Louisiana Weekly reported: "Smokey Joe Johnson, high stepping eccentric tap dancer, was featured with the band [Papa Celestin, the Municipal Auditorium] and his work was highly appreciated, he was forced to give an encore." In the 1960s, Johnson cut a couple of celebrated 45s for the "NOLA" label. Johnson's 23-years long association with Fats ended abruptly in 1993, after a stroke. Photo by the author.

Joseph "Smokey" Johnson (1936-2015), drummer and composer:
"I was looking for something (unique) to play on a record ["Big Chief"]. I turned the floor tom over on its side and played on the side of the floor tom (right hand) and I was playin' rim-shots on the snare drum. I also took two sticks full of Coke caps that I had nailed

on. I had two big ones that I overdubbed on that track. They used to let me do almost whatever I wanted to do on the session. That was a good session. That was the best thing that Professor Longhair ever did. That's Earl King singin' and whistlin." [50]

Curtis D. Mitchell (1926-2011), piano, electric & stand up bass, saxophone, and arrangements.

Tad Jones: You're on Big Chief with Fess.

Mitchell: Yes, I'm playing on it.

Jones: You know that lick Fess plays [sings the "Big Chief" piano lick]. *Did Earl* [King] *write that or did Fess write it?*

Mitchell: No, I think Fess just came up with that hisself [sic]. That's his style I think. But what happened, man. Fess had us in the studio [Cosimo Recording Studio, Gov. Nichols.] down there all night recording. He's the only one that couldn't read. Fess was supposed to originally sing it. But he couldn't sing it and play at the same time, so Earl wind up singin' it. That's Earl singin' and whistling. And then another thing with Fess. The man stopped Fess from playin' it left hand, 'cause he's playin' [sings the piano lick], just one hand, and the [piano] bass's interfering with the figure [hums it] I was playing [on the bass. Sings it]. He [Quezergue?] put a pillow down there by the foot, because he [Fess] had a habit of kickin' the piano. When he playing the Caldonia Inn years ago, they had an upright [piano] there, he kicked a spot in there. And see, them baby grands, he kicked the pedal where the pedal came down. So, what he doing there was interfering with what "Smoke" ["Smokey" Johnson] was playin' on the drum. So, they put a pillow down there. But it all come out good though. Before Wardell [Quezergue] did an arrangement on it, I had arrangement on it [sic]. But when I tried to get the cats together on it, I couldn't get 'em a rehearsal, and they think I know Earl and them got Wardell do another arrangement. 'Course it wasn't the same thing, arrangement wise [sic]. You know two arrangers don't think alike.

Jones: How did Earl bring the song to you? What did it sound like, when Earl brought it?

Mitchell: He singed it [sic] to me, like the same way he sang it on there [on the disc]. But I put my idea on how the horns's supposed to go. Jones: So that's all you heard Earl sang to you, he didn't play it on guitar?

Mitchell: Yeah, he split it [inaudible]. I was ahead of that arrangement you know. I don't know what happened if I had it man?

Jones: What was the difference from Wardell's?

Mitchell: Well, the horns. The bass figure was different plus the horns were arranged different [...] Mine was just as effective as his. You know you got to hear it. I remember we were rehearsing at, they had a place called: Blue Eagle [Club] on [2026] Felicity Street [Uptown], Big Emory [Thompson] and all of them was there.

Jones: The whole group was on a session?

Mitchell: No, not all of them, but a lot of 'em. You know this happened a year or so before the recording. I lived on Louisiana Avenue, man. All night long we used to be fooling with music. Matter of fact, we made Earl had a come together down there". [51]

George Porter (born 1947), el. bass, vocal and composer:
"I was a grown man when I got to play with Fess. Well, not really quite a grown man, but we had already been discovered as the Meters before I got to play with Fess. I was living upstairs here (Baronne Street), and Fess used to pass in front of the house all the time. That was just after he'd gotten out of incarceration. My wife, Ara, knew him, because she had lived around this neighborhood a long time. She'd call me and say, 'Look, there goes Fess!' He'd be riding his little bicycle in front of our house just about every day. I'd always say, boy I'd sure like to get a chance play with this guy.

So on that first day the Jazz Fest moved to the Fair Grounds [April 26, 1972], Zig (Modeliste) called me up and said 'hey man, how'd you like to close the Fair Grounds this year with Fess?' Man, I said

George Porter, Fess, and Earl Gordon, at the Mosebacke etablissement, Stockholm, Sweden. The band played there: Sunday, July 23 & 24, 1978. Photograph: Jan Ytterberg. Used by permission.

YEEAAHH! It was like a dream come true, y'know, finally getting to play with the Fess." [52]

"I've been uniquely pleased to only have one drummer in my life that I hated, I absolutely hated that motherfucker. I wanted to kill him. He wasn't my drummer, I didn't hire him, but I was on tour with him, with Fess in Europe for three weeks. He never let himself get alone with me 'cause he knew I would kill him. If I ever contemplated murder, that was the guy. He left New Orleans after that tour. I think he didn't feel safe in New Orleans no more after that (laughs)." [53]

Fird "Snooks" Eaglin Jr. (1936–2009), guitar & vocal:
"We did a session with Fess in the city of New York. First we did some audition tapes with Janis Joplin's band. It was hard to please him, because those musicians didn't really suit Fess, y'know. We were just trying different bands and Fess wasn't satisfied. So then we went to Hit Factory in New York and cut some stuff there and then we went to Baton Rouge and Memphis and cut some stuff that's on "House Party". [54]

"I enjoyed working with 'Fess [...] I was 12 years old [on the first gig with Fess]. Right off the bat I got his style. He was nice, drank that Muscatel wine. Oh yeah, he'd be sloppy but he knew how to handle himself.

Now Europe, that's where people really appreciate you. First time, I went to London in 1972 [1973] with Professor Longhair and a big package, Olympia Brass Band, Willie Tee and the Gators, another Dixieland group, the Wild Magnolias, it was a party for Atlantic Records [a James Goldsmith party]. It was really nice, that's my first time. Later on, I went to Holland with George Porter." [55]

Arthur "Art" Neville (born 1937), keyboards & vocal etc.:
"The piano style came from Fess who has a lot to do with every piano player who's ever worked out of New Orleans. Subconsciously you might not be aware of it but this is the man who was behind it all." [56]

"Fess was what I call cheeky—that's New Orleans talk for just some fly, nobody-else-could-do-it kind of stuff. – He's the man that really want me to play piano. I couldn't play like he did, but some definitely must have passed to me. He was playing stuff I couldn't figure out - the licks he was playing and the rhythm that he was playing them in... you just had to know where it would go. You couldn't count this stuff – you had to feel it because you gotta put it in a certain place for it to work. It wasn't anything to him – just another thing like walking.

When "Tipitina" came out [in 1953], I was in high school, and I was hangin' in what they called the sweets shops, the Happy Days shops. Just to hear Fess, listening to "Tipitina" on the jukebox – it was kickin', that's all I can say. It was serious music. It was a shame that a lot of people didn't hear it because they wouldn't play "race music" on the radio back then." [57]

Cyril Neville (born: 1948), percussion, drums & vocal:
"One of the most inspirational moments of my life was when I played drums behind Fess in San Francisco [September 1977?]. I want people to know how great that was to me, and I want it to mean something to my people. I want to brush the dust off of the history of a lot of other musicians who was not as well-known as Fess so that my children will know what went on." [58]

A poster, September 1977. The guys on the Wild Tchoupitoulas photograph were: Amos Landry, Booker Washington, George Landry, Carl Christmas, Thomas Jackson, & Norman Jackson. The author's collection.

Alvin "Mozart" Batiste (1932-2007), clarinet, saxophone, and composer etc.:
"Fess is a very important figure, as everybody knows in New Orleans. I went by Fess's house one day down on [South] Rampart Street to let him hear one of my songs. I was singing it in E flat minor, and he said

57

'You're not singing that in the right position; you need to sing it in this position.' He put it in A flat minor. It sounded much better. So it made me think about Ornette Coleman, because Ornette had evolved his own language in terms of describing musical events. As Earl King says, 'His own colorations of experience.'" [59]

Jessie Hill (1932-1996), drums, vocal & songwriter:
"See I been knowin' Fess all my life, we use' to open the curtain at The Blue Eagle ["a rough club and neighborhood", at 1824 Felicity St.], playin' in front of Muddy Waters, Little Willie John, Jimmy Reed, and all those guys. See I was so far advanced with my playin,' that only I could play with Fess. All this stuff you hearin' drummers play now, they's playin' what I was playin'." [60]

Jessie Hill & Pat Byrd, Fess' front porch, 1522 S. Rampart, mid 1970s. Allison Miner collection, Hogan Jazz Archive, Tulane University. Used by permission.

Henry Butler (1949-2018), piano & vocal:
"I could play some Professor Longhair when I was in High School", [61] "After graduate school, I got a job teaching at the New Orleans Center

for the Creative Arts, the creative arts high school in the city. Professor Longhair was around then. I knew the elements of the New Orleans style he was playing, but I'd never paid attention to them seriously. I mentioned to Mr. Bat [Alvin Batiste] that I thought I needed more work in that style, so he arranged for me to go to Prof. Longhair's house and just hang out with him. And I brought along my tape recorder. He obviously wasn't schooled professionally, but he didn't really need to be. He taught me some very down-to-earth things. He'd say things like, 'You play too hard. You need to soften your touch, because if you soften your touch you can move much faster.' Well, that really appealed to me because I wanted to start moving faster." [62]

David "Dave" Bartholomew (born 1918), trumpet, bandleader, & composer:
"Peter Goldsmith: Earl King says, the Rhythm is something completely special in New Orleans. Could you explain that and also the "Second Line rhythmfil"?

Dave Bartholomew: Yes I think, New Orleans has that certain something, a certain beat. Or let us say it in a better way. We had it. And we let it happen that other people changed it. We had a certain beat. We started with the "Funk" music; I believe Professor Longhair was first and the one who is responsible for what we today call the "funk beat". It was of course improved but Professor Longhair was the first one whom I heard using that beat. We have recorded a huge number of discs with this kind of beat [...]

Goldsmith: Do you think that Professor Longhair influenced nearly all piano players in New Orleans?

Bartholomew: No, I do not think so.

Goldsmith: Who did so then?

Bartholomew: One cannot say that for sure. There were so many people in those days. Like I already said, "Fess" originally brought the "funk sound" out, yes. I think that he is the most imitated piano player in this style in the country. Not only in New Orleans, but all around the

Dave Bartholomew's band, December 1947, "New Orleans' favorite jump-band". Clockwise: Earl Palmer, drums; Fred "Peelu" Lands, piano; Theard Johnson, vocals: Clarence Hall, tenor sax; Joe Harris, alto saxophone; Ernest McLean, amplified guitar; Frank Fields, bass; & Bartholomew, trumpet. Courtesy: Louisiana Weekly, January 3, 1948.

world people play the way the professor did. But the other kind of music came, I think, actually from the older musicians, who already had played in that way for many years. And I could not here mention just one musician, because all played with this Rhythm and beat [...]."
63

"[Fess was] a very good friend. The last time that I saw him was at the New-Victoria [Theatre], in London [1978]. I was on stage with Fats and I saw Fess passing in the wings! He died shortly after; I was at his funeral with Earl Palmer and others. He is the creator of what we call New Orleans Funk. I would say that Fats and me invented the "Back-Beat", but Fess, frankly, is the owner of the 'Funky-Beat'" [sic]. 64

"I think Professor Longhair was one of the greatest influence on New Orleans music piano players. You had another guy who played in the same vain, Toots, the late Toots Johnson [Tuts Washington]. I don't think Toots, I think his last name, I can't, I mean he was Toots, the great Toots." [65]

Ernest McLean (1925-2012), string instruments:
Excerpts from an interview conducted by Nina Falk Aronsen, March 9, 2004, Los Angeles, Cal., 2004.

Nina: Did you play with Professor Longhair?

Ernest: We had a packet [show]. Professor Longhair, Fats Domino, Jewel King [a vocalist], and let me see who else, it happened around '51. There were a few other guys, that were supposed to go out with us, but they didn't go.

"Nina: How long did you stay out, when you did those tours?

Ernest: A tour might last three, maybe four months. I call myself a jazz player, so I like all mines sound pretty similar [sic]. Like you get into the blues things, you might want to a more treble sound, but for playing jazz, you want that nice mellow sound, so that's different. (playing "Tipitina") That's Professor Longhair. A friend of mine played guitar with him, "Papoose". Every time you see them, they had a place that was closed during the week, it didn't open up until Friday, Saturday and Sunday, they used to get the key and go inside that place and rehearse. "Papoose" and a drummer man by the name of Charles Otis, and they had another Charles, who played drums before him. I just followed them guys go around and just listening, and I could sit down and just write down everything they played, you know, but I don't really want to copy, but I could do, and some of his ideas I would copy for Dave Bartholomew's band to play. We had just such a big variety of music, when I was playing with Dave Bartholomew, music for everything, society type music [playing Earl Garner's song "Misty"]." [66]

"Frankie Ford" (Francis Guzzo, born 1939), piano & vocals:
"Fess was like a cult, even then a cult figure and no one knew what Fess was playing (laughter). I mean no one REALLY knew what Fess was playing. I don't think that if you ever asked Fess what he was doing, he really knew. It was just in that feelin'". [67]

"Eddie Bo And His Band", Carnival Day, Club Riviera. Courtesy: Louisiana Weekly, January 10, 1959.

Edwin "Eddie Bo" "Spider" Bocage (1930–2009), piano, vocal, & composer:
"I was born and raised in New Orleans. My mother was a pianist and she played along the same lines as Professor Longhair. She introduced me to him and met him and then came along Ray Charles and stayed with us for about eight or nine years around the Dew Drop Inn. To be influenced by those people was something.

I heard music in my mother's womb, I could hear it so I had to get to doing something about it and I wanted to bring it to another level and do what I wanted to do with the music. The musicians who were around when I was young was Lloyd Price, Sugar Boy Crawford, James Black, James Booker and Professor Longhair. I sat and played with Professor Longhair [...] My dad knew [him. He] was a gambler, a straight gambler and he knew how to take the cards and do what he needed to do with them. So, he used to tell me about Professor Longhair and Tommy Ridgley and they would come to my dad's place all the time and he would bleed them out of their money." [68]

"I was too young to get in, but I would stand outside and listen to him at the Caledonia. I don't know if I can find words to describe his talent. Fess was not from the earth. I think he came from another planet. I've never heard anyone from this earth play like him." [69]

"There was only pianos when I was coming up. There must have been a piano in practically every house I went to. No drums, no bass nothing like that. What my momma played, that was the thing 'Fess played, what they called the 'Junker's Blues.' Man, you had to play that if you wanted anybody listen to you. Lots of them played that way, but 'Fess brought it out to the public. I sat around him a long time, man, we were very close. Now, he had a gift from God; they can imitate him to a certain degree, but they can't duplicate him. He could take a simple chord progression and run it from one end of the keyboard to the other, he could do so much with just that simple progression. Being around him like that, I learned a lot just from his way of thinking." [70]

"Fess and I were very, very close. We went out on gigs like you would never believe, in all these little towns – me and Fess and Ernest Chinn, Fess' son [a stepson, 1949-2002]. Chinn was a doorman. Chinn would knock a man out if he wouldn't pay, and draw his gun – oh, yes he would.

Fess and Tommy would go and bring all their money to my daddy. He ran games in what they called Shrewsbury [a New Orleans neighborhood] – that's where Tommy lived – and them two would go play catch with my daddy. My daddy dealt from the bottom of the deck. You know Saratoga Street, I used to jump the fence and come around to a place in the front, on Jackson Avenue, to see Tommy and Dave Bartholomew – Dave had a great big band, and Tommy was the vocalist [...] Fess used to sit in the back of Joe Assunto's One Stop Record's and Fess would play for hours. No money – he was cleaning up and stocking the place. Now here is a man that played so many polyrhythms that nobody's gonna equal it today. They can mimic him to a degree, but man, Fess played so many polyrhythms it was sickening. And you know they didn't pay him. Fess didn't start making a couple of dollars until after Allison (Miner) picked him up (in 1970), and even then, it took a long time. And he still didn't make it big – he made enough to survive, and bought a little house, but that was it." [71]

Allen Toussaint (1938-2015), piano, vocal, composer, & arranger:
"I didn't hear "Tuts" [Washington] until I was quite grown, but I came up playin' Professor Longhair since I was a very young kid. As a boy coming up I played exactly as Fess did. Because there were little rules, even though it seemed wild and random, there were little rules that you don't go against, when you're really doin' it.

I consider him havin' about five or six inventions, you might say. And simple as it might appear now, it was monumental at that time. One being [plays a couple of bars], and so forth and so on. That was "Hey Little Girl". And later on [plays a couple of bars on "Tipitina"]. And for a kid who's eight years old. *That is very exciting*, I want you to know. When you graduate to sliding [demonstrates on the piano], like that. And later on he did things like, [plays a couple of bars on "Mardi Gras In New Orleans"]. And after all of that, and many other things he came through [plays Fess's "Big Chief" piano lick], *knocked my socks off*, it never just flooded the airways. They were always going after something more sane, you might say, a little more where everyone know where one two three four is. With Fess it would be all kinds of ways. The crew comin' down the street, you could hear that. In Fess's music you could see the Mardi Gras Indians comin' down the street." [72]

Joel Dufour: We know that you were very close to the late Professor Longhair. There is a beautiful – and very sad – video in which both of you can be seen in the company of Tuts Washington ("Piano players rarely ever play together"). Can you tell us what Professor Longhair represents for you?

Toussaint: "Something monumental. Monumental. He had the greatest influence on the development of my music. When I heard Professor Longhair for the first time, I thought that I would be able to devote my life to playing exactly like him. Of course, I overcame that state of mind, but am pleased that I have kept an attitude, which assimilates

Allen Toussaint's band, San Jacinto Club, c. 1959. From left: Teddy Riley; Albert "June" Gardner, Peter "Chuck" Badie, Clarence Ford, Alvin "Red" Tyler, & Allen Toussaint. Courtesy Rick Coleman, used by permission.

all Fess's innovations as each record issued, one after another.

I consider him as our Bach of Rock, because he had the same kind of creativity. Of course, he has not been as prolific as Bach, but his inventions where so rich that you could have spent your entire life composing and playing on the basis of one of them. He had several periods. Thus at one stage you could have listened to one of his records and deduced it was Professor Longhair even though it was nothing like his previous work.

There were five or six of these innovations. For example, in the very beginning, he had Her mind is gone, then Baldhead, with that very special introduction. I would say that nobody ever has done anything comparable. And at the time, I was still a little boy so unable to conceive what could possibly make one think in such a way. Later on, he had other departures, the last one being "Big Chief". There's not a single record of which you could say that "Big Chief" originates. I can only relate to "Big Chief" through "Big Chief".

Jacques Périn: Under what circumstances did you meet Professor Longhair for the first time?

65

Toussaint: I first saw him on stage when I was a teenager. I could not get close enough to talk to him at that time. After that I didn't see him again for years. Subsequently he began to work with the stock in a record shop called "One Stop Record Shop". The owner was Joe Santo [Joseph Assunto]. He had more or less taken care of 'Fess in the sense that he was making a few dollars carrying boxes in the back of the shop. And one day as I had gone to "Basin Records" to buy a record, the salesman asked someone to get it from stock. The person who brought my record was none other than Professor Longhair! It didn't occur to me to say to myself 'Oh, he is a store man...', for that I am grateful, my reaction was 'Wow!' He was there, smiling from ear to ear. After this I often went back to this store to see Professor Longhair, but I didn't see him play. But it wasn't until much later, I must have been around 25 [circa 1963], that Professor Longhair came to my office at St. Philip Street and we actually could have a long conversation. And during that time, he had already spoken of me in interviews, after having heard certain records of mine where I made efforts to sound like him. He had mentioned my name, and that really touched me. A few times after that, I had the opportunity to look over his shoulder while he was playing, and I saw his incredible technique. That was a revelation. Subsequently I saw him now and again, up to the Montreux [Switzerland] concert in 1973 [...].

Périn: Did he perform regularly at the Dew Drop?

Toussaint: Not at the "Dew Drop". Not when I was there on a regular basis. He played in several other noisier and flashier places than the "Dew Drop". You see the "Dew Drop" was a little bit too refined for Professor Longhair. It tells you a lot about his life. But after that, I started to see him play, here and there. I went to the "Tipitina", when he was playing, of course." [73]

"Larry Appelbaum: I love how he sings [...] He has this, almost a yodel.

Toussaint: Professor Longhair, of course, he have the strangest yodel you'll ever heard. Also, he's the only one, I've noticed, that will, for some reason, feel the need to jump an octave on one whirl. Like he sing 'In The Night'. [Toussaint demonstrates, plays and sings a couple of bars of the song and jumps an octave on the word, "day"]. I hadn't heard anyone else think that music needs to go that way. I just thought that was fabulous." [74]

Bruce Raeburn (born 1948), former Curator, Hogan Jazz Archive, writer and drummer:
"There was this party several years ago [early 1977] over at Ed's house [Ed Volker], more or less to audition Reggie Scanlon [Scanlan] for Fess's band, and he had this deplorable set of drums, with towels all over the heads and brushes and everything. He had me sit in with Fess and I hadn't really studied his material, but Reggie had, and that was my most embarrassing moment as a drummer!
Fess just rode my ass incessantly! He'd say 'Watch my left foot, watch my left foot!' At one point he just had me clap. 'Don't play drums, just clap!' That was my opportunity to play with Professor Longhair, "he laughs, "and of course, Reggie got the job!" [75]

Reggie Scanlan (born 1952), bass:
"[Fess'] hands were amazing. When we played, I was always right next to his left hand. I used to like to watch him and it was hard to reconcile because it seemed like one person couldn't be doin' all that at one time. He was really quiet and withdrawn and soft-spoken and everything until he got on the piano and then he just really took over. His playing, to me, was everything.

The regular drummer who was playing with him when we got the gig, he was some guy from Canada [Earl Gordon]. So we got on the first gig and this guy tells me, he says, 'Look. This guy makes a lot of mistakes and doesn't know what he's doin' a lot of times, so just follow me and you'll be alright.' And I'm goin'. 'You got to be kiddin'!' This is Fess he's talkin' about! Some guy from Canada.

We were playin' Mobile, Alabama one time when I was playin' with him. Fess had this big Cadillac, pretty beat up. The guitar player was this guy Big Will Harvey. Before they got into the car, they each had a revolver that they brought into the car with them. And they both rode holding a gun underneath the armrest. And when I asked them why they were doin' that, they said, *Well, we're driving through Mississippi.*" [76]

"I could go see the Meters every night. I could go down to the Night Cap on [1700] Louisiana Avenue, and see George Porter, I could see George French ... you had options to see all this music and basically sit at the feet of the guy you wanted to emulate. And so as I came up, because New Orleans is kind of a small, provincial town–in the nineteenth century, yeah, it was the Paris of the New World, but that's, like, a hundred years ago–it really didn't take a whole lot for me to be able to start playing with people like James Booker and Professor Longhair and all these kind of guys.

You played with Professor Longhair?

Yeah, I did, for about a year and a half. I was playing with Eddie Money out in California–this was right before he was getting ready to get famous–and I got a call [early 1977] from Fess and he's like 'I need a bass player, you wanna' play with me?' Because I had jammed with them once before that, and I'm, like, 'I'm on the next plane, man'. So, I told Eddie Money, and he said, 'I can't believe you're going to quit my band to perform with a college professor'. I didn't say this, but I was thinking, 'you know what? That's why' [...].

You also played with Earl King. What was it like for you to play with musicians who had really made it?

I was in Earl King's band for three or four years. It was really interesting getting to work with people whose music you'd learned from the outside, actually working with them and seeing how the process is. It was a real learning experience. Playing with Professor Longhair's band was kind of like grad school for me. To me, any bass player who can keep up with him is doing all right." [77]

"Louis Armstrong had his jazz and stuff, but as far as the R&B, Fess deserves to have a museum, he deserves to have a foundation. He deserves to have his music available for people to either learn or learn about. It's like anything else you wanna learn about: You gotta go to the source." [78]

Theodore Emil "Bo" Dollis (1944-2015), vocals & percussion:
Dollis: "When we were rehearsing for those first two albums [The Wild Magnolias, 1974, & They Call Us Wild, "Barclay", 1975.] We would rehearse at Fess' house on [South] Rampart Street, the one that burnt down. He would get on piano, and you would have to turn and go the way Fess was going. It had that drive to it, irresistible.

You still perform his songs today, "Big Chief" and "Mardi Gras In New Orleans." It's like he wrote those songs for you!

Dollis: Oh yeah. He did so much with the Indian sound, Carnival tunes. Before there were Indian songs recorded, you couldn't wait to hear his music during Mardi Gras[...]." [79]

Alfred "Uganda" Roberts Jr. (born 1943), conga drums:
"Dick Gordon: When did you first get together [with Fess]?

Roberts: Maybe 72 [Perhaps, at the New Orleans Jazz Fest, 1972?]?

Gordon: So, you had eight years together.

Roberts: Yeah.

Gordon: And how did you find each other?

Roberts: There was a guy by the name of Quint Davis. And Quint Davis said, you know who you ought to be drumming with? I bet you'd sound good with Professor Longhair. So, when him and I got together, it was the beginning of a beautiful friendship. There was no rehearsin', we just played together. [A couple of bars is heard of Fess' April, 1974 version of "Tipitina", "Blue Star" / "Barclay"].

Gordon: What was it about his piano and your percussion that worked so well together?

Roberts: The Caribbean sound.

Gordon: Again, the Caribbean sound.

Roberts: 'Cause, he would have trouble with stick drummers, they would never play that rhumba/Caribbean sound that he would like to do [hums two bars of "La Cucaracha", etc.]. And they did never really satisfy him. When I came along, lots of time just him and I would play together, at different venues.

Gordon: And when you did, did you sit close together?

Roberts: I sat next to the piano so I could watch what he was doing and be able to listen.

Gordon: You would just be keeping the bass line for his piano, because it's all over the place. It's wild, it's exiting.

Alfred "Uganda" Roberts, and the author, the Ogden Museum of Southern Art, Camp St. New Orleans, December 11, 2014. Photo: Karina Engman. Used by permission.

Roberts: I would do no solo, no extra riffs no noting, just to keep that thing that made him happy. Because at one time, he used to play the piano and kick the side of it to keep the syncopation going. But the club owners didn't like that. 'He sound good but his tearing my piano, look at my piano it's all beat up' [giggle].

Gordon: How did you know when it was your moment for a solo?

Roberts: It was about one song I did a little solo, I think it was "Doing It". It's a like a strong back beat song [hums the melody]. And then when they had a break I had a chance to [imitates his congas], then go back. But most of the time I didn't solo, I just supported him.

Gordon: Was it OK with you not being the headliner, not being the number one guy?

Roberts: Wonderful for me.

Gordon: Why is that?

Roberts: I didn't get a chance to play with a Caribbean kind of sound band, most of the other bands were strictly jazz. But with Fess, that lil' kind of rhumba sound, and I was satisfied with doing a little rhumba thing, you know [imitates a conga rhythm].

Gordon: Bring out the best of you doing that, all right?

Roberts: Yeah.

Gordon: So, was it hard for you when he died and you didn't have that partnership anymore?

Roberts: Oh yeah, it was very emotional. But I had the capability to play other kinds of music with other people.

Gordon: You played one time for Paul McCartney, somebody told me this.

Roberts: We played at his birthday party on Queen Mary [March 24, 1975]. He gave a party for his wife [Linda]. Paul McCartney was a fan of New Orleans music, so he invited all musicians that were affiliated with Allen Toussaint, come out to Long Beach, California, to the party.

Gordon: So he was big fan of Allen Toussaint's music as well.

Roberts: Yeah. There was only one band to perform, Professor Longhair. Everybody else were special guests. [There were many other acts as well.]

Gordon: Wait a second! One band to perform, at this birthday party, and it was you and Professor Longhair

Roberts: Well, the band [Roberts, "Big Will" Harvey, Robert Harvey,

& Clarence "Juny Boy" Brown]. Allen Toussaint, he didn't go, he figured that after playing. [A couple of bars of "Tipitina" is heard, recorded aboard the ship, without the musician's approval. Released by
"Harvest" Records, UK].

*Gordon: Do you find now, that people now are paying more attention to you,
are any more appreciative of your music etc?*

Roberts: Yeah, 'cause a lot of them realize Fess is dead but they like to
carry his style on. And I am the closest thing that's available to help
'em. So they hire me just to support that sound. I guess they realize
that I was like a fire that enabled Professor Longhair to smoke, you
know. So many words!

*Gordon: I know those congas are big and heavy to drag around. I just wonder
if you ever walk through Congo Square anymore and think of that young
guy: "Bongo Al" sitting there by himself, years ago.*

Roberts: Oh yeah, I go there and look around. I even go to the neighborhood, although don't live in Treme now, but I still go there to see
the old cats and say, what's happenin'?

Gordon: Are there any little kids with little bongo sets playing, even today?

Roberts: No, they're more like traditional music, the second line bands,
trumpets, tubas, the marchin' band kind of sound, that's what they
like.

Gordon: So where's the next Uganda Roberts gonna' come from?

Roberts: That's a good question. But if he's comin' I'm willing to pass
it on to him. But I love it.

Gordon: It's deep inside you now, right?

Roberts: Everybody thought I was crazy, all the drummers in the
neighborhood used sticks, I'm beatin' with my hands, back in the
days.

Gordon: What would they say?

Roberts: Man, how can you beat on them drums with your hands? [A couple of bars of "Big Chief", is heard, including Roberts' congas, from Fess' Crawfish Fiesta recording session, "Alligator"]." [80]

Robert Palmer (1945–1997), writer, and musician:
Palmer roomed down the hall from Fess, South Rampart St., New Orleans, for a couple of days in the early 1970s.

"One night Willie Tee (Turbinton) [Wilson Turbinton: 1944-2007], one of New Orleans' finest soul singers ("Teasin You") and an all-round keyboard master equally at home with blues, classical music, and jazz, settled in for a powwow. He seemed genuinely thrilled when Fess suggested they play some four-handed piano on the battered old upright in our host's funky but comfortable basement rec room, and they jammed for hours. Not once did they clutter the music or get in each other's way. Fess chose the keyboard's bass end and provided tricky but clearly executed and rock-solid rhythm patterns–Afro-Cuban, walking basses, driving boogie-woogie. Tee embroidered modernist chord extensions, delicate filigree, and incisive push-pull counter-rhythms, weaving them into the very fabric of Fess's fundamentals. The feeling in the little room was one of mutual respect and love, fierce concentration, and more than a little magic. When they finished, Fess asked Willie to play "Stormy Weather"[by Harry Arlen & Ted Koehler, 1933] for him, solo, and the rendition that emerged rang in the air; a phantasm of latticework harmonics emerged long after Tee removed his hands from the keyboard.

Late that night, the tinkling, insubstantial ghost of sound woke me from a deep sleep, though the sound was too faint to hear clearly. I opened the door and tiptoed to the head of the stairs. It was Fess, two flights down, alone at the upright in the basement. He was playing some of the strangest music I had ever heard. The right hand-melodies and their bass-register underpinning strained to embrace each other, almost palpably yearning for union, yet the music's tenderness was more than matched by a fitful, bracing discord and unpredictably timed bursts of violent, jabbing frustration. After I'd taken a seat at

73

the top of the stairs and spent some time with this perplexing, other-worldly night music, it finally sorted itself out in my mind and I 'got' it. Fess was trying to play "Stormy Weather," but because he was so purely a bluesman, he was trying to fit the tune's harmonic modulations and serpentine melody into some sequence or combination of the tonic, subdominant, and dominant, the three chords that define the harmonic parameters of the blues. Of course it wasn't working, not in any conventional sense. Yet the effort was so noble, and the soundscape of grinding tonal collisions so expressive and fresh, it was much more than any perfectly articulated showpiece casually tossed off by a virtuoso. I must have listened for hours before I noticed my eyelids drooping and returned to bed, leaving the door open so that the music could insinuate itself into my dreams." [81]

"Johnnie Allen" (John Guillot, born 1938), singer:
"I've always been an ardent fan of New Orleans R'n'B / Rock'n'Roll music. Certainly, Professor Longhair, in my opinion, laid one of the cornerstones for this inspiring musical genre. The giants of this New Orleans sound have emulated and acknowledged his contribution. Sad to say, accolades came to him late in life. What a shame!

I met Fess at Ronnie Scott's in London in 1978 while on a promotional tour for Stiff Record Company. My version of Chuck Berry's 'Promised Land' was garnering attention on the British radio charts.

To relax from that week's arduous promotional tour, Charlie Gillet took me to hear Fess's solo performance. What a thrill that was! The Professor was in rare form. We chatted about everything from red beans and rice, to crawfish etouffée — we had never met until that night — to the impact that the New Orleans sound had on the development of Swamp Pop music in south Louisiana.

Then it was show time at Ronnie Scott's. This little Cajun sat in awe of his performance. He would have been an impossible act to follow. My favorite was "Bald Head". Rock on Fess, wherever you are. My only regret is that I have not been able to obtain any copies of the photos taken of us that night. Just one would be a treasure to my scrapbook collection. Though he's gone, his memory and songs will live on." [82]

Henry "Hank" Drevich (born around 1948), music fan and entrepreneur:
"I was hanging with Fess at the house on [South] Rampart St. with Steve Armbruster, one of my co-conspirators in the Alligator Ball and then Tipitina's. Steve had recently gotten an old piano and was trying to learn. He was asking Fess for lessons. So Fess gave him a lesson.

He sat down at the piano and said, first you have to have a good hip action and Fess rocked on his seat. Then you got to have a good shoulder action and Fess moved his shoulders up & down, side to side, together then individually, mixing it up. Then you need good wrist action and he rocked his wrists so thumbs then pinkies were striking the keys. He said you got all that your fingers will find the right notes, then he just burned it up, clowning a little for us as he looked like a dervish on that piano, all his actions in full gear. THE WHIRL-WIND! Fess had a way to pull more out when he wanted or needed to, he liked to surprise.

Besides Fess the other player who looked so totally physically at one with his music, to my eyes, is Zigaboo, the drummer of the Meters. Now when they were on stage together which was pretty frequent as I always tried to present Fess and the Meters on the same bill for Alligator Balls, the kinetics was awesome." [83]

Fess, and Joseph "Zigaboo" Modeliste (born New Orleans, 1948), at the Dr. John New Orleans Swamp TV Show (WTTW), Chicago, October 30, 1974. For the writer and musician Robert Palmer (1945-1997), Modeliste put it like this: "Fess is the foundation of all New Orleans music since WW II. Every drummer who's made regular gigs in this town has studied him". The late "Smokey" Johnson, was Zig's mentor. Photo and courtesy: Hans Andréasson, used by permission.

Stephen "Steve" Armbruster, (born circa 1950?), artist etc:
"Everybody says Professor Longhair would have been much more famous if he had early on agreed to travel. Only after he resurfaced in the early 1970s did he start accepting many out-of-town-gigs. But, even then, he always exercised caution. He knew the food would not be what he was used to, so he would carry his own supplies. He referred to these as his "Schwegs", after the local chain of the 'world's largest supermarkets [*Schwegmann's*]'. The story is told of how a stewardess once tried to interest him in one of her airplane meals. Fess eyed her suspiciously. He then produced his grocery bag from under the seat and answered, "No thank you, lady, I got my Schwegs." [84]

Alice Walton Byrd:
"We went out one night, and we in the kitchen fixin' a little snack, and we heard some rumblin' upstairs. So he took his forty-five and I had my little thirty-eight and went up there. A man had scaled down the back porch and got through the window. He holler, 'Ooh I'm in the wrong place at the wrong time.' I say, 'Oh yeah, you sure is,' and I wanted to shoot him in the foot but Fess wouldn't let me. He say, 'If you shoot him, you ain't gonna stop shootin' him,' and laughed it off. Fess tells the man, 'Now I want you to climb back out of this window and go the way you come in.' So he got out the window and scaled the back porch again, jumped the shed, and when he got halfway to the alley, that's when Fess stopped him. And he told him, he said, 'Now let me tell you, you go back there and you tell your daddy, your uncle, your brother, your cousin, and your granny about how I'm lettin' you off light but anybody else that come in here, I'm'na kill him.' I haven't had a minute's trouble with nobody tryin' to break in my house since." [85]

John Vidacovich (born 1949), drums, composer, & tutor:
"I was about 27. I had played with him before, substituted. He had a steady drummer for many years from Canada: Earl Gordon. Then Earl had a visa problem and when he left, I became the drummer. There were no rehearsals, I got on the van and we took off from Andy Kaslow's house and went straight up to Washington, D.C. The van broke and me and David Watson got in a little trouble with the police.

76

At first, I thought the gig wasn't going to work because Professor Longhair was so very used to playing with Earl. I was not playing that way at all and I did not want to play that way. I wanted to play the way I grew up hearing him. Once he got used to me and I learned the arrangements a little better, it was solid. Then Fess and I were just beautiful.

By the time '77 came around, I had taken a job with Fess steady, and pretty much the last two years of his life I was his drummer. We traveled all over, up to Canada, New England, New York, all over. We had three sax players, guitar, bass, drums and Fess. On sax we had Tony Dagradi, Andy Kaslow (he married Allison Miner, who managed Fess), and Jim Moore played baritone saxophone. Ronald Johnson played guitar. I played drums. Julius Farmer and then David Watson were on bass (both are dead now), and Alfred "Uganda" Roberts played congas.

He was a great guy to me, taught me a lot of stuff, spent time with me. He would play rhythms on my leg in the van when we were traveling. He was a tap dancer and a drummer, and he could play really fast stuff with his hands. Fess was very funny, liked to play lots of jokes, liked to tell me a lot of things that were not true and then laugh at me when I found out.

He was very much about drums and piano. There was none of this laying-back thing. Shit had to be dancing, it had to be moving, it had to be on the edge. Slightly contradictory to what people think music is around here. There wasn't nothing laid-back about his concept." [86]

"Robert Santelli: Speaking of tradition, you had the opportunity to play behind Professor Longhair. What was that like?

Well, It was cool, you know, 'Fess wanted everything with an edge. He didn't want it lay back into that blue - gray situation. He always wanted me to push it a little harder. If you listen to "Crawfish Fiesta" you'll hear a lot of tunes that are very snap, crackle and pop, but also greasy. There's one tune on that record called "Her Mind Is Gone "that's great. Usually when I listen to something I recorded, I don't like what I hear. But I can listen to that drum track over and over again.

John Vidacovich, on a gig with organ player Joe Krown, Frenchmen St., New Orleans, September 2008. Photograph by the author.

Santelli: Was playing with Fess hard?

At first, yeah. You've got to cop the style, the music has a style of its own; you are secondary. You have to make sure you're doing the music playing the style of the music the way the man wants it to be played. When you take a job playing with Fess you're not worried about expressing yourself, but about doing a good job. Through your good job is the way you express yourself.

It took me about three weeks of being on the road to learn the music; he was a very patient man. He also insisted that the drummer keep him going. Like he told me in the studio, 'Just keep kicking. Keep agoing [sic] right on me. Just keep pushing.' I'd say, 'Okay, Fess. Let's go babe.' [87]

"The rhythms he used, made you adapt to new sounds, like the claves (simulating wooden sticks). The drummer was responsible for more sound; you had to be able to create the effect of a tambourine. You always had to be aware of him rhythmically, especially with his left hand in the lower basic patterns. By using the rumba, he made more of a syncopated, Latino Beat". [88]

"The thing I'll never forget is probably the saddest. It was on a Saturday night, and we had just finished playing. I'd been with Fess about two years. We all went up to the dressing room, and me and David [Lee] Watson were drinking, and we wanted to go back downstairs and get another round of beers. Now Fess, he always drank Coca Cola. He used to call me 'Juwaski, I never knew why. So I said, 'Fess, me and David [Watson] are going down to get some beers, you wanna' Coke?' And Fess said, 'Hey Juwaski, could you get me a rum and Coke?' And I thought, he never had a Rum and Coke. But I said, 'Sure,' so I brought him a rum and Coke. It seemed strange to me right there. So we're up in the dressing room. And the piano he was playing was an old funky upright, and it made his fingernails bleed. And he looked at his hands, and just said, 'Man, when will I ever get to stop playing bad pianos?' And he drank his Rum and Coke and we all went home. And less than a week later, his last record came out, and I got the call that he died. It was his last record and one of his best; the sound was clean, the production was high quality. And he was gone." [89]

Erdine "Gerri" Hall (born 1935), singer; with Rick Coleman, music writer:
Hall: "I had an opportunity to look at a lot of the musicians that I had known. And I have an opportunity even now, to see some of the things about them I had never seen before. The ones that I all liked. Huey [Smith] is like Professor Longhair. They have the music in their fingers, the rhythm to the music is in their fingers […] We've only had three of them in the City like that, Huey Smith, James Booker.

Rick Coleman: Longhair and Allen Toussaint?

Hall: No, Allen adopted that. Excuse me, maybe I'm not supposed to say this. But Allen was not like Booker, Huey, and Professor Longhair. Those have the same type of building when they build the tunes. They put the rhythms with the music, with their hands. And then they give it to the musicians to play it. (Ponderosa Stomp, Friday, September 24, 2010)." [90]

Part two: In Search of Professor Longhair
by Jonas Bernholm *

My search for Professor Longhair started in 1965, when I found a 45' disc on "Watch Records" with Professor Longhair and the Clippers in a second hand store in Stockholm. Sweden's pro-Vietnamese politics made the country a heaven for deserters from the Vietnam War, and in their footsteps interesting records on small US labels followed. Any direct clue that this was a soul or R&B record couldn't be found in the artist's name, apart from the knowledge that many black artists hid behind thrilling pseudonyms like "Lonesome Sundown" or "Dr Horse". But the price was right ($ 0,10), and the title "Willie The Prince" gave association to a fine British R&B recording with Zoot Money ("Teach Me How To Uncle Willie"), so I laid out my money.

"Watch" label 45. Courtesy: John Broven. Used by permission.

Both sides of the record were interesting, and the organ playing [by Edward "Ed" Frank, 1932-1997] stirring. But meanwhile the Revolution of Soul-music rolled on. Every week a new classic was released with an ever-increasing number of fantastic artists. Professor Long-hair had to take a back seat.

A couple of years later "Sue" Records in England released a 45' with Longhair's "Looka' No Hair". I was a member of the "Sue-Island" Records Appreciation Society, and bought almost everything they had released, as my faith in Guy Stevens ability to put together out-standing issues was great. Their records with Huey "Piano" Smith on "Sue" ("ACE") and their fantastic rhythm and nonsense lyrics left me gasping with delight. And this Longhair record was much better than the one on "Watch". In footnotes and subordinate clauses Longhair's name started getting mentioned with reverence in the underground R&B and Blues press. His role as a true pioneer and innovator was getting attention.

When I came to America for the first time he was one of those I was most anxious to meet. The search was organized from my run down room at the Georgian Hotel on Canal, some ten blocks from Bourbon Street, upon my arrival in New Orleans, Monday the 15th of July, 1968. New Orleans was different from most other cities in America. The atmosphere and people were more like in a third world town – like in the Caribbean or in South America. The pace was slow. What didn't have to be done today was done the day after tomorrow, and appoint-ments and time were not kept religiously.

The first stop was the town's leading black radio station WYLD. The nice Gus Lewis, a top DJ, was well read in black history, black power and Soul music. But when hearing Professor Longhair's name he just shrug his shoulders - 'He has quit - it's been a long time since I heard anything about him etc.' In short – Longhair was a has-been. Allen Toussaint and "SANSU" records on the other hand was in. Allen's productions and compositions for Betty Harris, Lee Dorsey and many more had even found their way to Europe. It was my next stop. Allen was not in the office but a young frustrated man with tattoos on his arms, chest and face. It was Aaron Neville whose giant hit "Tell It Like It Is" ("Parlo" Re-cords) had not been followed up the way he wanted. Instead there had been massive legal and artistic problems in rather typical New Orleans fashion.

He took me to the Cosimo Recording Studios [748 Camp Street] where empty sleeves of his LP ("Tell It Like It Is") were scattered everywhere. It was a typical low-budget release where a handful of Aaron Neville's recordings had been filled up with other artist's recordings. Now, the empty sleeves served as hand fans in the summer heat.

Little Sonny [John "Little Sonny" Jones, 1931-1989] was in the studio with the Triple Souls [Inez Cheatham, Mercedes Morris & Sena Fletcher], the girl trio whose wonderful voices can be heard on all New Orleans Soul Classics from this era. Eddie Bo, [Edwin Bocage], the producer walked around with a briefcase and his processed hair neatly covered with a turban. Al Scramuzza, shrimp-fisher but also owner of "Scram" Records was there. Our spirits were lifted by some "Rock and Rye" [Whiskey] and before Aaron left, we decided to meet that night at the Ivanhoe piano bar [601 Bourbon, corner of Toulouse St.]. When Little Sonny finished, Wardell Quezerque showed up with a young black soul-singer. I think the finished recording was called something like "Mr Teardrop". I liked it slightly better than Sonny's tune.

At the Ivanhoe Aaron's brother Art and the Neville Sounds were the attractions. They did OK, but I felt that they were lacking that little extra something, and their version and new recording of "Bo Diddley" was pretty ordinary, compared to Bo's original ["Checker", 1955].

I was already feeling at home on the Bourbon Street. Appearing nightly was Clarence "Frogman" Henry, and at the billboard outside the club were large photos of "Frogman" and the Beatles taken during their tour. At the Court of Two Sisters, Roosevelt Sykes and Cousin Joe shared the piano while Frankie "Sea Cruise" Ford held residence at another piano bar. At "Al Hirt's", the top nightclub of Bourbon St. [corner of St. Louis], Fats Domino was with his band.

Despite repeated visits at the Sansu office [1211 St. Phillips St., Treme], Allen Toussaint had not turned up and Marshall Sehorn [1934-2006] was still out of town. But Clarence Henry told me one night about the Dew Drop Inn. Professor Longhair made no appearances at that time, but that was the place to find Huey Smith.

When I arrived, the stage was empty and the band of that evening was unknown to me. And Huey Smith was not sitting in the bar. I continued to the Night Cap, but drew a blank also there. At my next visit to "Sansu" I met Aaron again, and also his brother Cyril. We played some table tennis together and after a while soul-singer Eldridge Holmes turned up. He was not as together or interested in physical fitness as the Neville family members were.

Allen Toussaint finally turned up, but he didn't have time to talk but a few minutes. I still remember his characterization of Professor Longhair who really impressed him as a musician, but he felt that as a person I would find him boring and taciturn.

That night I went to the Sands [801 Jefferson Highway] at the outskirts of New Orleans. Irma Thomas was scheduled to appear there but not until tomorrow I was told. A Puerto Rican musician gave me a lift to the Dew Drop, but nothing happened there so we went to the Shadowland where we found Irma Thomas in the audience. And she was persuaded to go on stage and sing eight songs.

The artist of the evening was John Williams [1938 – killed in 1972], and Irma was not advertised. Johnny was also called "Scarface" after being attacked with a knife, but he didn't use it as his stage name. He had a past as a "Clown" with Huey Smith, but now he was a fine soul-artist building his show on James Brown.

Irma Thomas impressed me tremendously and when I told her about my disappointment that she had not sung "Ruler Of My Heart", she promised to do it at the Sands [801 Jefferson Highway] next day so I went there. After another unforgettable evening at the club with a rather large white audience, the singer Oliver Morgan, who closed his show walking around in the audience with an umbrella, gave me a lift home.

My visit to New Orleans was coming to an end. Next stop was Don Robeyland — Houston. I went back to the Cosimo studio where I met Joe Banashak ("Instant" Records), who produced a red headed Garland Hilton and the ever-present Triple Souls. The three girls were a little angry with Joe, as he had fallen behind in his payments

Inside New Orleans, February 19, 1966. Courtesy: Amistad Research Center, Tulane University. "The Professor Longhair show hit Mobile, Alabama with bang at the Jolly Pot [1213 Mobile St.]." Same source: June 5, 1965. "The Autocrat Club, it was a question of complexion—they'd hold a brown paper bag up, and if you was darker than the bag, they wouldn't let you in. The guy that ran it, he was kind of passé á blanc. And Edwin "Beansie" Fauria had something to do with it." Lionel Batiste Sr. September 2001. Courtesy: Keeping The Beat On The Street, by Mick Burns.

to them they felt cheated. After the recording we went to his of-fice/warehouse where all 45s were neatly piled up on the floor. He gave me a bundle of promotion 45s and the phone number to Huey Smith. That evening at *the Ivanhoe* I met Allen Toussaint with Mar-shall Sehorn who despite his young age already was a record busi-ness veteran who had worked with Bobby Robinson before forming a partnership with Allen Toussaint. Perhaps the two already then had the vision of producing a group like the Meters sometime in the future. We walked together to Clarence Henry's club before ending up at a West-Indian Club, where Allen sat down at the piano and played Caribbean Music for a while.

NOLA recording star Curley Moore is a former vocalist with Huey Smith and the Clowns. Curley is staring with Chris Kenner at the Blue Top Inn. He also toured with Etta James, Jackie Wilson and many other top stars. For many years Curley worked with Joe Tex, Earl King and Raymond Lewis. Working with these stars has made him a well seasoned and polish-ed entertainer, in fact, Curley Moore is one of the most dynamic personalities in show business today.

Inside New Orleans, May 15, 1965. Courtesy: Amistad Re-search Center, Tulane University.

After a while Fats Domi-no came in for a visit be-tween his own shows at Al Hirt's. I had also run into members of Domi-no's band visiting Clar-ence Henry. Fats was most elegantly dressed with his gigantic star shaped clock and ring with diamonds and sil-ver stains on his tie. Mar-shall wanted to buy me a Mint Julep (immortal-ized by the Clovers) [and many decades earlier Jelly Roll Morton], but it wasn't on the drink list.

At my last day in New Orleans, things finally started to happen. I called Huey Smith and we decided to meet late that night. He was going to rehearse with his new group "the Hueys" that evening. I went to Sansu to meet Marshall and "Curley" Moore [June Moore, 1943-1985], a singer of fine promise (and also a former member of Huey "Piano" Smith's Clowns). Then Marshall took me to Huey's small two-room flat where he lived with his light-skinned wife and two kids. Huey had heard that a young white kid was looking for him at the Dew

Drop and he was afraid that Johnny Vincent ("ACE" Records) or the Internal Revenue was out to get him, he told me. On his broken down piano Huey had an old publicity picture of himself that he gave to me after the, five hour interview. Huey, who had a fantastic memory, told me about his own career, and his idol and inspiration Professor Longhair.

It was Huey's opinion that if Professor Longhair had been better managed it was he, and

Huey Piano Smith. A publicity photo, late 1950s. Courtesy Jonas Bernholm & the Jefferson mag. Used by permission.

not Fats Domino, who would have had all those million sellers. We parted company at 3 o'clock in the morning. And I walked home.

Next day Marshall Sehorn took me to the airport. On the way we passed both Fats Domino's and Lee Dorsey's houses and paid a visit to Lee Dorsey's workshop/junkyard. Marshall was preparing a national tour with Lee to launch: "Four Corners Part 1 & 2" ("AMY") as the next major dance craze.

In [June] 1973 the Professor came to Europe for the second time. The place was Montreux, Switzerland and he was going to be backed by The Meters (with Art Neville).

The reputation as the Robert Johnson of New Orleans R&B had finally caught up with him, and everybody was excited.

During the day rehearsal, Longhair sat half asleep in a far corner be-hind the stage while the Meters practiced. Allen Toussaint was right. Longhair was a man of very few words, but he seemed very kind and gentle.

Art Neville, George Porter (of the Meters), and Fess, Montreux, Switzerland, Saturday, June 30, 1973. Photograph: Jan Ytterberg. Used by permission.

I guess Marshall Sehorn, who was there too, and the others in charge simply saw the Professor as an added attraction to the Meters who were going to be recorded live on stage. But when Longhair played the introduction to his classic hit songs like "Looka No Hair", or "Mardi Gras In New Orleans" the audience went crazy with delight before the Meters suddenly stumped in with their heavy bass-lines making it difficult to hear his singing and playing. This made the audience angry and they did everything to make the Meters play less obtrusive. And it was repeated several times until the Meters had to stop playing altogether, and Longhair could play all by himself to the delight of the audience.

Later we had the pleasure of hearing him many more times, as he became a frequent and very popular visitor to these shores. (Bernholm in 1999.)

Bernholm also added the following observation on the concert in Montreux, Switzerland, June 30, 1973.

There was a large cry out to hear Fess live. No one had heard him live before in Europe. He was just a legend. And nobody knew how good, or bad he was? Once we sat there in the concert hall, one heard his wonderful piano introductions, but then the Meters begun playing, and drowned both Fess' piano and vocals. They played just too loud. At the rehearsal earlier on the same day it was the Meters that only got to play. They went through all the bass lines and everything else, while Fess sat half asleep behind the stage. I don't think that he rehearsed at all. On the whole there was a lack of respect towards Longhair. Had he taken part of the rehearsal, they had obviously done a sound-check, and balanced the sound. Now, it seemed as they [the "Atlantic" records people], at all costs, wanted to record a Meters LP, but forgot Longhair. I think the audience understood that, and became angry. Anyway, that's what I became.

Jonas Bernholm and Ruth Brown (1928-2006), Stockholm, June 1980. Courtesy Jonas Bernholm. Used by permission.

* Jonas Bernholm was born 1946, in Stockholm, Sweden. He was one of the first to re-issue mainly black R&B from the 1940s and early 1950s with historically significant acts such as: Roy "Good Rockin'" Brown, Charles Brown, Paul Gayten, Wynonie Harris, Ivory Joe Hunter, Amos Milburn, Ella & Buddy Johnson, Julia Lee, Nelly Lutcher, Ruth Brown, Lucky Millinder, and Billy Wright, to name but a few. Bernholm's first label was formed in 1976. Over the years he released around 150 LPs of music that had been largely ignored by black music fans. Jonas traveled widely in the US in 1968 in a search for African-American R&B and Soul music artists. He also produced a couple live recordings while arranging European tours for a selected group of artists, for instance Roy Brown, Ruth Brown, Charles Brown, Floyd Dixon, and Nappy Brown. The Smithsonian Institution harbors "eight cubic feet of documents relating to Jonas Bernholm's lifelong interest and work promoting black American music". In 2016, a book on Bernholm was published: Resan mot rockens rötter, by Jan Kotschack, Premium Publishing.

2. WALTER NELSON SR. AND FAMILY

I.

Walter Nelson Sr. was an influential but little-remembered New Orleans guitarist, who went by, for instance, the nickname "Black Walter." [1] He and his wife Edna raised eight children in the Treme neighborhood, including musical sons Walter "Papoose" Nelson, Jr., Lawrence "Prince La La" Nelson, and daughter Dorothy Mae Nelson. She married singer, drummer and composer: Jessie "Ooh Poo Pah Doo" Hill (1932-1996). [2] Ostensibly talking about Walter Nelson, Jr., Fess was quick to acknowledge Walter Nelson, Sr. as a source of inspiration:

Papoose was with me in '49, he didn't stay with me but he lived around the corner from me. His daddy was a help to me, a pretty wise old man, his name was Walter Nelson too. And by him taking up so much time with me, showing me bars and different things through his guitar which [sic] I was playing the piano. So I didn't figure it was no more than right to help his son out. I couldn't teach him how to play his guitar with what he was doing, but I could teach him how the thing goes that I had in mind. But he was about the best guitar player, he was clever, it didn't take him long. His father still is a musician [in March 1978], *he can play majors, minors, ain't nothing to him. He's got that old lick, and he inspired me so much with his music as my mother's playing. All the way back in them days that's what they was playing, clear bass and straight strong picking.* [3]

Walter Nelson Sr. was born in 1904 in Verrettville (now Verret), Louisiana, in St. Bernard Parish, some eighteen miles east of New Orleans. [4] His older brother Henry "Stacks" Nelson (ca.1897-ca.1940) was also a guitar player. The Nelson family moved to New Orleans around 1914. Nelson Sr. started playing banjo and guitar in 1922. He eventually studied for half a year with Manuel "Fess" Manetta (1889-1969), who taught him how to read music. Manetta was a famous musician and music teacher who lived at 410 LeBeouf St., across the river in Algiers.

Nelson Sr. played his first professional job at the Silver Star (corner of

St. Bernard Avenue and St. Claude Street) with clarinetist "Kid" Ernest Moliere (ca. 1900-1952) and trumpeter Herb Morand (1905-1952). [5] The German researcher Karl Gert zur Heide, told that Moliere used to slap-tongue his horn, and his special stunt was to take the clarinet apart while still playing. [6] It is likely that Kid Ernest was the leader of a band that Jessie Hill used to sit in with on drums, around 1947. Hill called him "Kid Arnestine." [7]

In the late 1930s, Walter Nelson Sr., jobbed in a trio with singer-guitarist Smiley Lewis (Overton A. Lemons, 1913-1966) and Edward "Noon" Johnson (1903-1969). Nelson Sr. claimed to have taught both Smiley Lewis and Noon Johnson on guitar. Johnson also sang and played the bazooka, a huge, homemade trombone-like invention. They used to play for tips in the joints along South Rampart Street, and sometimes on Bourbon Street, prior to its heyday. Nelson, Sr. penned a couple of original songs, including "Walter's Blues."[8]

The mid-1940s saw Nelson Sr. perform with clarinetist George Lewis (1900-1968), drummer Joe Watkins (1900-1969), and bass player "Slow Drag" Pavageau (1888-1968). Another was Herbert Morand (1905-1952) of the Harlem Hamfats fame. The Chicago-based recording group and perhaps a precursor to 1940s and 50s R&B bands. "Kid" Morand returned to his city of birth in 1941, after traveling around and staying for some years in the Windy City. He recalled playing with Walter Nelson, Sr. at the Silver Star, St. Bernard and Annette (or Urquhart Street), in 1945. Joe Watkins was the bandleader for a while, and Pensacola, Florida-born Sadie Goodson played the piano. The celebrated New Orleans born reed player Sidney Bechet (1898-1959) sat in on a memorable night, early 1945.

In his Hogan Jazz Archive interview, Walter Nelson Sr. spoke about working at the H&J Bar with "Brother Cornbread," i.e., Joseph Thomas (1902-1981). Ralston Crawford captured "Black" Walter Nelson's band on a photograph, 1953, taken at the Club High Hat, in Treme. Rarely recorded Leroy Thompson (1913-1986) was on trumpet. He sometimes played with Nelson's band, at Picou's dance hall on N. Robertson St. I recall Leroy from my New Orleans sojourn 1969-70, kind and friendly, and always eager to jam. Nelson, Sr. stated that he taught many on guitar, including both of his musical sons and also

The H&J Bar, (St. Bernard Ave.?) 1948. Unkown, drums; James Ursin, Joseph "Cornbread" Tomas; Walter Nelson Sr., amplfied Gibson guitar. Photo: Nick Gagliano. Courtesy: *The Jazzfinder '49*.

the wonderful singer Smiley Lewis. In 1952, he went to Nashville, Tennessee, with Lewis, in a small outfit that included pianist Isidore "Tuts" Washington and drummer Cornelius "Tenoo" Coleman, (of the Fats Domino band). Lewis later cut a remake of the Harlem Hamfats big seller, "Oh Red!"

Bass drum player and singer "Uncle" Lionel Batiste (1932-2012) recalled that, "right there on St. Philip and Burgundy was a barroom called the Honey Dripper. That's where Smiley Lewis, Cousin Joe, and Walter Nelson [Sr.] played. Walter was living across the street, in a rooming house called Monkey Puzzle." [9] Around 1936, Nelson, Sr. linked up with jazz clarinet pioneer Alphonse Picou (1878-1961), the proprietor of Picou's Bar and Grill, Treme. He was a well-educated musician, comfortable with classical music as well as jazz. Nelson, Sr. played music and tended bar at Picou's. On weekends, Picou fronted a trio, and sometimes a larger band, in the dancehall section of the place – right up until the day he died.

While in New Orleans in the fall of 1957, the late "Big" Peter Deuchar, a British banjo player, then 25 years old, got in touch with Picou and Walter Nelson, Sr. In spite of the prevailing segregation laws of the time. Picou asked:

Walter Nelson, his guitarist and bartender and myself to accompany him [at Picou's place], and for about an hour he played soft, slow blues on his famous silver-belled clarinet, whilst his daughter, who managed the bar for him, and the customers stood enchanted, for he very rarely played.

I shall never forget the coolness of the room, which sheltered us from the blazing Louisiana sun, and the haunting notes that flowed from his clarinet, as he played the blues which he had known for so many years [...]

But the moment that stand outs more than any other was when one night quite late towards the end of my stay. Kid Sheik asked me to go with him round to Picou's place, as there was a dance and all kinds of festivities going on. So after a couple of beers at Local 496 of the Musicians Union on North Clayborne Avenue, we went round to have a look. The place was packed, and although I was the only white man in building, I was fortunately well enough known by then for there to be no objection to my being there, even from Policeman on duty. Walter Nelson invited me up into the high balcony bandstand that runs the down the side of the place, and I looked down on a veritable sea of black glistering faces.

The band was playing a tremendous rocking rhythm and blues beat which is the present-day music of that part of the Crescent City. And after a while there was hurried whisper 'High Society' and the band went into a half-tempo version of the old march [...] [10]

In January 1960, a fire destroyed Luthjen's beer parlor and dance hall, downtown, 1200 Franklin Avenue. Walter Nelson Sr.'s guitar and amplifier were also ruined. And the mother and son who ran the place died in the fire. [11] Nelson, Sr. had performed in the band at Luthjen's, the final Friday night. Its bandstand was suited for a four or five-piece band. Trumpeter Walter "Blue" Robertson, pianist Sammy Hopkins, and a drummer (by the surname "King") seem to have been Walter's fellow musicians. The place was commonly referred to as "The old folks home." UK trumpeter Ken Colyer described it in 1952, as a "wonderful, dingy old dance hall with dancing in front of the band and tables either side." [12] At the time of the fire, it was one of the few remaining neighborhood bistros with live jazz music on weekends.

Alphonse Picou's funeral in early February 1961 was one of the largest held in the city to date. Picou's bartender-guitarist was prominent

Picou building, Ursuline Ave. Nov. 2012. Photo by the author. The plaque on the wall states: "PICOU RES-IDENCE. Alphonse Picou (1879-1961), clarinetist, composer, and sometime bandleader, lived here at 1601 Ursuline Ave. from 1960 to 1961. He and his daughter, Olga Picou, owned the building which housed alternatively or concurrently many uses. These included a residence for Olga Picou, a private bar/hangout for musicians officiated by guitarist "Black Walter" Nelson on part of the second floor, a grocery store, and ultimately a restaurant and bar on the first floor. Picou was famous as an early pioneer of jazz, for his transposition of the "High Society" piccolo solo for clarinet, as a member of both the early Tuxedo Brass Band and the later Papa Celestin Band, and for his playing at the Paddock Lounge on Bourbon Street in the 1940's and 1950's, serving occasionally as the bandleader. N.O. Jazz Commission. Preservation Resource Center.

Walter Nelson Sr. Picou's funeral. Gift of Mrs. Abbie Kay, April 4, 1988. Courtesy: Hogan Jazz Archive, Tulane University. Used by permission.

in the funeral procession, and he can be seen in newsreel footage. [13] Photographs of Walter Nelson, Sr. holding Picou's clarinet were published in *Ebony* and *Sepia* magazines, [14] as well as various newspapers: "The Eureka Brass Band plays slowly a hymn to escort hearse with body of jazz clarinetist Alphonse Picou into ceremony for New Orleans, La., burial. Clarinet to be placed on grave is carried by Walter Nelson." [15]

Then tired old Walter Nelson [Sr.], guitar man in Picou's band and close friend for 30 years who slept on a pallet on the floor beside his maestro's bed in the last few months of his illness, sat heavily on the stone steps and declared with finality: "My old pal Peak has gone and left me here." In his hand, Walter held Picou's E Flat Clarinet [B Flat Clarinet] with the odd saxophone-like bell. He carried it through the streets thrust before him for all to see. It was Walter who remained to tell of the wonderful rapport Picou must have had with his Maker "long before he broke his arm six months ago and got sick." Said Walter: "Over the years I've heard him pray in the middle of the night and he called Jesus his 'darling'. Shortly before the wake of the night before. Picou's daughter Olga, her grown son Edward Waples of Los Angeles and Walter had sat in the nearby deserted room barroom to discuss what made Picou a great musician. "He was thorough in everything he did, whether it was music or building a house," Olga stoutly insisted. "I think it was because he played music out of his heart," his grandson said. Walter had shaken his head negatively and said simply: "God almighty made him a great musician."

Back at Picou's bar the post-funeral celebration continued in a way only New Orleanians know how to infuse with their suffering and pain. On the bandstand a group of musicians in their twenties were playing the hot Dixieland that was their heritage. And on guitar was Walter Nelson's son Bubu [sic],

taught to play by Picou whose first instrument was the guitar. ["Papoose"
Nelson was 29 years old, February 1961] *Below the stand was a tight mass
of dancers, sweating and undulating. There was "buck dancing" and, in the
midst of it all, was one of five white University of Pennsylvania students in a
Brooks Brothers suit trying to duplicate the gyrations of dancers around him.*

*At six in the evening the dancers and music stopped and all eyes turned to
the barroom television. It was time for the news and there flashed the parade
of that afternoon, followed by some film of one of Picou's last performances
[1958]. Each viewer automatically went into a dance on the spot where he
stood and someone shouted: 'I told you he ain't dead. There he is big as life!
Look at him!'* […] [16] *Ebony Magazine,* May 1961.

In April 1980, Nelson Sr. attended a funeral with music by a pick-up
brass band that included Milton Batiste and Kid Sheik Cola. He introduced the late Belgian New Orleans music buff, Marcel Joly, to Walter
Nelson, Sr. The band marched to the New Caldonia Inn. The local
writer Jason Berry, recalled Lionel Batiste's story of a funeral that he
organized for the Caldonia itself:

*With the destruction of 12 square blocks of housing in the 1960s to clear the
land that eventually became Louis Armstrong Park, the San Jacinto Club
and other hubs of the culture were bulldozed into memory. In an interview,
several years ago, Uncle Lionel told me of the memorial he organized for another casualty, the Caldonia Inn, a magnet for the second-line parade clubs.
Professor Longhair took his stage name at the Caldonia. Louis Armstrong
stopped there during his '49 ride as King of Zulu. Uncle Lionel Batiste had
a day job in a funeral home on Rampart Street "when they buried the Caldonia, tore it down" [ca. 1980?]. He orchestrated a funeral for the club as
it moved to another building, called New Caldonia. Uncle Lionel situated
a mannequin garbed as a weeping widow on a bench at the bar, borrowed
a casket from the mortuary and lined it with velvet. "I was the corpse," he
said dryly of his role, lying in the casket as pallbearers followed the Olympia
Brass Band playing dirges for the Caldonia Inn.* [17]

The Times-Picayune newspaper reported that Walter Nelson Sr. died
in his home, January 22, 1984, after a lengthy illness. He was 79 years
old. The guitarist was honored with a traditional brass band funeral.
[18] He left no known recordings.

II.

"Honey Boy Otis", the Dream Room, Bourbon St., 1958. He cut the "Federal" recordings. Photo Ralston Crawford. Courtesy: Hogan Jazz Archive, Tulane University. Used by permission. In NYC, April 1972, he was recorded with Fess, on a so far unissued session. The musicians included: Earl Turbinton, alto; Snooks Eaglin, guitar; & George Davis, bass, produced by John Hammond (Blues Unlimited, No. 92, June 1972).

Walter "Papoose" Nelson Jr. was Fats Domino's guitarist for some seven years. Fess claimed to have placed Nelson, Jr. with Fats, "because I didn't have any work. He'd come back if I needed him. The last place we played together was the High Hat Club,"(former Gypsy Tea Room). [19] The reason for his American Indian nickname, "Papoose," is open to speculation.

December 1951 marks the first time "Papoose" recorded, on a session for Fess. They cut the slow twelve-bar "K.C. Blues" ("Federal" 12061. Fess; Charles Burbank, tenor; "Papoose", guitar; "Bill" Sinigal, bass; & Charles "Honey Boy" Otis, drums). Unfortunately, the track was ruined by Nelson's out-of-tune instrument. On his friendship with Nelson Jr., Mac Rebennack related:

I started going down to watch Fats Domino playing at the Cadillac Club [Mike Tessitore's place, St. Claude St. and Poland Avenue], *I used to drive Papoose crazy standing in front of him all night, watching how his hands went. When the band came off I wouldn't let him go get high with the rest of the band, I used to ask him to teach me how to do that stuff. He'd be dragged because he was a guy who used to like to be high. He would get up in the morning and drop four bennies, five redbirds, drink a bottle of beer, smoke some weed and shoot some heroin, that'd be just to wake him up in the morning.*

97

I got to be tight with Papoose, and he was a cat who liked to enjoy life to the utmost. But he had a very miserable life, he was put down by everybody, cut loose by his family, and he had nobody but music. And his only side-kick from music was dope. But he was the most lovable sweet cat I have ever met. No matter how much I bugged him, he'd never tell me to get lost, he'd always show me something. Other people didn't like to have me around, they'd tell me get away from here white boy, what you tryin' to do, get me busted? From Paps I learned how to comp, how to play what was needed in a song. [20]

The late brass band drummer Lionel Batiste put it this way: "Papoose was a better player than his daddy, except for the blues – you can't beat those old men for playing the blues. He had a little brother – they called him Prince La La – he had in mind that he could play better than Papoose, but he couldn't ... People would come from outside the Tremé to play. Like the dance nights on the weekend. They used to go in the yard at the Monkey Puzzle and practice." [21]

Ten years after his initial recording session with Fess, "Papoose" recorded with Herb Hardesty's band (actually Fats Domino's band), maybe Nelson Jr.'s very last recordings. [22] His vocal on the shuffle blues, "Why Did We Have to Part," displays a confident singer and he executes some fine rhythm guitar. Composer credits are given to Hardesty and Nelson. The A-side is the Hardesty-penned "The Chicken Twist," a tight instrumental with a "Bo Diddley" type of beat. The idiosyncratic rhythm pattern, related to the clave beat, and common in almost all genres of New Orleans music.

Walter "Paps" Nelson Jr. died of a heroin overdose in the celebrated Theresa Hotel, Harlem, NYC, on February 28, 1962. He was found with a syringe in his arm – on a tour with Fats Domino. [23] Walter Nelson Jr. was only 29 years old – married to Earline Hall Nelson and the father of four children. [24] The large funeral took place in his hometown on March 10, with music furnished by Dejan's Olympia Brass Band. [25] In 1962, this brass band was the only one that dared venture into Treme, Mick Burns told. The other parade bands were too scared. [26] Invited were the family, relatives, friends, and members the American Federation of Musicians Local No. 496 and the Fats Domino band. [27] The funeral procession started at Picou's Restaurant & Bar. When the mourners came out of the bar, they met an enormous crowd. Fats's band was on tour; hence they missed the funeral. In the

Cornelius Coleman, Herb Hardesty, Fats Domino & "Papoose" Nelson. From the movie: "Shake Rattle and Rock", 1956. A publicity photo.

later part of the parade, a marshal known as "Little Eleven" became so "juiced" that he had trouble standing. [28]

Dave Bartholomew recalled "Papoose" as a "great guitar player. Oh he was out of sight. It was a shame, the boy died in his 20s, very young." [29] Nelson Jr. cut something like 70 recordings with Fats Domino, from 1951 until 1958. "Papoose" can be seen with Fats' band in a couple of films, among them "Shake Rattle and Rock" (1956) and "The Big Beat" (1958). "Papoose" toured Jamaica in early 1961 with Domino. The guitarist also waxed with Bartholomew and Clarence "Frog Man" Henry.

III.

Lawrence "Prince La La" Nelson, vocal and guitar, is mainly known for his fine recording of "She Put The Hurt On Me," cut in June 1961 for "A.F.O." Records. [30] Nat Perrilliat and Red Tyler, saxophones; Harold Battiste, piano; "Chuck" Badie, stand-up bass; and John Boudreaux, drums, were the session musicians. "La La's performance in the vocal booth was outstanding," said Battiste. "He exceeded all our expectations and invoked the spirit that made magic in the studio that day." [31] The song made it to number

28 on Billboard's R&B chart . In a 1979 interview, Fess told Andy Kaslow that he had trained Prince La La to sing, in the same way that he did many other kids, and some of them became pretty famous, too. [32] Fess pronounced his nickname as "Prince La Lá."

Courtesy Hogan Jazz Archive, Tulane, University (with thanks to Alaina Hébert). Used by permission.

Guitarist and singer "Deacon" John Moore (born 1941) recalled:

I used to go over by Papoose and Prince La La (Lawrence Nelson), who was his brother. I saw Papoose, Prince La La and his daddy passing the guitar around, drinking that white port and lemon juice, down at Picou's Bar. I was too young to be in there, but I would sneak in there in the daytime and just sit there and be watching them. One would be playing and one would grab the guitar and say, 'No, this is how it goes,' or the other one would take the guitar and say 'No, you playing that wrong – this is how it go.' [33]

Moore declared that he used to visit the Nelson brothers at their mother Edna's place. Deacon John claimed to be the guitarist on "She Put The Hurt On Me" (while Battiste cites Roy Montrell).

It seems Prince La La inspired Mac Rebennack's "Dr. John" persona. [34] La La's recording of the song "Need You" is an interesting illustration of that. [35] Rebennack suggested that the Nelson family "never wanted anybody becoming a professional musician, which was the lowest thing you could be in their eyes. I wouldn't be surprised if the family had something to do with his [Prince La La] being killed, there was always a lot of feuding among them." [36] Lawrence Nelson died in New Orleans in October 1963, only 27 years old. [37] The cause of death remains unclassified. His complete recorded output consists of around five songs. Like the rest of the Nelson family, he is buried in Holt Cemetery, near City Park.

Oliver Morgan (1933-2007), singer and pianist, was a friend of the Nelson family since the mid-1940s. He penned and recorded a song about Prince La La's death titled "Who Shot the La La?" Morgan provided Jeff Hannusch with this summary account of the Nelson family of New Orleans guitarists:

Papoose played more like his father... They played a lot of heavy chords. I wouldn't say that La La was as good of a player as Papoose — Papoose was a legend around here. But La La really played a funk style of guitar before funk got popular.

Believe it or not, I'd go by their house and play Charles Brown tunes like 'Driftin' Blues' and 'Trouble Blues' on the piano and they'd all play guitar behind me. It was something.

I never knew La La to do anything but play music. He played a lot at a place called Picou's which was on St. Philip. Miss Edna owned the joint – she was the woman La La's father stayed with. When I played in there with him and Jessie Hill, the place would be packed. [38]

This is a slightly reworked, and extended version of a piece, first published in: The Jazz Archivist: A newsletter of the William Ransom Hogan Jazz Archive: Volume XXVI, 2013. Thanks to Lynn Abbott, Hogan Jazz Archive, Tulane University, New Orleans La., for his invaluable help.

3. TWO INTERVIEWS

Fess at Quint Davis' home, Esplanade Avenue, October 17, 1974. Fess was once apologized to because the piano he had to play was out-of-tune – he answered that out-of-tune pianos were his specialty, so forget it! Photo by Hans Schweitz.

Hans Andréasson, Tommy Löfgren, and Hans Schweitz, from Stockholm, Sweden, conducted the first of the two interviews. It took place in New Orleans, October 17, 1974, at the home of Quint Davis, Fess' manager. Andréasson noticed Fess' trouble with his legs. Davis declared that Fess was very shy and disliked interviews; hence the manager advised the interviewers to hide the microphone! The result was, unfortunately, a recording with an extremely poor sound. A couple of decades later, Schweitz told how the interview came about:

"In October 1974, we made our second trip to the Crescent City and spent some days at Sansu Records/Sea-Saint Studios [3809 Clematis

Avenue], where we met and interviewed Earl King. We also got in touch with Quint Davis, who promised to set up a date for an interview. First he invited us to his home on Esplanade [Avenue] to give us a pre-listen to a new album that Longhair had just recorded, with Gatemouth Brown on guitar and violin on some tracks. It was produced for the French Blue Star label and produced by Philippe Rault ("Rock ´n´ Roll Gumbo", Blue Star 80.606). It sounded really good and we looked forward to meet Longhair the next day, October 15.

We heard nothing from Quint the following day and thought that he had forgotten us. Instead the evening was spent at Easy Eddie´s on St. Peters listening to Cousin Joe and when he finished his set at 01.30 the next morning we decided to give Quint another call. He had been at home together with Longhair all day but forgot to get in touch with us. We decided to meet in the afternoon the following day at Quint´s place. Until then we rented a car and took a ride into the countryside of Louisiana before heading back to See-Saint studios to interview Lee Dorsey. Then back to Quint´s place, with no AC. Here we met Longhair again, the last time was at the Montreux Festival the year before. He was as friendly as we remembered him and very relaxed. We conducted our interview and afterwards Quint said that he was a bit surprised as Longhair most of the time just answered questions with a short 'yes' or 'no'. 'Well, sometimes it comes to me,' he said." [1]

The indecipherable parts of the interview are marked: " / ... / "

Hans Schweitz: We don't know too much about you in Sweden. I think we could speak about the old times? When where you born?
Fess: I was born in 1918 in Bogalusa, Louisiana.

Schweitz: And how did you come in touch with music?
Fess: Well most of my family played.

Schweitz: Church music!
Fess: Both.

Schweitz: Did you start to play piano?
Fess: I started to dance in medicine shows, then I started to get interested in piano. I found out that you could get more money. All I was

interested in was work, at that time.

Schweitz: So you worked as a dancer first.
Fess: Yeah!

Schweitz: Was that on medicine shows.
Fess: I didn't like 'em / ... /

Löfgren: How old where you when you started on piano?
Fess: I was about ten.

Schweitz: Was there anyone you did listen to?
Fess: Oh yeah, I'd listen to quite a few. I had quite a few teachers. I took all of their ideas and made a gumbo out of it. I played a little from all of them first plus / ... /

Schweitz: Were you still in Bogalusa then, or?
Fess: Well, like I said I was born in Bogalusa, my mother [Ella Mae Byrd] [2] left there when I was two.

Schweitz: Who were the famous piano players in town during that time?
Fess: There were quite a few: Rocky Sullivan [3], Kid Stormy Weather [Edmond Joseph], Ray Charles wasn't around. "Tuts" [Isidore Washington], "Archibald" [John Leon Gross], but / ... / travelin' like Charles Brown and Amos Milburn.

Schweitz: Did you play as a solo act or did you have anyone backing you?
Fess: No, I was a one-man thing.

Schweitz: Did you play the same of type of songs as you later recorded?
Fess: No, I changed, I could take a blues and make a jump thing out of it. I'll take a jump song and make a ballad out of it.

Löfgren: Did you play blues?
Fess: Not for myself. I like to listen to other people's struggles, yeah that's all blues is struggle, struggle music, to give it a termination.

Schweitz: To me, your records have some kind of Latin feel in the beat!
Fess: Take your mind off from being blue, huh!

```
WATCH FOR THE GRAND OPENING
CALDONIA NITE CLUB
Formerly Japanese Tea Garden
UNDER SAME MANAGEMENT
MIKE TESSITORE, Prop.

ST. PHILIP AND ST. CLAUDE STS.        MA. 9114
VISIT NIGHTLY THE CALDONIA INN
```

Louisiana Weekly, January 15 1947. Courtesy: Amistad Research Center, Tulane University.

Schweitz: Did you call yourself Professor Longhair then?
Fess: No, not at that time. I was known as 'Little Lovin' Henry 'til I started to record. I got the name Professor Longhair /.../ It all started at the: Caldonia Inn, where I wore long hair, the guys I worked with they started to let their hair grow. They /.../ Professor already. Some guys came around /.../ the guy with the long hair. Professor Longhair and the Four Hairs /.../ the combo I started /.../ Professor Longhair, Professor Shorthair [Clarence Fritz].

Löfgren: How did you pick up this Latin influence?
Fess: Well, I was teachin' at the time. I was teachin' the average fellow, help him with his, whatever he was playin' /.../ what I was doing, so he could spread out. When I first had the Hungarians.

Andréasson: Why Hungarians?
Fess: /.../ Robert "Barefoot" Parker on saxophone. Sometime I would change the drummer. They are so hard to keep in line for steady work. So, whenever I would get a drummer. I would switch Al [Miller] from drums back to trumpet.

Schweitz: What was the first record you made?
Fess: Hadacol Bounce.

Schweitz: How did you record that?
Fess: A fellow sellin' Hadacol medicine came through lookin' for tal-

ent. But you know he heard that I was, you know, /.../ rhyme, to help them sell his medicine /.../ came back here once again. That's when I met Mr. Ervins, he came down with a recording machine. He wanted to record a song, the Hadacol Bounce. He didn't have no license. That's why it flopped /.../

Schweitz: Did you record that for another label?
Fess: They wouldn't let you play it unless you paid the station /.../ The Hadacol medicine or anything like C. J. T. /.../ that's when I first started with the C. J. T, selling stuff in a bottle, doing anything /.../ [C. J. T. was a medicine and a Medicine Show]

The Daily Oklahoman, Thursday, June 29, 1950. "Hadacol was a mixture of vitamins B1 and B2, iron, niacin, calcium, phosphorous, honey, and diluted hydrochloric acid in 12% alcohol."

Schweitz: Did you work in other places in New Orleans at that time?
Fess: I worked quite a few places here in New Orleans when I started to record /.../ band /.../ didn't have so much money to pay you, so I got most of the jobs.

Schweitz: Did you do any touring?
Fess: Never liked touring /.../

Schweitz: Did you do any recordings before the "Atlantic"?
Fess: Yeah, I did one for "Mercury", "Star Talent" /.../ "Wasco".

Schweitz: Were they all cut in New Orleans /.../ "Federal".
Fess: Yeah!

Schweitz: Which was your biggest hit?
Fess: /.../ no money either.

Schweitz: Did you always use your own band?
Fess: Yeah!

Andréasson: You recorded this song about the Mardi Gras, were you ever involved in that?
Fess: If I marched in it? I never participated, I never liked it, I tried /.../ before I got off the streets.

Schweitz: They still play the record every year, don't they?
Fess: It'll be 25 years /.../

Andréasson: Did you get any royalties for it?
Fess: I hope I will!

Andréasson: But you never got any so far?
Quint Davis: /.../

Schweitz: Isn't there anything you can do about that?
Davis: We tried to sue them.
Fess: Do it again, let them start suing.

Schweitz: What about that thing, you went to England for a private thing a couple of years back?
Fess: That was a party.

Schweitz: And they brought you from here to England?
Davis: We took 32 people, took the Preservation Hall Jazz Band, Fess, Snooks Eaglin, the Wild Magnolias and Willie Tee.

Schweitz: A hell of a party [chuckles].

Davis: Yeah, a hell of a party!

[This extravagant society party is detailed in chapter: 5, Professor Longhair Is Back.]

Schweitz: When you play nowadays, do you play as a solo act or do you have anyone backing you?
Fess: I've got away from solo 'cause I'm expecting, I've got so many things / ... /

Schweitz: When you did this [Blue Star/Barclay] *album, was it the first time you played with "Gatemouth"* [Brown]?
Fess: It was the second time. I played with Gatemouth around '50, '52 / ... / When you can keep up with the beat, tempo [strikes a beat with one hand] then you know a man is qualified.

Guitarist Edgar Blanchard (1924-1972) was the leader of the Gondoliers, one of the two house bands at this classy nightclub at: 2836 LaSalle St. "After completing two consecutive week-ends as the feature star in Dew Drop's Grove Room, the master of guitar and mad vocalizer of the blues, Gatemouth Brown moves into the Dew Drop's swanky lounge nightly for an indefinite period. The real treat comes in the fact that 'Gatemouth' will be presented in the lounge with an 'Admission Free' door. This is considered a grand treat and it's best that those desiring to see the masterful guitarist should make reservations early for tables. The Gondoliers will support 'Gatemouth' with their jumpy music." Louisiana Weekly, November 8, 1947.

Schweitz: Yeah, we heard parts of the record here and it sounds like you played quite a while.
Fess: /.../ it's a natural thing if you've been here a long time like "Tuts" in the '30s /.../

Schweitz: How did you catch up with Gatemouth in the '50s.
Fess: Well, he /.../ every band that came here. I brought him on /.../ I would ask him coming to town.

Schweitz: That means you played with a lot of people coming to New Orleans.
Fess: Oh yeah, I believe I played with every musician that was worthwhile.

Andréasson: Did you play mostly at the Dew Drop Inn?
Fess: No, I never did work at the: Dew Drop Inn /.../ treat me like these people did /.../ $3 or $4 dollar gig.

Löfgren: Did you play regularly in the 1950s and 60s.
Fess: Yeah /.../ nights /.../ Saturday /.../ those places.
Fess: /.../ been drinking /.../

Andréasson: Why did you call your band the Shuffling Hungarians?
Fess: Well, I had a little fellow played drums, we called him a Hungarian /.../

Schweitz: Sounds pretty wild, Professor Longhair and the Shuffling Hungarians.
Fess: /.../ at that time I was training /.../ Fats [Domino] and his band /.../ stayin' in the background /.../ working around the city.

Schweitz: If your new album turns out to be a hit record, selling a lot of records, will you do more extensive touring then?
Fess: [Probably nodding yes. Laughters].
Davis: /.../

Schweitz: Will you put out a single from the album?
Davis: I hope so. [4]

Sincere thanks to Hans Schweitz for the tape recording plus photos.

Stuart Colman (1944-2018) conducted the following interview, un-known date, in March 1978, for: *It's Only Rock & Roll*, a BBC Radio One Show. The series was broadcast each Saturday at 5.30 in the af-ternoon, from London, UK, and ran from 1976–1979.

Colman: Going back to the old New Orleans days. What happened after your real busy days in the 50s?
Fess: I quit playing for a while, you know, I wasn't makin' any money out of it so I decided to let go and help other people with their things and make something out of it.

Colman: When actually was this?
Fess: Was around '50, say from '57 to around 1970.

Colman: And then the New Orleans Festivals came along. How did they come about?
Fess: Well, I met a good friend. He was a friend and his name was Quint Davis and he was in charge of the festival. He hires all the mu-sicians and performers every year and he offered me a tremendous amount of work. I was working with him on the festival and he in-sisted on me went back in the business and record. Which I did, so he got me a session with Warner Brothers, "Barclay" album, which we did a session for. Well, and from then on I've just been going steady, you know.

Colman: We haven't seen your album from over here until the recent Queen Mary live set. What was the story behind this?
Fess: Well, really, that was cut live on the Queen Mary. And, it was Paul McCartney who did that you know. It was a surprise to me that everybody liked and enjoyed it.

Colman: Your style of playing seems to range from barrelhouse, even to Latin American. Who actually influenced you?
Fess: My mother [Ella Mae Byrd] started me off when I was very young, with the swing-based music at the time. And well, I was with her from seven years old up to when I got 15, 16 years old. When I could get out, like any other big young boy and see the town and get off of her apron strings, eh! And I started to layin' around barrooms and barrelhouses, dives, and 'hole in the walls' as they call 'em, and

started to listen to their type of music, which I really enjoyed. I think that the first man's music, which I got into, was a fellow they called 'Sullivan Rock'.

Colman: Really!
Fess: He had a real crazy barrelhouse style of playin', you know. So I started to practice behind him awhile, and run across a fellow they called [Kid] Stormy Weather. He had some licks and things, working the elbows and shoulders. I got carried away with these kind of things, it inspired me. So I took those two things and put 'em with what my mother had showed me and I said. Well, now, I'm ready to start to put me a gumbo together, and looking out to meet a man they called Bertrand. He took a little time with me. And Tuts Washington, he had very strong fingers and a tremendous reach on the piano. I couldn't reach as far as he could I couldn't make that spain he probably meant span]. So he taught me how to where I wanted to get, and back.

Colman: A rolling style.
Fess: Rollin', yeah! So this is the way it got together. I just started to make a Gumbo, Rock and Roll out of it.

Colman: From all accounts your mother was pretty talented too.
Fess: Ah, she was professional she played all over the world during her time. She played piano, drums, guitar, bass, danced. Her time was beyond me, when she was comin' up.

Colman: Well, we better move on now, so how about we hear one of your really early numbers?
Fess: 'Bald Head' is one of the earliest numbers, that was around 1950.

Colman: Would you do: "Bald Head" for us now.
Fess: Yeah, I sure will.

With sincere thanks to Dave Clarke, Warrington, UK, for the tape recording.

The most important Fess interviews are:

—Hudson Márquez: New Orleans, May 30, 1969. (An excerpt of the interview is found in Up From the Cradle of Jazz, by Berry, Foose & Jones, 1986).

—John Broven & Mike Leadbitter: New Orleans, April 10, 1970: Blues Unlimited, No. 76, October 1970.

—Tad Jones: New Orleans, November 13, 1975: Living Blues, No. 26, March-April, 1976.

—Bill Greensmith and Bez Turner: London, UK, March 1978: Blues Unlimited, No. 130. May 1978.

—Andy Kaslow: New Orleans, November, 1979, released on the CD: Professor Longhair: fess' gumbo, "Stony Plain" SPCD 1214 (Canada, 1996).

—Allison Miner conducted a couple of interviews, for a Fess biography, kept at the Hogan Jazz Archive, Tulane University.

—A conversation at the piano with Fess, Tipitina's, January 1980 (two days before he died). Fess Up: two DVDs, plus a book. US, 2018.

4. "ROCK JAMAICA ROCK" – FROM NEW ORLEANS TO JAMAICA

"You cats from New Orleans ain't nothing but a bunch of West Indians." Pianist James P. Johnson (1894-1955). [1]

I.

Fess: If you take 'Mardi Gras In New Orleans,' that's also instrumental with saxophone, but with 'lyrics. No, it's not really jazz — a little Latin and rumba and a little calypso.

Max Jones: The mention of calypso is significant because the importance of the West Indian influence in New Orleans music and on the city's culture and subculture is often forgotten or minimized. Longhair agreed that a great many Black Americans came into Louisiana from the West Indies, adding that most of his people were West Indians. His grandfather he said, was from there. Did the Caribbean music rub off on him at all?
Fess: Yes, because my mother had a lot of that in her and she taught me, as I told you. I guess this is where I really get most of the feeling from for my tunes, and words, you know. Because she played professional all around the world; she was in her prime then. [2]

The New Orleans R&B influence on Jamaican music is often mentioned in articles and books, but only incidentally. Fats Domino's Jamaican sojourn, and his recordings, serves as good examples. [3] Fats' recordings of "My Girl Josephine" (1960), and "Let the Four Winds Blow" (1961) made it to the *Jamaican Hit Parade*. The rhythm patterns of tracks have a certain Rock Steady/Blue Beat feel. The lively Ska and Rock Steady/Blue Beat music of the 1960s, were forerunners to the slowed down Reggae genre. The Jamaicans often turned to the southern US radio stations to pick up the music. In New Orleans, the hip voices of Clarence Hayman/Hamann aka "Poppa Stoppa" and Vernon Winslow aka "Doctor Daddy-O", came through the radio waves with their local brand of R&B. Winslow had even taught Hayman how to "talk Black".

In the 1970s, Fess sometimes expressed an interest in Reggae music.

He was without doubt a popular recording artist in Jamaica in the 1950s, yet his influence on the islands creative music scene was limited. A Fess track like, for instance, "Cuttin' Out" ("Ron", 1959) was reissued in the early 1970s in Jamaica on "Pop Rank International", a bootleg label. *"We start imitate the Rhythm and Blues songs by Smiley Lewis or Professor Longhair, Louis Jordan you know, those kind of beat. We tried to imitate it. It didn't turn out that way so we decided to keep it as our own type. That's how the Ska come in* [sic]." The Jamaican music pioneer Derrick Morgan (born: 1940) declared. [4] Cuban born singer and composer Laurel Aitken (1927-2005) performed and recorded in Jamaica during the 1950s and 60s. In 1999, he recounted:

We used to listen to American rhythm & blues from New Orleans. Everybody used to dance to that music in Jamaica, but in the '50s our music there was Calypso [Mento], *which come from Trinidad, and we took Calypso and mixed it with the rhythm & blues and we turned that into Ska. So part of the roots of Ska music is from America. Ska music is American rhythm & blues and Jamaican calypso and it went from there - that's where Ska come from. We used to listen to men like Smiley Lewis, Joe Turner, Roscoe Gordon, and all these guys in the '50s and we were influenced. I was influenced, by Roscoe Gordon* [1928–2002] *because he played a downbeat boogie. Roscoe Gordon is an American Black singer* [...] *Not only me, but other guys during that time was influenced by him because it was very popular – the boogie-woogie stuff. And as I said, we mixed the boogie-woogie stuff with calypso and that's where Ska came from, as simple as that.* [5]

II.

"Island" records founder Chris Blackwell, was once deeply involved in the Reggae music business. In New Orleans (2005), he accounted:

In Jamaica we heard a lot of music from New Orleans, the kind of music that was played by the sound systems. 'Cause' reggae is probably the only music that was born in the studio. You would never hear reggae music played in clubs and bars and even live. The whole music scene in Jamaica started with sound systems. And sound systems would play R&B records. And the labels that they liked, a lot of them were from here. "Imperial" records was a big label that they liked, Fats Domino was on "Imperial". Fats Domino was the biggest star in Jamaica. And a lot of his music did have a kind of shuffle rhythm. Ska, which was, sort of, what the music was called before reggae, really is shuffle, accept with the accent on a different - yeah. New Orleans music was very influential to Jamaican music. It was Jamaicans trying to play New Orleans, but just having that Calypso in the blood, I guess […]. [6]

The Jamaican sound systems were predecessors to the 1970s discothèques, and in time the rap music fad. The roots of the rap music are partly Jamaican deejays, who used to "toast" ("rap") to the records they spun on the turntables. Fess' 45s were sometimes spinned on the sound systems, among them: "Bald Head" ("Mercury"), and "Misery" ("Ebb"). In 1962, Lloyd Williams waxed an excellent Jamaican remake of the latter song, with the composer listed as "R. Byrd" ("WASP"). It follows Fess' version rather closely. Williams, a rather obscure singer, was one of the local acts on Shirley & Lee's 1961 Jamaican revisit tour. Williams cut "Misery" in the late 1950s, backed by the Celestials, a band formed by Trevor Aljoe (born 1944). Aljoe was eventually dubbed as "Jamaica's Fats Domino", with the nicknames "Al T Joe"/"Jamaica Fats". He waxed a couple of remakes of Domino's chart hits and copied the Domino vocal style to the bone. In 1970, Lloyd Williams cut a 1970 remake of the Domino/Bartholomew penned "Hey Little School Girl, Are You Going My Way" (a song with provocative lyrics). It's a New Orleans-rumba-type track, as Rick Coleman pointed out, inspired by Fess' "Hey Now Baby (Hey Now Honey Child)".

Jamaican singer Prince Buster cites: Thomas "Tom" Wong ("Tom the Great Sebastian"), as the king of sound systems. He was of part Chinese, and part African descent:

I can remember Tom playin' on the sidewalk in the evenin', an' he play a Fats Domino tune, "Mardi Gras" ("Mardi Gras in New Orleans") - I went totally freak out, an' kept tell Tom: play it back, play it back! Some line in the song jus' carry me a step beyond an' I jus' went with it. Duke Vin was with Tom, an' I was a follower of Tom's sound system, and Tom was THE sound system. Tom went into sound system duels with people like Count Nick and Count Buckram - these are good sound systems in those days, top cream, and Tom won it beca' Tom was the perfect thing, the MODEL, y'unnerstand? [7]

Left: Fats' remake of "Mardi Gras In New Orleans" (September 1952), a 7-inch 45 rpm, with the composer listed as: "D. Longhair" (the line-up was: Domino, "Wendell Duconge", Herb Hardesty & "Buddy" Hagans, "Papoose" Nelson, Frank Fields, & "Tenoo" Coleman). Courtesy: House Of Oldies record store, Stockholm, Sweden. Right: Trevor Aljoe. Early 1960s. Courtesy The Daily Gleaner, Jamaica.

III.

Louis Jordan (1908–1975), the influential reed player/singer and bandleader, was the first US R&B artist to tour Jamaica. His six-piece band played for sold-out houses in March 1951. "Saturday Night Fish Fry" was one of Jordan's most popular items, penned by the New Orleans born drummer and singer Ellis Walsh. Reed player "Capt." John Handy (1900-1971), born Pass Christian, Miss., yet, mostly associated with New Orleans jazz bands. He once revealed: "Both these players, Louis Jordan and Earl Bostic, used to listen to me. Jordan really was older than Earl Bostic, and when I was playing in Texas in the early 'thirties, I knew Louis Jordan was there listening. Of course, he was a young man then, but everywhere we played Louis Jordan was there". John Handy, 1966. [8]

Smiley Lewis never made it to Jamaica. But his recording of "School Days Are Back Again" (1957), reached position ten on the *Jamaican Hit Parade*, early 1960. He cut it with Dave Bartholomew's band, in New Orleans. Another Jamaican singer: Justin Hinds (1942-2005) told:

The people that really influence my way of life in music is really the American artists. I used to listen to rock and roll sound. That's where I get ideas. I listen to B. B. King, Louis Jordan, Smiley Lewis and those guys. I listen to a

great pianist, Professor Longhair. The reason why I called my group Domi-
noes – I used to listen to Fats Domino. I like the man's song [sic] and I used
to like the game, dominoes. [9]

IV.

As the crow flies, there are some 18.000 kilometers from New Orleans to Jamaica's capital city Kingston. In 1959, it was an island with
only around 2.5 million people, still ruled by the Brits. In that year,
Fess was scheduled for a Carib-
bean sojourn. The arrival date
was set in the summer of 1959.
Huey "Piano" Smith was to be
the head-act in a package show,
including singer Bobby Marchan, (1930–1999). The Ohio-born
artist, sung lead for the Clowns.
He and made many recordings,
backed by Smith's band, in the
1950s, early 60s. Marchan's characteristic high-pitched voice
is easily recognizable. He was
gay and a female impersonator.
Some of Fess' recordings sold
in good quantities in Jamaica,
among them: "Baby Let Me Hold
Your Hand" ("Ebb", 1957).

"Looka, No Hair" was cut for the "EBB" label
(121x) in 1957. The A side was: Fess' superb up
tempo remake of: "Baby Let Me Hold Your Hand"
(The 1951 Ray Charles eight bar blues). The Fess
"Oldies 45", reissue (stamped "Made In Jamaica") was most likely a bootleg disc. The author's
collection.

Huey was born January 26, 1934 in New Orleans, and started to play piano
at an early age. Dixieland and big bands were popular In New Orleans at
that time. Professor Longhair and Smiley Lewis where the most influential
R&B players. Huey formed his first group, the Honey Jumpers, when he was
about 13-14 years old. He remembers one night when the Professor walked in
the place where Huey played. Professor was so good that Huey didn't want
to play anymore that night, and he started to practice a little more. Apart
from Professor, it was Ray Charles who really inspired him to play. Jonas
Bernholm, 1971. [10]

I see Smith's unique brand of funky Rock & Roll/R&B, as a prototype
for the 1960s and early 70s funk music.

Pianist Huey "Piano" Smith & the Clowns, plus Fess, and the rest of the troupe was supposed to arrive in Jamaica, late July 1959. Radio Jamaica (RJR) was involved in the: 'Rock Jamaica Rock' show. This is how the local newspaper, *the Daily Gleaner*, described the coming musical 'Five-Star' show:

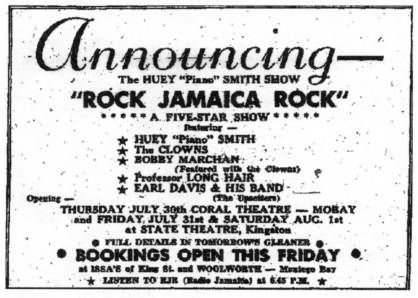

The Daily Gleaner, Wednesday July 15, 1959.

'Huey Smith ... Prof Longhair coming in'

Another American Musical Show, featuring five recording stars, will perform a series of engagements in Jamaica when Huey "Piano" Smith – popular Ace recording artist brings in – a show titled "Rock-Jamaica-Rock" at the end of the month. [sic]

The show will open in Montego Bay [Mobay] at Coral Theatre on Thursday, July 30, with two shows at 7 and 9 p.m. The Kingston run opens at State Theatre on Friday, July 31, and continues on Saturday August 1, with three shows each day 4.30 p.m. 7.00 p.m., and 9.00 p.m.

The other four stars in addition to Huey "Piano" Smith, are the "Clowns" who are always featured with Huey Smith recordings; and Bobby Marchan, a featured singer with the group.

Then there is Professor Longhair – a comparatively new star in the musical firmament, but whose first two recordings "Baby Let Me Hold Your Hand" and "No Buts, No Maybe" have skyrocketed him among current bestsellers.

Sold Millions

Rounding out the musical package is Earl Davis and his Band who performs under the name of 'The Upsetters'. The Davis Combo will supply the orchestral backing for the show. This group is remembered most for the musical accompaniment they have to Frankie Ford in his hit "Sea Cruise". Since then Earl Davis has been the band heard on all the hit discs turned out by Huey Smith and "The Clowns".

Huey Smith's recordings have sold in the millions, and his better-known hits are "Rocking Pneumonia" and "the Boogie Woogie Flu" [sic]; "Sea Cruise" with Frankie Ford; "High Blood Pressure"; "Don't You Just Know It"; [sic] "Yockomo", and "I'll Be John Brown" [sic]. His latest release is stated to make the best-selling charts shortly. "Rock-Jamaica-Rock" is the second of

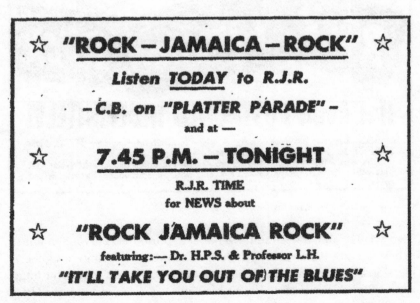

A Radio Jamaica Rediffusion (RJR) ad. Courtesy the Daily Gleaner, July 14, 1959.

the popular summer shows scheduled for Jamaica. The first, Lloyd Price's "Stagger Lee Show" [in June 1959], was one of the year's big smashes, and Huey Smith, aware of this, has packaged his show with outstanding performers who can deliver what is known in their trade as a "Sock-O" job with plenty of punch.

The arrangement of working in the show with a Montego Bay opening, worked so well with the [Lloyd Price] "Stagger Lee Show" that the promoters have decided to repeat this method again.

It has been pointed out that Montego Bay patrons who buy tickets for the 9 o'clock show should endeavor [sic] to arrive at 8.45 so that they can be admitted to the foyer of the theatre and thereby avoid getting caught in the crush outside the theatre.

The bookings open this Friday at Issa's of King Street, for the State Theatre performances [in Kingston] and at Woolworth's in Montego Bay for the Coral Theatre show. [11]

Courtesy: The Daily Gleaner, Monday, August 10, 1959.

Two weeks later the same newspaper reported a "postponement of 'Rock Jamaica Rock' owing to the public preoccupation with general elections." [12] Earl Davis and his Upsetters, was based in Baton Rouge, the capitol of Louisiana. The Davis band never recorded with Huey Smith. The story of his life, unsuccessful struggle for royalties etc., is narrated in John Wirt's important Huey Smith biography. [13] "Whatever preoccupations the Jamaican public may have had with the island's elections, Huey Smith and the Clowns' Jamaican engagements were in reality, scrapped to meet domestic demand for the group." Which was much more lucrative for the artists booking agent, in New York, though not for the artists. Fess' view of the subject is not known.

V.

Owen Gray (born 1939) is a singer who grew up in Kingston's shantytown, called Trenchtown. He's said to have a light voice with a cutting edge. At an early age, he attended the important Alpha Boys School, alongside many other islanders, who were to gain fame as musicians. Among them the crucial guitarist Ernest Ranglin (born 1932). In 1962, Gray recorded,"Let Me Go Free" ("Starlite"), described as, melodically an almost exact copy of Fess' 1953 version of "Tipitina". I find Gray's track as, something in between "Tipitina" and "Misery" (Ebb). Two eight-bar songs, but without the Calypso/Rumba rhythm (the 45rpm disc is incredibly rare). Owen Gray was one of the first artists to be produced by Chris Blackwell. In 1971, the singer cut a reworked version of: "I Hear You Knocking", the Bartholomew/Domino creation. First waxed by Smiley Lewis, and then by Fats Domino.

Owen Gray, alongside several of the Jamaican top acts, were invited to sing on Fats Domino's farewell performances. It took place at three different theaters, on February 9, 1961. In August, that year, Gray had appeared on the Shirley & Lee return shows in Jamaica, as well as the Sam Cooke and the Ray Charles, early 1960s Jamaican concerts. Reportedly, Gray lived in New Orleans for a while in the 1970s, yet, there's no information to be found on his stay in the city. The singer eventually moved to the UK.

Jamaican singer Jimmy Cliff, born 1948, told:

When I was growing up, I listened to Professor Longhair, and I think Smiley Lewis is from New Orleans too, and of course Fats Domino. Fats Domino inspired me, and I was inspired by some of the jazz people like Louis Armstrong. I think New Orleans music inspired Jamaican music, which has become known as reggae, because a lot of the musicians were jazz musicians and they always talked about New Orleans. New Orleans was such a mecca, inspirational and a fertile ground for musicians all over the world.

I'm so grateful I had the opportunity to hear the radio when I was a child. It's so great to know that live music is still going on in New Orleans. When I get there, they will be getting the whole nine yards. I'm going from ska right up to dancehall. [14]

Allen Toussaint, mid 1960s, a publicity photo.

VI.

In October 1957, a handsome 19 years old pianist toured Jamaica with Shirley & Lee (Shirley Goodman & Leonard Lee). The teenager was Allen Toussaint, hired as a replacement for Huey Smith. This was the young man's very first tour in, and outside the US. It's a tour he still vividly recalled, in 2009. The low-key legend was quite surprised when I mentioned it, in the summer of that year. Reportedly: "Each band member of the [Goodman/Lee support] band was paid $22.50 a night, in dollar bills, out of which they had to pay for their own food and lodging." [15]

"I tried to learn every piece Professor Longhair ever came out with", Allen Toussaint said. [16] The profoundly Fess-influenced piano of Toussaint, sounds very inspiring on many of his 1960s productions, for instance the many Lee Dorsey tracks. Another great illustration to this is Jessie Hill's: "Oogsey Moo", co-written by Fess. Dorsey's successful recordings were usually composed, arranged and produced by Toussaint. They sold very well in Jamaica. According to the *Daily Gleaner*, Shirley Goodman's singing partner Leonard Lee never showed up. As a substitute, bass player Roland K. "Cookie" Cook (1935-2000) sang Lee's vocal parts. He was also leader of the support group. The Jamaicans loved Shirley & Lee, therefore the singing duo made it back to Jamaica twice. There was even a Shirley & Lee sing-alike contest. It was in this context, Millie "My Boy Lollipop" Small (born 1946), learned to mimic Shirley Goodman's nasal vocal style. In the UK, Small waxed a 1965 album, consisting of some bland remakes of Fats Domino's chart hits.

Roland Cook, fender-bass, piano and vocals, was a schoolmate of Earl King. In the 1950s, "Roland Cook and I started out playing music together", Earl stated. [17] "Cookie" waxed with Allen Toussaint for "RCA", 1957, under his own name,

The Shirley & Lee Show, Jamaica. Courtesy: The Daily Gleaner, October 13, 1957.

same label; and also for Johnny Vincent's "ACE" label. Eventually for Earl King, with Huey Smith on piano. George French recalled Roland Cook working with pianist Emile Vinette, and drummer Joe Fox, at *the Backstage 500 Club*, Bourbon St., in the 1960s. Cook joined Fats Domino for an indefinite time in 1970. Cook lead his own orchestra; and for a short time worked for Ernie K-Doe, and Dave Bartholomew.

"Completing the outfit is 'Screaming Jay' Hawkins, who was also with Fats Domino, but now is on the success ladder with his own group". *The Daily Gleaner* reported. Hawkins had a short stint with Domino as a vocalist. Around ten months before the Jamaican visit, Hawkins had cut his own fabulous creation: "I Put a Spell On You" (a R&B track in ¾ time, including a banjo comp). Eventually, a song with many remakes. Cleveland, Ohio-born Jalacy Hawkins, caught quite a stir in Jamaica with his wild songs, on-stage theatrics and self-created brand of voodoo jive. In 1969 Hawkins waxed the album "Constipation Blues" ("Philips" records), which included New Orleans guys such as Earl Palmer, Ernest McLean, Plas Johnson, plus his brother Ray. It's an album with an odd cover-photo: Hawkins in a casket! He died at 70, in the year 2000.

VII.

Louis Jordan made his very first recordings, in 1932, with Louis Armstrong (1901-1971). Armstrong was perhaps the first major New Orleans born musician, to tour Jamaica, with his All Stars in 1957. It was also the same year as a 20 years old Clarence "Frogman" Henry performed in the island. Henry was riding high on his chart hit "Ain't Got No Home". "Satchmo" was the Jamaican singer Kendris Fagan's favorite artist – she performed under the epithet: "Girl Satchmo". Her vocals display an obvious influence by her idol. But she sang in the R&B/Rock Steady/Blue Beat idioms and recorded a couple of times in the 1960s. Fagan migrated to the UK in the late 1960s.

Successful vocalist, Lloyd Price and his band, did several shows early June: 1959, in Montego Bay, and Kingston. He was living in NYC then, therefore mostly Northern guys in Price's ten-piece band. The heavily Armstrong inspired trumpeter & singer Louis Prima (1910-1974) was another New Orleans born artist who became extremely popular in Jamaica, but he never made it there.

Fats' band in Jamaica, February 1961. L-R: Clarence Ford, baritone saxophone; Arthur "Duke" Reid, a famous record producer, sound system Dee Jay, and label owner; Domino; and two unknown guys. Below Reid, the head of great drummer: Cornelius "Tenoo" Coleman (1928-1973).

In February 1961, Fats Domino did a row of sold out concerts in the island. Read Rick Coleman's book *Blue Monday: Fats Domino and the Lost Dawn of Rock 'n' Roll*, for more about his in Jamaican sojourn etc. The successful Bartholomew/Domino ditties inspired many Jamaican artists to do reworks of the tunes.

These are some of the New Orleans acts that toured the island:

Lloyd Price's "Stagger Lee Show", including his ten-piece band, performed in the island in June **1959**.

Shirley & Lee returned, on behalf of their extreme popularity, in August **1961**, and July **1962**, backed by Byron Lee and The Dragonaires.

The white teenybopper: Jimmy Clanton toured the island in May **1962**. He had recorded at Cosimo's with mainly Black musicians, among them "Red" Tyler. In Jamaica, Byron Lee and The Dragonaires backed Clanton.

Soul music pioneer Sam Cooke (1931-1964) conquered the island in: **1960**, **1961** and **1962**. The drummers in his bands were New Orleans born Albert "June" Gardner (1930-2010), and Leo Morris, aka Idris Muhammad (1939-2014).

In, December **1961**: Ernie K-Doe made it to Jamaica with "Joe Jones & The Joe Jones Band", the lineup was: "Teddy" Riley, trumpet; Reginald "Reggie" Hall, piano (Fats Domino's brother-in-law); Alvin Robinson, vocal & guitar; Harold Battiste Jr., alto?; Morris "Moe" Bachemin, tenor; possibly "Acy Fairman" (James "Preacher" Fairman) bass, Leo Morris, drums. It was a package-show and the outfit also backed the powerful singer "Big Maybelle" (Smith); the Shirelles (Addie Harris, Shirley Owens, Beverly Lee, & Doris Coley); and "Little Anthony"

(Jerome Anthony) of "the Imperials". Bachemin cut with Fess, and Mac Rebennack etc. in 1959.

Vocalist Jean "Mr. Big Stuff" Knight toured Jamaica in December **1971**.

A Choice of Jamaican Remakes of New Orleans Recordings:

The bulk of this list is drawn from the website: "Skaville Cover Versions In Jamaican 60's Music", in addition Rick Coleman's biography: *Blue Monday: Fats Domino and the Lost Dawn of Rock 'n' Roll*. Additions and certain adjustments have been made.

Larry Darnell, "For You My Love" (*Regal*, 1949); Nellie Lutcher & Nat King Cole Trio, "For You My Love" (*Capitol*, 1950); Paul Gayten, "For You My Love" (*Chess*, 1957). — Shenley Duffus, "For You My Love" (*Dodd*, 1962).

Louis Armstrong & Louis Jordan, "(I´ll Be Glad When You´re Dead) You Rascal You" (*Decca*, 1950). — Sheridons?, "You Rascal You" (*WIRL*, 196?). Composed by New Orleans born Sam Theard.

Jewel King, "3 times 7 = 21" (*Imperial*, 1950). — Slim Smith, "3 Times Seven" (?).

Fats Domino, "Going To The River" (*Imperial*, 1953). — Eric "Monty" Morris, "Going To The River" (*Blue Beat*, 1962); Prince Buster & All Stars, "Going To The River" (*Fab*, 1967).

Shirley & Lee; "Feel So Fine" (*Aladdin*, 1955). — Derrick Morgan and Patsy (Millicent Todd), "Feel So Fine" (*Duke Reid's*, 1961).

Shirley and Lee, "Let The Good Times Roll" (*Aladdin*, 1956). — Derrick and Patsy, "Let The Good Times Roll" (*Duke Reid's*, 1961).

Clarence "Frogman" Henry, "Ain´t Got No Home" (*Argo*, 1956). — Shenley Duffus, aka "Country Boy", "I´m A Lonely Boy" (*Blue Beat*, 1964).

Dave Bartholomew, The Monkey Speaks His Mind (*Imperial*, 1957). — Denzil Thorpe "Monkey Speaks His Mind (*Coxsone*, 1966).

Professor Longhair, "Misery" (*Ebb*, 1957). — Lloyd Williams: The Celestials, "Misery" (*the Wasp*, 1965).

Chris Kenner, "Sick and Tired" (*Imperial*, 1957). – The Techniques, "Oh Babe", (*Treasure Island*, 1966).

Little Richard (Penniman), "Good Golly Miss Molly" (*Specialty*, 1958). — (Basil) B. Gabbidon, "Hully Gully Miss Molly" (*Blue Beat / King Edwards*, 1962).

Lloyd Williams' remake of Professor Longhair's 1957 song "Misery". The author's collection.

Huey "Piano" Smith & the Clowns, "High Blood Pressure" (*Ace*, 1958). — Prince Buster "High Blood Pressure" (*Prince Buster/Island*, 1965).

Fats Domino, "Margie" (*Imperial*, 1958). — Clue J. & His Blues Blasters, "Margie" (*Coxsone*, 1959).

Fats Domino, "Be My Guest" (*Imperial*, 1959). — Millie Small "Be My Guest" (*Island*, 1965).

Jimmy Clanton, "Go, Jimmy, Go" (*Ace*, 1959). — The Wailers, "Go Jimmy Go" (*Dodd*, 1964).

Clarence "Frogman" Henry, "But I Do" (*Argo*, 1960). — Al T. Joe, "But I Do" (*Wasp*, 1962).

Joe Jones, "You Talk Too Much" (*Ric*, 1960). — Gaylads, "Talk Too Much" (*Studio 1, Dodd*, 1964); Delroy Wilson; "Talk Too Much" (*Fat Man*, 1974).

Chris Kenner, "Something You Got" (*Instant*, 1961). — Hortense & Alton Ellis, "Something You've Got" (*Reid / Treasure Island*, 1965); Lee "King" Perry: The Sensations with Lynn Tait & His Band, "Something You Got" (*Wirl/Doctor Bird*, 1967).

Lee Dorsey "Ya Ya" (*Fury*, 1965). — Fitzroy Campbell "Waiting For My Rude Girl" (*Buster*, 1967).

Lee Dorsey, "Get Out Of My Life, Woman" (*AMY*, 1965). — Tony Gregory "Get Out Of My Life Woman" (*Dodd*, 1966).

5. PROFESSOR LONGHAIR IS BACK

On my second trip to New Orleans, fall 1969, I had the pleasure of meeting Peter Haby, a researcher, writer and profound New Orleans music buff. Since then, we have kept in touch, on and off. In January 2002, I received a letter from my friend in Melbourne, Australia:

"On my first trip to New Orleans in 1969 I met Allison Miner [1949-1995] who worked at the Jazz Archives at the Tulane – I was very interested in finding out more about Brass Bands, the Church Parades,

Allison Miner & Fess, New Orleans Jazz Fest, late 1970s. Courtesy: Allison Miner collection, Hogan Jazz Archive, Tulane University. Used by permission.

John Leon Gross aka: "Archibald" (1916–1973), New Orleans, May 1969. Photo and courtesy: James Stuber (Zurich, Switzerland). Used by kind permission. "Archibald was a swell piano player. I got some ideas from him. He was the first one to come out with 'Stagger Lee' from the style that I put out. 'Cause you had a bunch of 'Stagger Lee's'. 'Stagger Lee' was out when I was a little boy". Fess, in Blues Unlimited, No. 130, 1978.

the [Mardi Gras] Indians, a number of piano players – Archibald [John L. Gross], Fats [Domino], Tuts [Washington], Burnell Santiago, and Longhair – Allison was very supportive and would let me know where and when some of the more obscure parades and musicians would be at – I met up with Jules Cahn at some of these events – He was also extremely helpful. I got to hear Archibald at the "Court of the Two Sisters" [613 Royal St.], and one of the big hotels on Royal [St.] – He was fascinating to hear play and he talked a lot about Santiago and Longhair. Referring to Longhair, Archibald said, Longhair had an original approach on piano. He had his own style with Latin rhythms, Cuban touches, and he often used a drummer to emphasize a parade like syncopated beat played in a lot of Barrel Houses for good times and dancing. I saw Longhair on South Rampart St. He played a little piano in a record shop there [Joe Assunto's One Stop]

– Demonstrating certain styles. He seemed quite reserved, very frail and up against in some ways."

"On my next trip, in 1974, I endeavored to hear more of Longhair [...] He played on Stage 3 and closed the Jazz Festival that year. Doc Paulin['s] and Kid Thomas [Valentine's] band preceded him. They stayed to listen to Longhair and seemed to know him. If my memory serves me right, only about 60 people were listening to Longhair. It was extremely windy and about to rain but Longhair was fantastic. Playing all his well-known tunes. He lost his house during Jazzfest being burnt down? A benefit for Longhair was held at the Warehouse. An amazing night of music with Dr. John, Olympia [Brass Band], Mardi Gras Indians, Willie Tee [Turbinton], Earl Turbinton, Toussaint, etc. I was fortunate to hear Longhair play at a number of pre-Jazzfest parties and one for his local neighbours. That was an amazing experience for someone like myself. Dodie Simmons and Allison would let you know about these. I did not see Longhair after the benefit or if he was playing gigs around" [...] [1]

Burnell Santiago, late 1930s (playing with a guitar and bass player). Photo: George Hoefer. Courtesy: Hogan Jazz Archive, Tulane University (with thanks to Alaina Hébert). Used by permission.

New Orleans born Burnell Santiago, died only 29 years old, in 1943; when Henry Roland Byrd was 25 years old. Local musicians acknowledged Santiago, from a family of famous musicians, as the city's most technically advanced pianist. No doubt, Fess must have been familiar with Santiago, but why was he never ever referred to by Fess? *Burnell was a genius. He would win every contest—he could beat the jazz pianists and the honky tonk ones. He could play any kind of music and he could beat them all. He could have had a wonderful career in music, but somehow he didn't care to play for money. Anyone in New Orleans will tell you that he was the greatest. Pity he never made a record.* Alton Purnell (1911-1987).

Two Burnell Santiago items, privately recorded acetates, were released in 1992. Earl Palmer accounted:

Steve [Angrum Jr.] *and I used to stand and watch Burnell Santiago play in that little barroom behind the Donze brothers' grocery where they had this old upright. Stand there for hours watching this mother play. Burnell looked like a little Filipino. Fantastic! Man! Back then when I was little, they said Paul Whiteman wanted to take him and he wouldn't go. He was a junkie and not a very brilliant kid. Playing for fun, making a little money. He was always taken care of by somebody–his brother* [Lester], *broads, Harold Dejan. I think he died of consumption. Goddam he was something.* [2]

* * *

Next morning, after Mike Leadbitter's and John Broven's first day in New Orleans, April 1970: "James La Rocca told us about an interview he'd made with Polka Dot Slim who plays locally and listened to a tape by Prof. Longhair... who sounded as good as ever playing some fine boogie woogie solos. After a huge breakfast, we went down to 1522 S. Rampart to see and hear his story.

Roy Byrd, also known as 'Baldhead' or Professor Longhair, lives in a decaying street alongside an extremely noisy bar. He's in poor shape at present; a slightly built Negro, Roy is neither bald nor has overlong hair. He doesn't drink now but looked as if he was suffering from a massive hangover. One eye was closed, the other wept gently. He walked carefully as one knee is just liable to give away. Obviously, the guy was having a bad time physically and financially and I felt sad that a man who had made hit records was ending his life this way. Talent rotting away because nobody

James LaRocca, and Monroe "Polka Dot Slim" Vincent (1919-1981), New Orleans 1972. Photo and courtesy: Hans Andréasson. Used by permission.

cares is a situation I've came across many times; but it still upsets me. Roy settled down to talk about the hows and whys [...]

Today he works spasmodically in a one-stop record shop [Joe Assunto's One Stop Record Shop, S. Rampart], plays weekends in the 1st Bass Club at 3rd & Baronne, or just hustles. No-one is interested in recording him and he's not over- enthusiastic himself unless he can see some good front money. His music, which he describes as a mixture of "rhumba, mumbo and calypso", is as good as ever and it would be nice to hear him with just a rhythm accompaniment. Nobody has yet put his talent as a boogie pianist on wax, and this also should be done. We left him with faint hope, if nothing else. (Anyone with a genuine wish to help artists like this, please contact B. U. [Blues Unlimited] for leads.)" [3]

The Leadbitter/Broven piece was, possibly, the first major magazine or newspaper Fess feature. Some blues scholars are of the opinion that James LaRocca must take some credit for rediscovering Fess, and not only Quint Davis.

John Broven recounted: "I can remember we were planning to see 'Fess play one Saturday night in April 1970, but were 'advised' against not going because of the racial tensions of the time. So near and yet so far... As Mike mentioned the '1st Bass' it may have been that club, I don't know. Just a thought, I wonder if the club should be 'First Base' (as in baseball...)." [4]

* * *

"First time I [Bruce Raeburn] heard Professor Longhair was in 1970 at a place called The Nutcracker in a strip mall on Veterans Boulevard in Metairie, so named because its proprietors – two musicians, but really evil-minded comics in practice – specialized in a song called "Hot Nuts" and had a skit poking fun at audience members while they were using the, a-hmmm, 'facilities.' Once people were in there, a red light would start flashing and the comics would make outlandish jokes about what was going on inside.

When the unwary victims came out, everybody would be staring, pointing, and laughing uproariously. After the skit things calmed down a little, and they brought out a piano player. He looked kind a dignified, an older guy, so I thought, "Oh that's nice, at last a moment of sanity." Little did I know. As Professor Longhair liked to put it, 'I'm a little rowdy with my playin'.' That's like describing a hurricane as 'a little wind and rain.'

Can't say I was ever the same again after that night, 'cause Fess could mess with your brain, not to mention the other body parts, the ones that like to dance. Once he started playing, you just had to move to it – the rhythm just took over. At the time he was working as a janitor by day, sweeping up at the One-Stop Record Shop on South Rampart Street, and taking whatever musical work he could find – which wasn't much considering that he was playing at The Nutcracker as the filler between flatulence jokes." [5]

Fess first Jazz and Heritage Festival performance took place in 1971, with the dates as Wednesday, April 21, to April 24. It was staged at the impressive Municipal Auditorium (erected, 1930), and the adjoining Congo Square/Beauregard Square.

"One of the most amazing performers at the second festival [1971] was Henry Roeland Byrd a.k.a. Professor Longhair." Until the festival I had only heard him through recordings of music and an interview that were on file in the archives [Hogan Jazz Archive]." Allison Miner, narrated: "The sound of the interview was so bad. They must have been on a front porch with cars going by. Quint [Davis] also had a recording of Fess's most renowned songs, "Big Chief." Even though the recording was poor, the talent on it was obvious. [Presumably a taped live recording?].

When Byrd came out to the festival, he was carrying an aluminum folding chair for a woman who was supposed to one of his managers. He referred to her as "Miss Terry." [Jeff Hannush stated that one T. Terry, was Joe Assunto's wife. Was this the same person?]. His suite was so shiny. It must have been pressed so many times that it practically wasn't there.

He wasn't performing anymore. He was working as a custodian, sweeping the floor at the One Stop Record Shop in the 1500 block of

Fird "Snooks" Eaglin, spring 1961. Courtesy, the Danish magazine: Jazzrevy, October 1961. Photo by Erik V. Krustrup, who also conducted an interview with Eaglin, at 9127 1/2 Palmetto St., Metairie. Krustrup was utterly surprised to find out that Eaglin wasn't a "street singer". He and his band played in nightclubs and dance halls like, for instance, the San Jacinto.

South Rampart Street. That day he got up on the stage with just one drummer, Edmund Kimbro [Edward Kimbrough]. Snooks Eaglin was playing on another stage. Quint asked Snooks to come and perform on stage with Fess.

When the three of them started to play, the entire festival stopped and everyone came over to see and hear these great musicians. It was truly amazing, even at that early stage in Fess's 'comeback'. He was definitely a presence, but was he wasn't yet what he was to become.

He was malnourished and run-down. He had had such a hard, hard time.

From that time on, we were Byrd's friends. He came to our house almost every day; he became part of our lives, Quint and mine. Fess and I had a talkative relationship as only a man and a woman who are close friends can have. He said I was a lot like his wife, Alice, who was also a Libra. They had been together since the 1930s. [sic] We became an extended family." [6]

Fess' re-created band, the "Four Hairs Combo", did two gigs at the 1971 Jazz Fest. Tickets were $3. On its first day, he played with drummer Edward "Shiba" Kimbrough (once tutored by Fess). On the next day, Fird "Snooks" Eaglin was added, he sang a couple of tunes with the band as well. Parker Dinkins (of the 'Ahura Mazda' label) described the Festival as moderate success. And according to Dinkins, the blues acts etc. comprised:

Babe Stovall, Bongo Joe, Clancy "Bluesboy" Lewis, Snooks Eaglin, Roosevelt Sykes, Archibald, Allen Fontenet & the Country Cajuns, Robert Pete [Williams] *all interesting. But PROFESSOR LONGHAIR 'was far and away the best on Friday playing with Eaglin who redeemed himself from an earlier stint using, of all things, 'California Dreaming'. Scott Dunbar couldn't be persuaded to attend, but [Gospel singer and pianist] Annie Pavageau moved a wheelchair patron enough to donate $ 20... more next time.* [7]

From 1971, henceforth, Fess became a regular performer at this important festival.

* * *

Lars Edegran reviewed the 1971 Jazz and Heritage Festival:

The greatest benefit of the afternoon concerts was probably Professor Longhair and Snooks Eaglin (and a drummer), who played a couple of songs together. Eaglin showed an up to date style and he was also an excellent solo guitar player (Chicago type). Longhair plays with a strong sense of rhythm and he is a nice singer. [8]

"The Heritage Fair in Congo Square each day will begin at noon with the James Rivers Quartet and Professor Longhair's rhythm and blues. It was impossible to cover all of the afternoon activities, but individual performers and groups were notable for one reason or another. One pleasant surprise was the New Orleans Ragtime Orchestra. Drawing perhaps the largest crowds was an early rock'n roller of some fame. Professor Longhair, who contributed mightily to the general aura of good-feeling." [9] Paul Lentz, 1971.

James Rivers, with his own band, Bourbon St., November 2012. Photo by the author.

In 1962, James Rivers (born 1937) cut a couple of tracks on tenor saxophone, with Fess, for Ripolle Roberts' "Rip" label. Rivers had also played with Sam Cooke. James' funky tenor saxophone was caught on "Sea Cruise", the original recording of it with Bobby Marchan and Gerri Hall ("ACE"). This was prior to the version with Frankie Ford's replaced vocal. Al Johnson's "Carnival Time" is another celebrated track with Rivers' saxophone. This multi-instrumentalist was still an active musician in his hometown in November, 2012. By spring 1972, the New Orleans Jazz & Heritage Festival had moved to the ancient: Fair Grounds Race Course & Slots, at 1751 Gentilly Boulevard. This is the Mid-City area of the city, approximately, a thirty- minute walk from the French Quarter.

"After a long period of inactivity and abortive mismanagement, Fess Longhair is performing again. In April at the New Orleans Jazz and Heritage Festival, he made his first large-scale reappearance, accompanied by bass, drums, and Snooks Eaglin on guitar. Fess literally stole the show with his highly infectious dancing music even to the point to where some of the carryings-on offended some of the older gospel singers. Eaglin who has lately taken on a Jose Feliciano approach to the guitar, was dynamite in the lead-rhythm contaxt [sic], accompanied by Fess, and played some 'screaming' blues licks. Although the two hadn't played together in years, Blind Snooks was sensitive to Prof's music, and enhanced and emphasized in its fine points. Tra Lo Walla!

Longhair's past R&B career encompassed a few works which are not generally known to be of his origin. Fes [sic] wrote "Over and Over" the flip of Bobby Day's hit "Rockin Robin" on Chess, and co-authored "Buzz Buzz Buzz" by the Hollywood Flames on Ebb. "Oogsey Moo" by Jessie Hill on Minit is a tune written by Longhair, with Jessie and it is far superior to the well-known hit "Ooh Poo Pah Doo". Prof. never liked "Ooh Poopsey Do", as he calls it because of its inane lyrics and scream - type vocalizing. Others like Fats Domino and Mack Rebennack collaborated on a friendly basis, obviously learning a lot. Fats even copied his style (mumbo for mumbo) on his "Mardi Gras in New Orleans" number for Imperial.

The upsurge in interest in his music, and the reality of playing and being 'on the road' has greatly affected Fess' physical and mental outlook. He doesn't want to stand still on past achievement but wants instead to earn respect and fans by what he is doing now. Fess is a remarkable individual – very straight–forward, with an incredible smile that reveals two gold front teeth. The music flows from him and he creates many songs on the spot, as his mind is a storehouse of lyrics. One of his least-lauded but most unique features is his whist-ling. On record ("Big Chief "), it's done by Earl King but Fess taught Earl and outshines him to this day. Fess' whistling is very bird-like (Byrd like), and full of subtleties unperceived by the casual listener.

Planned appearances this summer in the East will give a larger audience the chance to hear and appreciate his music. Tippitina! [sic] NB (Nick has recorded Professor Longhair (Roy Byrd) and an LP will soon be released...)" [10]

Nick Buck's recording remains unreleased. Fess did not compose, "Over and Over", and he's not the co-author of: "Buzz, Buzz, Buzz."

* * *

These are excerpts from, perhaps, the first major local newspaper article about Fess, February 1972.

"Rockin' Along with the Professor" by Jennifer Quale:
"His cheeks bubble in and out as he whistles the refrain to "Go to the Mardi Gras." Professor Longhair, unsung father of the local rock'n'roll sound, first recorded this perennial favorite in 1948 [1949]. Originally titled "Mardi Gras in New Orleans," the well-scratched recording billed on scores of local jukeboxes sent Professor Longhair on a roller coaster ride to sporadic fame and misfortune.

Having cut "Tipitina," "Baldhead," "Hey Now Baby," and many others, Professor Longhair became known as "King," in the early '50s, says Quint Davis, the musician's manager. 'His recordings aren't easy to find, but they were real big hits in their day,' agrees Dick Allen [1927-2007], Tulane's jazz archivist. 'All the jazz bands used to play these numbers... I see his name in blues magazines, now that he's making a comeback.' Davis explains 'it's been only in the last couple of years that Professor Longhair had any recognition. While playing publicly for the first time in nearly 10 years at a recent New Orleans Jazz Festival, he really surprised everyone,' says Davis, 'Fess just knocked them out. George Wein (producer of the Newport Jazz Festival) signed him up for Newport as a discovery'.

'Fess' as he's called by friends and jazz aficionados, performed last summer at the annual Festival of American Folk Life, sponsored by the Smithsonian Institute in the nation's capital. Of that appearance, the rock publication, "Rolling Stone," reported: 'A terrific half hour of rocking piano and singing was produced by Professor Longhair, a New Orleans bluesman few people seem to have heard of, whose playing makes a magic lantern slide of Elvis and most everything that followed'.

What 'Fess does is to take a basic blues and jazz hit up by changing the tempo and the keys. He calls it rock'n'roll. 'I've been playing this same thing since '37 – '38,' says 'Fess. 'I was father of this stuff – nobody else was playing it. Back then, nobody knew what it was. In those days there was just opera, blues, sentimental, jazz and Dixieland [...]

'My Mother played the drums, the guitar and the piano,' Fess recalls [...] 'She took me to church when I was little. That's the best place to begin learning music, for getting soul up. We used to make our own instruments when I was a kid – like trap drums out of boxes. We'd take cigarette papers, put them on the back of a comb and play on that; we got all kind of noises out of that...

'I used to play all the rhythm instruments. I started out on drums, but I didn't have any real ones. I'm glad I quit playing them, because one leg went bad. I switched to piano because people had them – they were readily available and you could play them.'

Fess, who acquired his own sense of rhythm before the age of 10, used to hang around speakeasies and jazz clubs when he was growing up.

'He would shine shoes and sell papers while listening to the music out through the doors,' explains Davis. 'He went to school for a while, but his mother tutored him mostly. They were very close' […]

What follows is the common story about Fess' life and career, narrated by Quint Davis. Dave Bartholomew and Ray Charles are mentioned. Davis indicated that Fess met Ray Charles in 1952, at the J&M studio. [11] 'Fess admits he admires the blues singer probably more than anyone playing today. I like anything he does. Says Fess, but I got all my feelings from the old-timers. They aren't around anymore.' Fess also revealed that he worked as stevedore, unloading bananas, on the riverfront: "I toted them, there was no conveyor belt then. Those bananas, whew... I don't even want to eat them anymore. Actually, I never had any intentions of playing music for a living just for pleasure. I really wanted to be a preacher. Still have that nature; that's the blues for me. But I don't like to play straight blues. I put rhythm in it—otherwise it's too sad. Who wants to feel bad?' [12]

* * *

"Resurrecting New Orleans: The Gulf Coast Originals Never Left Home" by Timothy Crouse, May 1972:
"No pilgrimage to New Orleans is complete without a visit to the dwelling of Professor Longhair, the brilliantly innovative pianist who

is one of the offhanded founders of modern day popular music [...] He isn't just playing the piano when he's sitting there; that's a lot of things going on. The Professor lives on [1522 S.] Rampart Street, only a block from the former home of Louis Armstrong, in a peeling but dignified single-story white frame house. He prefers not to sun himself on the decaying five-column porch but to hide in front of his battered Buick station wagon, like a salamander under a rock. His features, moreover, are reptilian; he is lean and lithe as a cobra, with enormous yellowish bug-eyes, a flat nose and two buck teeth made of gold that stick out like blunted fangs. Late on a warm afternoon, the Professor was dozing in his car, cap pulled over his eyes, trying to recuperate from a three-night jag of poker-playing at Happy Jack's Social and Pleasure Club.

'See how my eyes are runnin' water,' said the Professor, wiping away a pool that had formed on his eye pouch. 'Strained 'em. Them dim lights. Them cats fallin' into differences, walkin' the pot, and pullin' cards from under the bottom of the deck when they should be dealin' off the top. Strain your eyes.'

Although he still composes and does occasional lounge dates, the Professor played his last paying recording session in 1964, and has yet to collect on it. 'I just give it up' he says. 'All I wanted to do was to make some money, and I got nothin' but alibis. So I went back to my old thing of playin' cards.'

In recent months the Professor has been subsidized by the producer of the New Orleans Jazz Fest [sic], an earnest young man who has provided a telephone, vitamins, and an RMI electric piano. "It's really a sensitive, dignified piano," says the Professor. "Keeps you with your tie up all the time." He is revamping his old material on his new piano. "My old records sound kinda draggy to me now. You gotta' keep up with dances if you want to make some money. Now everybody jumpin' and hoppin', they ain't dancin' no more, so you got to rig this stuff up to suit them." The Professor's new mentor has yet to receive an adequate recording offer.

Professor Longhair's place in local musical history has been secure ever since the night in 1936 when, playing in the Vieux Carré with a band fancifully named the Shuffling Hungarians ("I had one Hindu in the band but there weren't no Hungarians"), he slipped a new and stiffer beat into a shuffle called "Bald Head." "That's why they call me the father of rock 'n' roll—cause nobody ever hearin' it before like that. I don't know what inspire me, I just got happy that one night.

In the fifties, when the record industry descended on New Orleans, the Professor had several hits and a manager who kept all the money. About the time the Professor retired from recording, the big record companies retired from New Orleans. But the Professor doesn't see that as the end. 'The music never die,' he says. "There are millions of piano players here now. I believe there are more musicianers now than there are just plain ordinary laborers. To tell you the truth, the music's already comin' back, you just don't have nobody to push it." [13]

* * *

Bill Wyman (William G. Perks, born 1936), bass player for the Rolling Stones: 1962 - 1992:
"On June 26, 1972, while we were on tour in the USA, [and in New Orleans] I went out to a dinner with Charlie Watts, Mick Taylor, Ahmet Ertegun, and Truman Capote. We had an excellent meal and then went down to an old barnlike recording studio [Matassa's Jazz City, 748 Camp St.]. Mick and Keith were already there, along with the rest of the tour party. Ahmet had arranged a wonderful party for us, where Snooks Eaglin, Professor Longhair, and a New Orleans Street Marching Band performed [most likely Dejan's Olympia Brass Band]. Best of all though, was Roosevelt Sykes [1906-1983], who played brilliantly and reminded me of Ian Stewart, our piano player. You would never have thought he was 66! I finally got back to the hotel around 2:30 am." [14]

* * *

"Rock: Prof. Longhair in Concert, And Foghat." by Jon Newlin:
"When Professor Longhair hobbled on to the Warehouse stage, it was like the descent of one of those deities who, at the end of Greek tragedies, would come down assisted by stage machinery and put aright all of the clumsy and miserable affairs of men.

But as always, the more splendiferous forms of etiquette much in evidence and the crowd was baffled and respectfully bored. They knew whom to they were listening, but they didn't know more than that. In his green and silver turban, and filmy pea-green suit that would probably match within ten feet of it, he launched into "Mardi Gras In New Orleans."

Spotty applause, but the professor and Snooks Eaglin (plus a bassist: Will Harvey and drummer James Black) seemed relaxed, like they'd be happy playing some juke joint the size of the Warehouse Stage. Every time Longhair opened his mouth there was a dazzling flash of gold. His playing is both highly sophisticated and highly primitive—endless variations on a theme, some infinitely subtle. What he knows, he knows perfectly.

A surprisingly ascetic reading of "Stagger Lee", Eaglin's amazing guitar work on "Jambalaya," pure Storyville ragtime for the bridge on "Look A-There (She Got No Hair) ["Bald Head"], and a version of "Tipitina" (there must be a thousand different variations on it) arrived like a train at the station, steam and all.

These were some of the highlights that soared over the crowd's collective gooky craniums. I guess they didn't want to go back to the womb, but also they didn't realize that if it wasn't for Longhair, there wouldn't be anybody like Foghat to top him on the bill. In contrast to the applause at the end of Longhair's set, Foghat did seven encores" [...] October 1972. [15] UK writer, commentator, and photographer Valerie Wilmer described James Black (1940-1998): as, "one of the major exponents of the unique New Orleans funk beat." [16]

Fess premier tour to Europe was a very brief London, UK, visit in January 1973, his sole Euro-gig this time. Fess' band was a grouping of five New Orleans bands. Their overseas flight started on January 7, for a show on Wednesday night, January 10. The employer was James "Goldenballs" Goldsmith (1933-1997), a controversial Anglo-French tycoon. [17] He threw a party for his 18 years old daughter Isabel at the "poshest of posh": *the Ritz Restaurant and Hotel*, at 150 Piccadilly, Westminster Borough. Goldsmith usually lived here when in London. In *Blues Unlimited*, Fess was described as: "Resplendent in lurex turban, bright green suit and pink shirt when Mike Prince met him in Carnaby St. with Parker Dinkins, and Snooks Eaglin! Goddam. Luckily they'll be back for Montreux this year with luck." [18]

Besides Fess, the bands were: Percy Humphrey's Preservation Hall Jazz Band; the Eureka Brass Band (well, sort of); the Wild Magnolias (Mardi Gras Indian tribe); plus Willie Tee & The Gaturs. If one excludes the gospel music idiom, the musical genres of the bands might be seen as representatives of 20th century African-American New Orleans Music.

James "Goldenballs" Goldsmith, late 1970s. Unknown photographer.

"Professor Longhair came to this country [UK] only twice during his career [...] only a privileged few saw him perform at the now legendary millionaire's party [...] The day before, scheduled for rehearsals, he spent a half hour or so just playing solo piano amidst the hustle and bustle of tables being laid, sound men tinkering and back drops being erected. At no time did he appear to be overwhelmed by the awesome event, in fact he spent a little while walking out in London, a fair guess the lunchtime shoppers wondering who the turban clad figure was" [...] Tom Stagg, in his Fess obituary, spring 1980. [19]

* * *

"Puttin' on the Ritz: TOM STAGG reports on an historic jazz jam." by Tom Stagg, January 1973:
SHROUDED in an air of mystery more befitting the Allied landings on D-day, 28 of New Orlean's' [sic] finest musicians spent four days of last week holed up in London's plush Royal Lancaster Hotel [at Lancaster Terrace, Hyde Park].

Their presence in the country was supposed to be secret. They slipped quietly in and out of the country, and they were under the constructions not to be photographed or speak to news-papermen [...]

Indeed, the whole affair had more than a vague flavour of the Twenties and the Jazz Age.

Among the musicians were the legendary Professor Longhair [...] *and his band* [plus three acts, including] *the incredible Mardi Gras Indians.*

It was a jazz (and blues) fan's dream come true — or should have been, because security guards in the Ritz made it virtually impossible for "outsiders" to penetrate either the party on Wednesday night or the rehearsal which preceded it on the Tuesday.

The rehearsal, which was ultimately more rewarding for the music than the party, took place in one of the Ritz ballrooms, some floors below street level.

There, among the clatter of workmen, technicians, and flower-arrangers, the first musical strains came from Longhair (a.k.a. Roy Byrd), trying out the piano.

Next, rehearsing their route through the tables to the strains of "The Saints", were the Eureka Brass Band — led by trumpeters Percy Humphrey and "Kid Sheik" Cola, with Clement Tervallon [Tervalon] *(trombone), Raymond Burke and* [Paul] *"Polo" Barnes (clarinets), Earl Turbinton (soprano sax), Lester "Boot[s]" Alexis (snare drum), and Nowell "Papa" Glass, carrying the old Olympia Brass Band bass drum.*

For a few minutes, the sobriety of the Ritz was shattered—as hotel employees jived and the Mardi Gras Indians second-lined. It took a couple of bourbons to cool down before Humphrey rehearsed the Crescent City Joymakers, with Tarvallon [sic], *Burke, Barnes, Narvin Kimball (banjo), James "Sing" Miller (piano), Chester Zardis (bass), and Dave Oxley (drums)* [...] [20]

Dave Oxley (1919-1974), "sang hauntingly on 'Georgia'". He was Earl Palmer's predecessor as Dave Bartholomew's drummer, and Palmer's uncle. Trombonist and bass player Clement Tervalon (1915-1989), had played in big bands lead by Lucky Millinder; Buddy Johnson (at the Gypsy Tea Room, with Johnson's band, December 1945); and the Paul Barbarin Dixieland unit. Tervalon was the bassist on a couple wonderful Roy Montrell, "Specialty" tracks, cut in New Orleans, August 1956.

Next in the line was Longhair's band, and what a shattering experience! There was no stopping Fess as he romped through "Professor Longhair's Blues", "Go To The Mardi Gras", "Everyday" ["I Have The blues."], *"Meet Me Tomorrow Night", "Professor's Boogie", "Tipertina"* [sic], *"Looka No Hair"* ["Bald Head"], *and "Cry To Me". With him were the truly outstanding Snooks Eaglin on electric guitar, Erving Charles (bass guitar), and Lester Alexis (drums).*

But time was tight, and the Mardi Gras Indians showed that their act is vocal as well as visual. A friendly group of young men, they were only too happy to explain the ancient customs of the Indians, and their role today. Among their ranks they had Chief of the Golden Eagles [Joseph "Monk" Boudreaux, born 1941] *and Chief of the* [Wild] *Magnolias* [Bo Dollis], *and their instrumentation — just tambourine, woodblock, cowbell, and bongo — made a fantastic sound on "Iko Iko."* [21]

The percussion players and singers probably incorporated: "Gator June" Johnson Jr.; "Crip" Adams; "Quarter Moon" Tobias; "Bubba" Scott; "Gate" Johnson, and James Smothers.

The final show-stopper at the rehearsal was Willie Tee and his band. Organist Willie (Wilson Turbinton) had his brother Earl on Soprano and alto saxes, Raymond Randolph on guitar, Charles on bass-guitar, Larry Panna (drums), and Lewis Clark (bongos) [congas].

The following night was the party, and the ballroom was bedecked with regal splendour — chandeliers and drapes proliferating, something like an old-time society ball in New Orleans.

Suddenly, the Eureka mob erupted though the drapes, plus the Indians, and with Anderson Minor [Sousaphone, 1901-1973] *and 91-year-old Henry "Booker T" Glass* [1888-1981] *as Grand Marshals. The guests were quite unmoved by the "Saints"— chock, or simply incomprehension?*

As Longhair mounted the stage, a group of girls clustered around the steps, but sadly the set was not the equal of his rehearsal performance.

By the time Willie Tee and the Gators closed the night's music, the audience was tired and some a little the worse for drink. But the band's professional approach provided a memorable finale.

There may never be a "next time". What a shame a more sympathetic and knowledgeable audience wasn't given the chance to hear these fantastic musicians. [22]

The local Jazz fan Richard Milward, recalled a *Royal Lancaster Hotel* party, after the Ritz bash.

"One or two people tried to get into the Ritz and if I remember correctly [UK, reed player] John Defferary was successful by posing as a waiter. I remember asking Booker T Glass if he had seen Buddy Bolden. He said: "yes, he was good" but said little else about Bolden. I think the guy who ran the New Orleans Jazz Festival [Quint Davis] was overseeing the visit of all the musicians to London and he was a bit shocked at the Alcohol bill when they checked out from the hotel. £1,200 seems to come to mind, which was a lot of money in those days." [23]

In the early 1970s, Bo Dollis and the Wild Magnolias used to rehearse in a house at 1713 S. Rampart, sometimes with Fess sitting in on piano. It was rented by Quint Davis, and mainly used as a practice hall, situated at 1713 South Rampart St. In April 1973, this wood structure was severely damaged by a fire – and ultimately torn down.

"The Ritz is in Picadilly, possibly the best location in London [...] Green Park is just around the corner [...] To enter Ritz is to step inside a world of grandeur created by its founder César Ritz, and opened in 1906." [24] Geoffrey Wansell's book: *Tycoon: the Life of James Goldsmith*, gives more details on the spectacular Ritz party. Many of the guests came from the British aristocracy, among them: Sir Max Joseph, Lady Melchett, Lord Antony Lambton, Lord Goodman, the Duke of Marlborough, and Lady Annabel Birley. A couple of UK music celebrities were invited as well for example: singer and keyboard player Georgie Fame [1943-], and in addition the eccentric, legendary singer and writer George Melly (1926-2007).

In all the sixty–seven years of its distinguished history the Ritz hotel in London had seldom seen such a fuss, or extravagance, for a party. The magnificent mirrored rooms in its basement echoed to the shouts of a team

The "poshest of posh": The Ritz Hotel and Restaurant, 150 Piccadilly, St. James's, London, October 2018. Photo and courtesy: Jon Guthrie (with thanks to him). Used by permission.

of anxious florists busily removing all the hotel's own flowers and replacing them with orchids and palms that Jimmy Goldsmith had ordered to be brought in specially. He was determined that his 250 guests should leave the chill Piccadilly air behind them and descend into a tropical night in Louisiana. To sustain the illusion, he had arranged for five jazz bands to be specially flown in from New Orleans to provide music for the evening. The floor was to be covered in chopped wine corks to give an impression of sand […]

When the first guests arrived […] Isabel Goldsmith played her part. She smiled and shook hands, thanked the guests for their compliments, and danced with whoever asked her. There were more of her father's friends than her own, but she did not mind. [25]

Imagine the chosen people dancing to Fess' songs like "Tipitina" and "Go To The Mardi Gras". Which they unlikely had heard, yet, even more doubtful, had shaken their butts to. Wansell ended: the guests "stumbled out into the first rays of dawn [...] the party had been a success".

Fess allowed Tom Stagg an interview for the *Melody Maker*, published, April 1973, **"Professor rock"**: *Professor Longhair, the legendary and elusive New Orleans pianist, is slowly winning the recognition he deserves. Tom Stagg tells the story [...]*

Tom Stagg, 1973. He is long time New Orleans resident. Courtesy Pete Lay. Used by permission.

The sad fact is that the great Fess has been sadly neglected over the years, and while he has sat at home in quite obscurity, the jazz historians and record producers have passed him by. In the past it has been difficult to pin down this man's career on paper, the little that has been written has had a fair share of inaccuracies, but now Longhair is on the threshold of real success with one trip outside the U.S.A. already under his belt. [26]

The story of Fess's career was narrated, partly with content from the Leadbitter/Broven piece in *Blues Unlimited* (No. 76, October 1970). Stagg's article ends:

A turningpoint [sic] in his career came in January this year, when for a private function Professor Longhair left the United States for the first time, and came to London with his band to play at the Ritz for a party. Fess stayed a lot in his room sleeping, he was tired after the long journey and was not very keen about flying anyway. On his few trips out sightseeing nobody knew who he was, but many wondered, who was the guy in the turban and green suit looking at the sights and sounds of Carnaby Street!

Shattering: *He made two appearances at the Ritz, the first an early evening rehearsal when immediately he tried out the piano and some shattering blues and boogie woogie sounds emanated through the old building. Later in the evening he rehearsed his "regular" band—Snooks Eaglin (gtr), Erv-*

The New Orleans born bass player Erving Charles Jr., (1941-2003), Mediterranean Café, Decatur St., May 1989. The lineup included Leroy Jones, trumpet; Elliot" Stackman" Callier, tenor saxophone; Sadie Goodson, piano & vocal; and Joe Lastie, drums. Erving Charles Jr. was the son of guitarist, and bandleader Erving "Buddy" Charles Sr. Fats Domino was Erving's bandleader for many years. Erving Charles Jr. died of heart attack. Photo: Marcel Joly, courtesy Katy Joly. Used by permission (thanks to Katy Joly).

ing Charles (bass gtr) and Lester Alexis (ds) — and this proved without any doubt that Fess is now at the peak of his power. He likes the strong amplified rhythm behind him as he literally pounds away at the piano, and once he started his set he would have gone on for hours.

His repertoire has not changed nor has his voice, and everything stopped and everyone listened to "Everyday I Have The Blues," "Looka No Hair," "Tipitina," "Go To The Mardi Gras" and many others.

In many respects this rehearsal was more satiesfying [sic] than the actual party gig. On the second night the amplification was a little amiss, too much feedback, but still nothing could overshadow the tremendous rendition of "Big Chief," complete with vocal and whistling. Longhair returned quietly home, but good things are in the wind.

He is now getting the odd job on Bourbon Street again and is booked once more for this year's Jazzfest. He has also had an offer to appear at the New-

Lester T. Alexis (1914-1990), on a gig with Danny Barker's band, partly hidden: Frank Naundorf, trombone; Joe Rouzon, reeds; and Frank Fields, bass; New Orleans early 1980s. Photo: Marcel Joly. Used by permission. Alexis was brought up in a family of 14 children. His 20 year older brother Ricard, a trumpeter & bassist, "raised Lester to manhood". Paul Barbarin, started Alexis on drums as a teen. (Ricard Alexis, interview, Hogan Jazz Archive, Tulane University). Lester first cut for Fess in 1949. In Rick Coleman's ("Bear Family" LP) liner notes, the drummer told: He [the Mercury talent scout: William. B. Allen] knowed how good we was [sic]. He wanted to invest some money. So he used Fess, Alma [Mondy] and all them recording and we backed all of them up... We started playing early that night and recorded all night, man. We ate and drunk and everything. Lester was nicknamed as: "Duke", alternatively: "Boots" Alexis.

port Jazz Festival, and has been booked for the blues festival in Montreux, Switzerland, July, along with Snooks Eaglin. [27]

Things for him are a little better but they could be better still. He will still take on a three-day card game in preference to playing a gig with no guarantee, but when at home he will greet visitors in his friendly way and talk freely about his music. The majority of the time he just sleeps on the front seat of his battered car outside his house. He is still neglected and it is time now that this situation was finally remedied. [28]

Margaret "the Iron Lady" Thatcher, died early in April 2013, at a Ritz Hotel suite as she sat up and read.

* * *

The Warehouse, was New Orleans' premier 1970s rock venue, a bare-bones, 30.000-square-foot music venue (demolished in the late 1980s). On Friday, January 26, 1973, Fess performed there at 'the Second Annual Grease Ball'.

The Warehouse last Friday had the cleanest, most homogenous cross-section of suburbanites I've ever seen at a rock show, and the most enthusiastic. One might have thought himself at Uncle Sam's, Nutcracker, Your Father's Mustache or even the LSUNO University Center for all the para-collegiates and post-grad types that packed the building.

They had come to see their childhood fantasies and/or memories set to the glorious music and mime of Vince Vance and the Valiants. What they got was really three shows in one – for the perennial Professor Longhair opened the show, and the second "Annual Grease Ball" dance contest for best rock 'n' roll couple took place before the Valiants performed. Longhair and the dance contest was nothing short of sensational. The professor was hot again. Dressed in a dollar bill green gabardine suit with green and white striped pimp socks, he rocked his electric piano through his standard repertoire of rhythm and blues classics:"Stack-O-Lee", "In The Night", "Mardi Gras In New Orleans", "Tipitina", et al. To my amazement, the 'fess' seemed foreign to these people. You got the feeling they were asking themselves, "...who is this funky old man?" So little of what he played struck a familiar chord to them. They liked him, for certain, and applauded wildly (four encores), but there was a reserved air about it that twenty-eight and thirty-odd years of suburban cleanliness couldn't hide. Word has it that Longhair was just as great the next night at an uptown benefit for the Free School. [29]

"New Orleans Jazz & Heritage Festival" by Terry Pattison:
The fair closed Sunday with Professor Longhair, the king of New Orleans R&B. With Snooks Eaglin on guitar and rhythm section from the Meters, he created a funky, swinging blues sound. Naturally he did all his hits— Mardi Gras, Bald Head, Tipitina, and Big Chief. He is one of the all-time great New Orleans pianists and his performance here showed that he's still the king of Mardi Gras music. Of course the crowd was dancing for his entire set. They hated to see him stop at the sunset. All in all an extremely satisfying festival. It is hoped that it will be even better in 1974. [30]

The summer, 1973 issue of *Living Blues magazine,* reported Fess jamming with B. B. King, Roosevelt Sykes, Bukka White, and the Meters' rhythm section, at the New Orleans Jazz Fest.

* * *

"Montreux '73", by Norbert Hess:
Atlantic Records' 'Night in New Orleans,' in my opinion the high point of the festival featured Dr. John, Allen Toussaint, The Meters, and the legendary rock 'n' roll founder Professor Longhair (Roy Byrd). Amplification difficulties destroyed the Meters' usually clean, compact sound, and an intolerant (mostly Swiss) audience whistled and cat-called until the group left the stage. Longhair played an interesting mixture of blues, boogie and Latin American rhumba, and standing ovation brought the old man back for three encores. Dr. John's set featured several R&B classics along with his own recent material. One of the finest piano pieces I heard was from the New Orleans piano man, Allan Toussaint, accompanied by the great tenor saxophonist Gary Brown. Dr. John, Toussaint, Brown and Longhair all returned for more encores, and everybody went home satisfied around 2 a.m. [...] [31]

In 2012, George Porter was interviewed by one Michael Limnios: "What was the worst moment of your career?"

That might be along the same lines as what happened in the best moment as once again the Meters were getting booed off the stage. We went to Montreux

Montreux, Switzerland, Saturday, June 30, 1973. Photo: Jan Ytterberg.

Jazz Festival to be the house band for Professor Longhair and Dr. John. We did our set with Dr. John and then there was a short break and Fess came out as the headliner. Well, the baby grand piano was acoustically miked and we were an electric band. The blend of the two did not work very well and the audience could not hear Fess's piano. So once again the Meters were being booed off the stage. This time we left the stage and just let Fess play. [32]

From his Montreux visit, photographer and blues fan: Hans Andréasson, reported for the Swedish *Jefferson* blues magazine. This is the last part of his piece.

Late at night, [after the TV cameras were off], *when almost everybody had left, I lingered at the bar. Then I heard piano music from the Concert Hall and went to find out what it was. A group of fans had persuaded Professor Longhair to do a couple of encores. It was a marvelous moment, with just a few listeners around the piano, and 'Fess' was moved to tears by the overwhelming reception. He played a couple of songs by himself, including his signature 'Mardi Gras in New Orleans'. After that Dr. John showed up and played a couple of tunes, and he was so much better than earlier in the evening. Then Allen Toussaint and his saxophone player Gary Brown joined the party, and improvised a couple of numbers.*

A lovely spontaneous ending of an evening, which had been disappointing in many ways, at least for me. [33]

* * *

At the end of April 1973, John Broven and James LaRocca held a huge party at the (Louis C.) Mason's Americana Motel, South Claiborne Avenue, New Orleans. Broven did research for his future book: *Walking to New Orleans* (1974). Fess was invited, plus an impressive number of local acts, among them: Alvin "Red" Tyler's Gentlemen of Jazz, including vocalist Germaine Bazzle, and versatile pianist & arranger Edward "Ed" Frank; Tommy Ridgley; Ernie K-Doe; Milton Batiste; Art Neville; George Porter; Chris Kenner; Earl King; Gerri Hall (of Huey "Piano" Smith fame); Alvin Batiste, and his drummer Herman Jackson; bass player/singer Roland "Cookie" Cook; singer Tony Owens, plus the rock band Greased Lightnin'.

Longhair? What more can be said. He's loved by everyone in New Orleans. 'It's so good to see him doing well at last. Said Red Tyler, 'after all the bad times he's had.' He's an originator, the father of New Orleans rock 'n' roll and still drenched in the blues. He had to do an encore (a regular thing these days), and it's only at times like this that you realise how well numbers like "Baldhead" slot naturally into a club atmosphere. George Porter was mad that he missed Fess's set [...] John Broven, summer 1973. [34]

* * *

"Professor of rock", by Robert Partridge, September 1973:
The Professor, they say, influenced just about every musician in New Orleans. And it's not a claim he's about to deny. "I taught most of the youngsters," he comments. "I had so many kids comin' to me wanting to play drums, horns... they wanted to play music, y'know. I'd go along with them an' give them work." Roy Byrd, a/k/a Professor Longhair. It's been a weird year for the Professor. For most of his life he's been in New Orleans, playing in bars and dives but mostly just being neglected.

And then he starts off 1973 playing for a private party in London, coming back to Europe this summer for the New Orleans package tour with Dr. John, the Meters and Allen Toussaint.

It's taken 25 years, but at last things are looking positively up for the Professor — a name he's had ever since he started to play the piano.

"The fellas I taught, they started callin' me Professor Longhair. The girls, they, don't know me too well. I don't go too much for ladies, you know, for peace sake. They can cause a lotta trouble. The best way to keep peace with the fellas is to keep away from their ladies. So the girls started to callin' me Longhair, an' the words got together in some kinda way an' the name stuck," he says.
Back in 1948, Professor Longhair and his band, the Shuffling Hungarians, were playing a number called "Bald Head" in New Orleans' Pepper Pot Club [across the river, in Gretna].

It would be convenient, of course, to be able to point to one man, one record or one year and claim that was when rock 'n' roll began. But history's not like that. It's not so simple.

Many people nevertheless, would claim that "Baldhead" contained at least the essence of rock 'n' roll. There was a stiffer, more potent beat slipped into that New Orleans' shuffle rhythm.

"Well they say it was rock 'n' roll. I really don't know what it was — they can call it what they want, though," says Longhair. "To me that tune was a ballad, but they say it was too rough an' rugged to be called that." The Professor's interest in music started in the Twenties. "It was my mother that got me started, I used to listen to her in churches an' different places," he comments.

"After that I tried dancing, seein' if I could make some money. I didn't care what I played or did at that time. I was dancin' in the beginning, but there wasn't much money in it. I did so many funny things. Acrobats, an' things, you know, runnin' up the wall an' all that." He also formed a duo with Champion Jack Dupree. "We worked together for many years. When I first met him he was basically a comedian. He'd sing an´ vocalisin', an' then do the comedian bit while I played the piano, drums, anything I could make a livin' at, you know," Longhair recalls.

And perhaps the best Roy Byrd could make a living at was playing piano. He put together a whole series of blues combos, including the Shuffling Hungarians, in the late-thirties, "That name was built around one of the guys in the band who had a funny accent, a Hungarian accent, you know. I had to get a name for the band an' the first thing I could think of was the Shuffling Hungarians. We done a lotta shufflin' in those days," says Byrd.

"At that time we had Robert Parker on saxophone. Al Miller was originally playing drums, but after I met [the drummer] Milton Stevens, I switched Al over to trumpet." That band also included Walter 'Papoose' Nelson, a legendary New Orleans guitarist, who later became one of the primary sources of inspiration for Mac Rebennack.

"Robert Parker, after he'd thought he'd learnt as much as he could from me, left the band. I never tried to hold him. So he drifted off an' started buildin' his own little outfit. An' I made another group, although right now, it's real difficult to remember all the names, there were so many."

He had to wait until the late-forties however, before his first recording session. Jesse Erickson, owner of the Star Talent label, persuaded Longhair to record "She Ain't Got No Hair" (which was "Bald Head") in 1949. The label was eventually forced out of business for holding non-union sessions.

"That label didn't get no place. You don't see them 'round no more, I don't know what happened to them, but I do know they didn't give me enough to get a sandwich with for that session. They didn't rent a studio, so they couldn't have had no money.

"They had a little recorder in a place right behind the [Municipal] Auditorium in New Orleans [the Gypsy Tea Room No. One?]. That was the first record to hit the streets, an' it disgusted me."

There are two aspects to Roy Byrd's recording career. One — he created some of the most dazzling music to come out of New Orleans, while, two, he saw hardly a cent for his efforts.

"After Star Talent I met a guy who got me on Mercury. The records seemed to be doin' all right, but the money wasn't going to me. I left Mercury, that's when I met Jerry Wexler and Ahmet Ertegun. But after a while I didn't see them no more. So I started hittin' from label to label, tryin' to hit lucky."

Byrd rejoined Atlantic in 1953, coming up with the extraordinary "Tipitina," although he had to wait until 1959, and the Ronn label ["Ron"], before he had another chart success, "Go to the Mardi Gras." He went back into the studios and in the mid- sixties to cut "Big Chief."

He's been with six or so labels throughout his recording career, although Byrd claims none of them paid him for his records. His recording career had started about the same time Fats Domino brought out the classic 'Fat Man'.

"I broke up my outfit to make his outfit up. Well, little Walter Nelson, I taught him, trained him 'cos his daddy [Walter Nelson Sr.] helped me a lot."
"It looked as though Fats was gonna make some money, an' I thought if he had some of my musicians, I would've been the first friend he would've thought of. I thought that. But I been thinkin' wrong over a lotta things, looks like everythin' I was thinking was wrong, so I just quit," Byrd comments.

For a long period during the Fifties and indeed most of the Sixties, Byrd virtually quit the business. "I gambled to make some money, cooked, washed

cars, anything to make some money 'cos I had children to raise, you know,"
he says.

He still played the occasional club gig, perfecting those weird piano synco-
pations which have subsequently become part of New Orleans musical vo-
cabulary. [35]

He talks about the second line—that 2/4 rhythm—which forms the basis of
New Orleans music although he professes not to know why the city has such
a rich musical tradition. "I imagine there were more people in New Orleans
that wanted to play music than in other places, it's really a music town," is
his only comment.

But throughout the whole period of his exile from the recording studios
during the Fifties, he still retained his "professor" credentials.

"Yeah, I was teachin' all the guys in New Orleans. Practically all of them, I
helped Toussaint, Sugar Boy [James Crawford], Guitar Slim [Eddie Jones],
Fats [Domino] any of them that come to me for help," he comments.

And so he could have remained, a revered New Orleans musician with a
legendary past, but no future, if it wasn't for a young blues enthusiast called
Quint Davis, the organizer of the New Orleans Jazz Festival.

"I just figured the Festival had to have Professor Longhair. So I finally found
him and asked him to play. One day he showed up at the [1971] Festival, just
him and a drummer [Ed Kimbrough], in black suit, black shirt and black
glasses," says Davis.

"I'd never seen him play before, but people at the Festival, musicians, were
knocked out. You see a lot of people in New Orleans thought he was dead an'
gone.
You think people in Europe thought he was gone. Well, people right in New
Orleans, black people who knew him, thought he was dead. And when he
started playing they said it wasn't him. People were saying 'that's not the
real Professor. I knew the real Professor an' he's dead.'

But he just sat down at the piano and it was electric. Everybody just gathered
'round the stage and he was fantastic, incredible, hot rock 'n' roll piano."

That was in 1970, Longhair's first major gig in over a decade [sic]. *The next step was to find a record contract. Davis took Longhair, together with Snooks Eaglin on guitar and a bass player and a drummer to Baton Rouge to cut 30 demo tracks* [September, 1971].

The tapes were sent to Atlantic. Davis knew the company was planning to a reissue album of Longhairs old material, and thought Atlantic would be interested in the Professor's new songs. Eventually he landed a recording deal with Albert Grossman's Bearsville label.

Grossman, however, wanted the album re-recorded using Bearsville musicians. The way Davis tells the story. Longhair waited around for six months until finally they decided to cut the album with Zig Modeliste and George Porter from the Meters and Snooks Eaglin in Memphis.

"That session is now lying dead in the Bearsville vaults because Grossman wanted white musicians — more commercial on it. He wanted his people, like Rick Danko from the Band, to play, but we waited six months for them to set it up," claims Davis.

The Bearsville contract has now expired. And still no new Professor Longhair album.

There's hope yet however, because Buddah taped the New Orleans Jazz Festival and Atlantic are preparing an album from the recent Montreux concert. So the Professor will, at least, have some sort of record out.

And Mac Rebennack too, he plans to record the Professor. Quite when or how have yet to be decided, but partnership has a special significance. Rebennack, you see, was one of the Professor's pupils back in the Fifties. The Night Tripper meets the Big Chief of New Orleans. [36]

The Baton Rouge, La. sessions were released in 1987, and 1991. Multi-instrumentalist George Davis (1938-2008), played electric bass on the June 1972 recording. The Memphis recordings were released in 1987 and 1991. The destiny of the "Buddah" recordings, cut at the New Orleans Heritage Festival, is still unsolved. Bob Dylan, plus the Band, Janis Joplin, Paul Butterfield, just to mention a few, were all managed by Albert Grossman (1926-1986). Guitarist Nick Gravenites, meant that, the trip of Grossman was money. "He was no tap dancer, no musician, he was a business man and the business he took care best of was his own." [37]

* * *

"Professor Longhair In New York – 'Byrd's The Word'", by Anton J. Mikofsky, 1973-1974:
Hearing Roy Byrd, alias Professor Longhair, live at Kenny's Castaways [157 Bleecker St., Greenwich Village], *could have been a disappointment. After all, how many 55-year-old singer-pianist sound as good (or better) in 1973 as they did in 1949-53? Well, "Fess" was not only a disappointment, he was great.*

His singing features maniacally off-center tonality, deliberately, for grabbing attention. "Honey child!!" he bleats, cracking the "correct" note at the front of the phrase quite wide open. He is certainly capable of crooning in perfect pitch, as he does in the unfractured nonsense lyrics of Tipitina. And he does as much hula hoop rollin' and waterfall tumblin' on the piano keys as he does with his acrobatic vocal arpeggios. One trick that flips me for a loop is his trilling his way stepwise up a treble scale. Or Mr. Byrd will take off on sudden flights of fancy in the middle of a steady-rolling piano blues. Bits and pieces of Here Comes the Bride or ancient military marches flash into his musical consciousness. But it's not a medley; it's an effortless recreation. And although Fess is infinitely entertaining, he's about as far from an "entertainer" as Thelonious Monk is from the cocktail pianist at Hilly's (not to pick an example!).

In short, Fess is a musician. Well rounded in blues, R&B, boogie, rock and soul, he can play anything — in his style. Thus he took on (and took over) Solomon Burke's Cry to Me, Ray Charles's Mess Around (sans vocals), the folky Junco Partner, his New Orleans colleague Antoine "Fats" Domino's Going Home Tomorrow. And of course he's on home base with his own inimitable dawn-of-rock material like Tipitina, In the Night, Mardi Gras, and (co-authored with Earl King) Big Chief. But thrill that he is for certified 50's freaks, Longhair doesn't limit himself to a revival of his old hits. Ball the Wall, one of my favorites from his Korean War-period oldies (on his Atlantic LP) isn't even in his current repertoire, "It's not rehearsed," he said, refusing a request: Fess works with a band. At Kenny's he had only electric bassist Julius Farmer and

*conga drummer Alfred Roberts, two strong Louisiana dudes. Home in New
Orleans, the Professor works with a larger class of "Blues Scholars" (as his old
singles called his sidemen), including the R&B group the Meters and Snooks
Eaglin, the blind guitarist of some renown. At Kenny's, Longhair's trio was
plenty much gumbo as it was. Zipping, eccentrically swinging rhumba-rock-
ing through pianistic roller coasters, he poured glissandos, trills, and all sorts
of unnamed ornamentations over a base of dance provoking solid rhythm. And
his singing and whistling wigged everyone out.*

*No longer need anybody tell me of his pasts glories, about how he "tutored"
Lee Dorsey, Huey Smith and the Clowns, Allen Toussaint or Ernie K-Doe. I
don't need to read any more rave reviews of his reissue album, as fine as it is.
I have heard the Byrd, and the Byrd's the word.* [38]

* * *

"Professor Longhair's Rock And Roll Gumbo", by Robert Palmer,
March 1974. Excerpts:
*During the past year, he has made three New York appearances, one at the
Newport - New York Jazz Festival and two at Kenny's Castaways, and con-
verted the initially curious to believers [...]*

*In person the Professor cuts an unassuming figure. He is a slight and quite
man who often works in a leather jacket, blue jeans, and a tee-shirt. In conversation, he reveals a dry wit. At Kenny's one night I asked him if he had
ever played for a sanctified church service, "No," he said, "You've got to have
plenty of patience to have religion, but I've seen sanctified church service.
But I've seen sanctified people when the spirit hits them. Whoooooo! It hits
'em so hard it knocks 'em out!"*

*At the piano Longhair displays the rhythmic acuity of a master drummer.
He has developed a system he calls cross-chording for playing his percussive
brand of music without destroying his hands. "That's putting alias keys in
there," he explains. "You don't have to use them, but it gives you a better
blend. See, when I started on the piano I couldn't reach an octave; my hands
were too small. That started me to jumping, and jumping, and from jumping
I had to come across other keys that I didn't need. So I have to cross chord to
get the natural keys I want." When talking about music, he uses the terms
"pitch" and "beat" interchangeably, and he seems to judge the relative suc-*

cess of a particular performance by how many metric subdivisions he is able to feel within a bar of music. "I was up to 16ths," he said of one set at Kenny's, "and I was trying to see if I couldn't get up to a 32nd."

Later at the Chelsea loft where Longhair, his band, and manager Quint Davis were staying, 'Fess lectured his conga drummer ["Uganda" Roberts] on the importance of maintaining an even rhythmic accentuation. "If you give me the pace, and feel that I've got the feeling, and you got to keep it there, I don't need drums," he said. "See, I can do a thing and maybe I'll have to do it again to express my feelings. That's how I'm letting people know that I'm not just simply lucking up on this, I'm executing it. And I like to do things so that other musicians can see how high they're being done. I don't mostly play for the audience. I can keep them happy, but I've got to give another musician something to analyze." Longhair's patented cross rhythms and accentual patterns are indeed fascinating subjects for analysis. Like the music of West African drum orchestras, they are additive in principle. Once a foundation is established, 'Fess, like Elvin Jones and other masters of polyrhythm, is capable of infinite digression, split-second shifts, suspensions, and variations. Any number of cross-rhythms is theoretically possible as long as each player understands the pattern of basic accents which, as Longhair suggests, is perhaps best understood as a series of dotted 16ths and 32nds [...]

"'The blues guitarists I heard played just what they felt the way they felt it," he recalls. There wasn't any certain time or air. You just produced a sound to fit the verses in a line of blues. But I didn't care for that feel. I like to be happy or just jolly; just let me around some dixieland or jazz or some way out beats. I like those beats, those movements. I used to listen to Perez Prado in those days. I liked his movements." [39]*

By this time [around 1953] he had pupils and followers aplenty. "I wasn't exactly a teacher," he explains, "but I would give the younger musicians ideas and help them learn what they needed to know. It was the younger musicians who really liked what I was doing.

There's very few people in the younger generation in New Orleans that have recorded that I haven't done something for or helped. I helped Fats Domino when he was sounding exactly like me, when I was teaching him how to play the songs and let him produce them. I figured I could make enough just staying in the background so that I wouldn't ever need to again what I'm doing now. Then he got somebody else to do these things for him, after he got where he could do them without me. He started off with one of my vocalists and one of my guitar players. I broke my band up to complete his band, just to work with him or be involved. But none of my ideas worked out [...]

"Papoose" Nelson played guitar. John Broven thinks that Fess referred to Jessie Hill as the vocalist. [40]

Domino and many of the New Orleans musicians who backed Little Richard, Huey Smith, and other rock and roll stars of the 1950s simplified Longhairs rhythmic innovations considerably. The multiplicity of beats Fess had worked so long to develop became "the big beat." I asked him if Domino was principally to blame for simplifying his approach. "No," he said. "They were all doing that. That's why so much of the music now sounds like it does. Nobody's really staying together anymore it's crackin' up. The best of the youngsters I've heard is Zigaboo (Zig Modeliste, drummer with the Meters), has a pair of hands and imagination. He's well acquainted with what I do" [...]

As Jerry Wexler has noted, Professor Longhair is now "singing and playing at the very top of his power — better than ever. The spirit of his music is a physical force that hits his listeners. It hits 'em so hard knocks 'em out! [41]

* * *

Tad Jones, on the New Orleans Jazz & Heritage festival, April 18 - 21, 1974. Excerpts:

For me the festival began on a high note Friday morning with an unscheduled appearance by Professor Longhair. What began as a sound check on Stage 4 became an impromptu 15-minutes concert, featuring old favorites How Long, Big Chief, Mardi Gras In New Orleans, and a few odd improvisations. Though rarely heard as a soloist, Longhair held up well without his own group, much to the delight of the small crowd which had gathered [...]

No one could have planned a better climax to the festival than bringing together Clarence "Gatemouth" Brown and Professor Longhair. Gatemouth had already done a set earlier in the day. Though I was expecting something more in the vein of his old Peacock recordings, what I found was an old artist with a new direction. He played blues guitar with brilliance and Cajun fiddle with a fire that would make your heart stand still. He and Longhair performed together as if they had spent hours in rehearsal. Gatemouth's mellow guitar fit perfectly behind Byrd's keyboard syncopations. I don't think I've ever heard anyone complement Longhair as well as Gatemouth. Some 4000 spectators were on hand to catch this final set [...]

Though the festival ended Sunday at dusk, there is an epilogue. Shortly before the fest, a fire destroyed Professor Longhair's home, piano, sound equipment and many personal items. A relief fund was quickly established and a benefit concert was planned for the Monday after the festival. Held at the Warehouse, the benefit featured an almost unbelievable lineup of talent— Dr. John, Allen Toussaint, the Meters, Earl Turbinton, Tommy Ridgley and Earl King just to mention a few. While the town's musicians seemed to pull together in the wake of the tragedy, the people of New Orleans didn't. Less than 1000 showed up for the benefit and only $4500 was raised. The Jazz & Heritage Festival had another successful year. Too bad it had to end on such a sour note. [42]

Tad Jones, fall 1975:
Dear Living Blues, In regard of to the review of the Professor Longhair LP ROCK 'N' ROLL GUMBO ["Blue Star" / "Barclay"] by Robert B. Sacré in LB # 22, I'd like to correct a few details which Mr. Sacré is not aware of. He states in his review that Mr. Byrd had a good reason to have the blues because three days before the recording session his house burned to the ground. This is far from the truth. What did catch fire (but was not totally destroyed) was a house in the 1300 block of South Rampart Street which his manger had rented as a practice hall. True, Longhair did have some personal belongings in the building, but, all was not lost. Today Longhair lives at 1522 S. Rampart St., in the same house he's been in for the last 15 years or more. Keeping the record straight. [43]

"Three items were left in the rubble, and they turned up only after an extended search: Fess' diamond stickpin, a briefcase containing important papers, insurances policies, car title, etc.—and one scrapbook. Everything else—clothes, piano, sound equpiment [sic], furniture, memorabilia—was gone." The *1974 New Orleans Jazz & Heritage Festival* program-book.

James Black. In public school, Black, "Smokey" Johnson, and John Boudreaux had the same music teacher, the very influential Yvonne Busch (1929-2014). James was to record with jazz celebrities like: Yusef Lateef; the Adderley Bros.; local acts like Eddie Bo; Lee Dorsey/Allen Toussaint, and even a Bourbon St. Dixieland unit. Black was also a pianist, singer, plus an accomplished composer. When Fess died (30/2-80), Black was abroad, during January - March, 1980. He toured all over a wintery Sweden, in the vaudeville stage show: One Mo' Time. This was perhaps Black's sole Euro visit? A heavy drug habit ended his life, in his home town. Photo: courtesy: New Orleans Heritage: Jazz: 1956-1966.

In 1987, singer "Benny" Spellman (1931-2011) commented the Fess concert, March 24, 1975, aboard the retired RMS Queen Mary. Since 1967, she remains permanently moored in Long Beach, Cal. Fess and his band was invited by Paul and Linda McCartney. They were host for a party, a celebration for a soon-to-be-released LP album (Paul McCartney and Wings, Venus and Mars), waxed in New Orleans. Fess was recorded live. The other acts were: Ernie K-Doe; Robert Parker; and the Meters (also recorded live). Spellman narrated: "It was the greatest trip of my life, man. They gave us a 20-gun salute when we went on the ship. Everybody that was somebody was on that ship. I'm talking about Paul Williams [Paul Newman?], Michael Jackson, Frank Sinatra, Dean Martin–everybody! Professor Longhair went up there and he killed the people, man. It was as if he knew–hey man, this is my last big show." [44]

"I consider Mr. and Mrs. Paul McCartney my friends because they came a long way to meet me." Fess told. "They invited me to California to play a session for a party they had on the Queen Mary. But I really didn't know they was recording the album [...]" [45]

In 1975, Tad Jones wrote a New Orleans report for an Australian blues magazine.

In the Uptown section Jed's [University Inn] has experienced two SRO dates in November and December with Professor Longhair. The club itself is small and intimate and generates just the right kind of atmosphere for Byrd's mood. On the stage with him were Alfred Roberts (congas) and James Black (drums). [46]

* * *

"Professor Longhair: The Man Who Taught New Orleans Music," by Bunny Matthews, June 1977:
Last August [in 1976], I found myself at dance given by Civil Defense Post 714 (Both Fess and his wife, Alice, are active in the organization) in the basement of some old building up near Melpomene. The celebrants were mostly black couples in Civil Defense khakis.

Dr. John, who was at the time coasting down from being a Famous Rock Star and heading for England to work with Van Morrison, stood in a corner, still absorbed by Fess after all the years. A couple of us attempted to talk with him but it was clear that this was his Affirmation of Faith, following the licks and eventually, sitting in—singing old Roy Brown songs for Fess.
I know how it is because when I get too strung out, frazzled by all these deadlines and NOPSI bills and the oppressive summer oxygen, I like to sit at Fess' feet and loose myself for a little while. Professor is a particularly apt name for the man. No academician has taught me more. Lately, things have been looking better for Fess. Paul McCartney recently bought the rights to a tape of Fess, recorded a couple of years ago on the Queen Mary. Fess got a $5,000 advance (which is nothing compared to what the latest punk group gets but still it's still about twice any amount he's been offered before), and the McCartneys seem intent on releasing the album. Lots of people have shown interest in Fess—Bob Dylan's manager, Albert Grossman flew Fess and Snooks Eaglin up to Bearsville, N. Y., several years ago (Snooks, being

blind with acute hearing, couldn't sleep at night because the sound of the snowflakes falling kept him awake) and recorded some tracks, which Grossman apparently never quite decided what to do with. It seems that non-Orleanians are a bit overwhelmed by Fess and just can't figure out what this Professor Longhair is all about it.

FORTUNATELY, Fess has an extremely dedicated manager, Allison [Miner] Kaslow, who seems to spend every waking hour trying to get Fess' music broadcast to the world. The McCartney deal was the result of a couple of years work, negotiating with the McCartney organization, securing the publishing and wading through the shambles left by Fess' former manager Quint Davis. (Quint, the director of the Jazz Festival, and Allison were partners for a long time. Allison no longer works with the Festival and admits that this year's event reduced her to tears. "It was as if your only daughter turned out to be a whore.") Fess' career suffered while Quint's flourished.

There have been numerous other human monkey-wrenches in Fess' continuing saga-in fact, it seems that just about every major figure in the New Orleans record industry has screwed Fess out of one thing or another. When Allison contacted Joe Assunto, a well-known record distributor, to arrange for Fess' appearance at the very first Jazz Festival, Assunto told her that Fess was dead. Actually, he was sweeping out the back room of Assunto's warehouse [One Stop Record Shop?]. This sort of stuff continues to this day apt name for the man. No academician has taught me more. Fess still doesn't receive royalties for "Go to the Mardi Gras," he has never seen any money from the French Barclay ["Blue Star"] album recorded by Philippe Rault and likewise for the "Mardi Gras in New Orleans" album ["Mardi Gras Records", MG 1001] released this year by Rault and Warren Hildebrand.

Now to me this is pretty outrageous because I am friends with Philippe and Warren and I believe they love Fess and they certainly aren't cigar-chomping magnates way up in New York or something. It just seems that people won't give Fess a fair deal. (Fess confined that Jim Russell is one of the few honest men in the New Orleans record industry—too honest, it seems. Fess recalls that back in the '50s, Russell would pay musicians before the gigs and the musicians would split with the cash and never show up to play)...

And how is it working outside New Orleans?

"That I haven't really had the opportunity to acknowledge because I be so busy trying to keep the men on the right track, on time—it's such a headache tryin' to deal with something and all the responsibility falls on you and the whole thing is shabby and shakey. What we really need is to get somewhere and relax for about three months and work on something.

"Everytime you go to do something, you gotta train somebody else —it just gets to be a headache — it's worrisome... I'm just like a music teacher. Everybody I get they're brand new... first, you gotta get what he's been playin' out of him to play what you want him to play."

Will Harvey is about the steadiest player you've got...

"Will? He plays good... I keep him with me because he keeps the band happy a lot. He'll imitate the average one of 'em out there if you'll really keep him goin'... if he got something to work with. Like I said, we keep breakin' up and re-hiring and re-teaching..."

"People think you can go out there and cut a record because you can sing a song and well, that's true . . . But to continually do anything, it starts to get monotonous: you get sick of the same tune —you gotta change your beats as well as your tune. If you can't do something right, you just as well not bother with it."

"I was soloing once and everybody thought I should have a band. —'Wow, you got too much going, don't kill it, stretch out ...' So I got a band and then the guys tell me: 'Wow you've got too many pieces.' So I'm right back where I started. Now I gotta forget about the big-band arrangements and start thinking solos of my own. And then somebody comes along and says: 'You got to do another album' and I gotta look for more musicians. I don't know how many bands I've had since 1970 ... how many I've used."

Any favorites?

"I like 'em all. I don't believe they have a band aound here that's been workin' steady for ten years — I'm not talkin' about Dixieland or at the Blue Room over at the Roosevelt [Hotel, 123 Baronne St.] *— they can afford to keep 'em working all year round. I had a break like that at the Royal Sonesta* [Hotel, 300 Bourbon St.] *and all the guys froze up on me and I lost that gig..."*

You like to record fast, I've heard.

"If you go in there clowning around, somebody in the bunch is gonna get awkwardly around the fourth or fifth hour—you gotta go in like a gig—fresh—and do it in as less time as possible—I know you can do six songs in an hour."

Six songs in one hour! Most of the rock groups do one song in six months!

"Well you know that's them ... not me."

Finally, can you clear up the mystery of Tipitina —where does that come from? It's not somebody's name, is it?

"Oh no ... that comes from way back. I was reading in the paper about this volcano exploding—I don't know where it was ... I think maybe in Hawaii— and it was called Tipitina. I liked it and wrote my song."

"I get titles in a lot of strange ways—like that song 'Baldhead'—I had this girlfriend and the guys were making fun of her 'cause she was baldheaded and Mike Tessitore, who ran the Caldonia Inn, got me playin' this song about her and we were laughing and having a good time and she walked in and well, she went right back to the house that night and packed her bags. The song became a big hit." [47]

Mardi Gras In New Orleans, "Mardi Gras Records" (MG 1001) was a compilation album, including Fess' "Go To The Mardi Gras", 1959; and the original version of "Big Chief", Parts 1- 2, 1964. Jim Russell (1920-2014), was a manager and agent etc., who moved to New Orleans in 1955. In 1969, he opened *Jim Russell's Records*, 1837 Magazine Street. It was a store with an impressive amount of records, among them, a large quantity of local vinyl discs. The store closed down after Russell's death, late 2015.

* * *

SAN FRANCISCO • *Professor Longhair, Gatemouth Brown and the Neville Brothers along with ["Big"] Chief Jolly [George Landry] of the Wild Tchoupitoulas performed extensively throughout the Bay Area after their*

Monterey Jazz Festival appearance. The group, sans Gatemouth, performed at the Boarding House five nights (Sept. 20-25), including an opening night bash hosted by producer David Rubinson, who offered barrels of crayfish and beer to the press, musicians and record people. Afterwards, all were treated to a concert performance which opened with the Nevilles' funky New Orleans renditions of "Shake Rattle and Roll," ["Baby"] "What You Want Me To Do," and "Tell It Like It Is." They stayed onstage to back Longhair and proceeded to drown the poor man out, but he nonetheless managed to convey some of his unique musical charm with "Bald Head" (a la 1949), "Big Chief," "How Long Has the Train Been Gone," [sic] and a nice solo opening to the classic "Tipitina." Dr. John joined in for a few numbers and added some nice blues touches while staying rather inconspicuous. By the end of the Longhair set, the piano had become more audible. Ending the show were the Wild Tchoupitoulas. Actually, the real Tchoupitoulas, with the exception of Chief Jolly, were not present at all. Substituting for the group were the Nevilles, who did a splendid job replete with wildly colored feathers of red, gold, blue, and pink and so forth. Gatemouth, who brought along his own band, remained in San Francisco about a month [...] [48] Tom Mazzolini.

Fess did a show at the *Monterey Jazz Festival*, Saturday afternoon, September 17, 1977, supported by the Neville Brothers rhythm section: Renard Poché, guitar; Roger Poché, bass; and Newton Mossop Jr., drums. The concert, billed as: *Mardi Gras In New Orleans*, was sold out months in advance. The Neville Brothers comprised: Art, Aaron, Cyril, and Charles Neville, Gerald "Professor Shorthair" Tillman, keyboards (1955-1986), plus the rhythm section that supported Fess as well. [49]

* * *

Maxwell "Max" Jones (1917-1993) started out as a musician, but he gave it up for music journalism. He ultimately became the dean of British jazz and blues music writers, and befriended, and wrote about the elite of UK and US musicians.

"Professor Longhair talks to Max Jones", London, April 1978:
ALWAYS a pleasure to meet a legend, and New Orleans' – singer – pianist – songwriter – influence Professor Longhair has been called a "living legend" and such things more often than most.

I missed him when he paid a brief visit in 1973 to play at a private party given by James Goldsmith—although I did catch his New Orleans sidekick, guitarist Snooks Eaglin, also performing at the shindig—so it was hotfoot over to publicist Tony Braisby's place last week to meet the creator of "Tipitina," "Mardi Gras In New Orleans" and "Professor Longhair Blues." A very nice legend he is, too.

The professor, known to intimates as Fess, is a softly-spoken man, tall and rather slow on his pins, who has the deeply engraved sad streak of someone familiar with bad feelings times and tough times.

Max Jones and daughter, circa 1949. Courtesy: Orkesterjournalen, March 1949, Sweden. Used by permission.

He does smile, however, and I think his one concert appearance in Britain last Sunday was the source of much pleasure. His first public performance here, and only one date! It seemed to be a long journey for one show.

No, I don't think so. It was so nice of the man to invite him, and he felt that this kind of exposure was good for him professionally. Besides, as he told me with absolute conviction, he loves playing.

I knew Longhair was also promoting the release (on March 23) of his first in concert album. Harvests's 'Live At The Queen Mary' [sic] made at a Paul McCartney-hosted celebration on the Queen Mary in 1975. But the chance to publicise a record had not been the clincher. He was coming over for the record, he said, before he'd learned of the album's release.

When you come to think about it, the release looks a bit overdue at that. But Fess (if he'll pardon the familiarity) is used to hold-ups, hang-ups and cock-ups, personal crises too, and speaks quietly about disappointments past and not so distant.

PROFESSOR LONGHAIR

Fess, aboard the RMS Queen Mary, 1975, a publicity photograph. "Dear folks, Please find enclosed a single ["Harvest" HAR 5154] by Professor Longhair. We met when we were doing [the album] Venus and Mars in New Orleans, and he eventually played at a party on the Queen Mary, [...] Hope you enjoy this record, and help to make it the success it probably deserves to be. Long Live Fess! It's a hit. All the best Paul McCartney." Courtesy Alan Balfour (with thanks to him). Used by permission.

A number of titles were cut a few years back with Snooks Eaglin on guitar, and Longhair said he thought them good. Albert Grossman, it appeared, had the recordings but was not ready to release them.

"I would have put them out myself," said the pianist. "Music is something that can get out of date, and when you hang onto things too long you sometimes find that you've missed the boat."

In the past, not surprisingly, he has earned very little from recordings—or anything else—and his story echoes that of only too many jazz, blues and folk performers who are relegated naturally (like book writers, if I may say so) to the league of the clipped.

Today there is more than hope that the worst is over. He will be receiving royalties on his "Queen Mary" album, naturally, and he's beginning to collect on some of the oldies also.

The grinding poverty is behind him and he left me in no doubt that the experience scarred him and made him feel the futility of going on with music.

He likes to see the royalty checks and, in one of his phrases, "get some pleasure out of myself." Is he getting payments on only a few of his records or most of them? He smiled slowly, showing the gold in the front of his mouth, and I thought it was about the only gold coming his way.

"Just about most of 'em," he said in answer to the question. 'We're catchin' up now, since Miss Allison joined us." She is manager Allison Kaslow, a petite and pretty young woman with knowledge of jazz gained from work in Tulane's Jazz Archives for two-and-a-half years. Unlike most managers I've come across she carries a very young baby around with her.

"We got a few more yet to catch up on, but it's been pretty fair since I and Miss Allison got together," Longhair continued. I said it must be a nice feeling after so many years of neglect.

His most successful songs and treatments of traditional material such as "Stag-O-Lee" (called "Stagger Lee" on the new Harvest album), have 'been picked up by or have influenced musicians in his hometown and halfway round the world, and his strange, rhythmically animated piano playing has been highly regarded by, dozens of star names from Dr. John, Clarence Frog-man Henry and Fats Domino to Huey Smith, Allen Toussaint and various members of the Stones and Beatles. I guessed that the Doctor ("Well, all the boys call me Doctor Professor Longhair, the girls all call me a little old lovin' man," he sang on one of his down-home blues) was aware of the potency of his particular medicine.

"My numbers, they got around," was all he'd say. Was Jack Dupree one player who heard him in the earliest days? "Well, he used to work with me around 1935, He was a comedian then, see, and both of us did some dancing. He was helping me to learn how to sing, to control my style, and I was giving him a hand on the piano.

"He had been fighting before then, he told me. But he was a comedian when we got started. I haven't worked with him since then, and '36 was the last time I saw him, you know. At the time I'm talking about we didn't have any idea we were going to make any records." [50]

William Thomas Dupree, aka "Champion" Jack Dupree, London, UK, 1959. Photo and courtesy: Tony Standish (1931-2017). Used by permission.

Longhair, born Henry Roeland Byrd [sic], has been around music all his life. His mother started his interest in music when he was very small —"five, six or seven years old" —and this expressed itself first of all in dancing with local street bands.

"I started out professionally as a dancer, and she taught me guitar and drums, harmonica and jew's harp, and I wound up playing piano and decided to stick with that. I used 'to travel with her, to the outskirts of town, and when I was about 18 years old I started to travelling. I was in and out of New Orleans from a kid up."

Was he able to live comfortably on the royalties, I wondered? He was managing now, he replied, and felt he was going forward these days instead of just standing still or falling back.

"I feel like I'm going to prosper at last. I still love to play. It's in my blood. It's just that I don't care to be out in public playing if I'm not going to make any money, because it embarrasses me when I meet my friends and have to bum cigarettes off them, or a quarter or something of that kind. It's no good.

"See, 'I have a lot of poor friends in the neighbourhood where I was raised up at, and it's no more than right that when they think they've got a genius in their neighbourhood they wanna honour him and respect him, and yet I couldn't offer them a coke or a cigarette because I was in the shape they was in, or worse. I mean, I needed them to give me something."

To put the matter bluntly, did he think this situation existed largely because he was black? He adjusted his shades and thought for a while.

"Well", he said, "That had never occurred to me because I was raised up mostly around white people. There were few coloured people that I was around too long at a time, and it didn't seem like there was a colour line where I was. Just everybody was friendly, and I've always been friendly with people that I've met. They didn't seem black to me, or any colour."

One extra stroke of bad luck came Fess' way, early in '74 so far as I recalled the date, when his house in the 1800 block on South Rampart Street burned down.

"It was one of my wife's relatives' places that she had made her a present of, and it burned to the ground. We lost it all, and I needed a benefit which got me back some of the things though I couldn't recover everything I'd lost, such as clothes, instruments and things that I'd gathered 'round me. So it put me behind a little."

Shortly after the fire, Longhair was able to put some of his emotions down on record in a new studio in Louisiana. Paul McCartney, too, stayed in New Orleans later that year and got to hear the pianist in a club. Later they met in Toussaint's Sea-Saint Studio and a friendship was struck up, though I gather the Prof. had no idea who McCartney was until he told Allison about the encounter afterwards.

"He was down about six or seven months, and some months later this party came up on the boat in Long Beach, California and he invited me to come over and play for the party and we cut the album live at the party.

"We had, I think, Clarence Bell [Clarence "Juny Boy" Brown] *on drums, Big Will Harvey on guitar, Little Robert Harvey, bass, and we had Alfred Uganda Roberts on conga. They're all people I'd taught."*

A Longhair album which earned him glowing reviews (including one from me) was the French Blue Star set recorded in his birthplace, Bogalusa, Louisiana, I wondered if he also thought it a good album. He nodded and said he liked that record.

Why had it been made in Bogalusa? For sentimental reasons? If so, Fess looked unimpressed by them.

"It's where I was born, year of 1918. There was a studio out in the country, and they thought that would be a grand thing to take me back there 'cos that was my hometown.

"But I know nothing of it, you know. My mother left there when I was a kid, maybe two months old, so you know how long that's taken since then. I've been in and out of New Orleans ever since. "We had Gatemouth Brown there on that date to help me out with some tunes, and Snooks Eaglin was up there — yeah, but he didn't play on anything, 'cos Gatemouth Brown took it over.

"But I always kept Snooky with me in case there was something they wanted did. I'd taught him already and he knew the mix and all that. And of course I had Shiba [Ed Kimbrough] *on the drums, "Uganda" Roberts on congas and Julius* [Farmer] *on bass."*

Today, Longhair works normally with a seven-piece band, and he's regularly to be found at Tipitina's, a place on Tchoupitoulas and Napoleon in New Orleans named (after his hit tune). Tipitina's and Professor Longhair's Piano And Juice Bar.

His line-up contains old friends Will Harvey on guitar (he has also played bass with the Professor) and Alfred Roberts on congas.' And they are the only New Orleanians. The others are younger musicians who like the style. Earl Gordon is the drummer; the occupant of the bass-guitar chair has not quite been decided at present; and there are two tenors, Tony Dagradi and Andy Kaslow. The latter is married to manager Allison Kaslow.

Nowadays, Fess has a fancy for working with larger groups — larger than a combo, that is — but he explained that size brings difficulties. "You see, there are only certain musicians I can play with because I do things according to the way I feel, and arrange the numbers the way I feel. It's not like music you would play or hear anywhere.

"They don't have written music; they have to memorise these things and make them come out the same way next time. I'm just breaking in a couple of horns now, been workin' 'em in maybe six months — I'm not exaggerating.

"I feel like now I can pay them; the people who engage me will give me enough to hire 'em, if they want to hear what I have in mind and am trying to bring forth to express to them.

"So far we only have the one regular club in New Orleans, but work a variety of places such as the Superdome Stadium and auditoriums, and we've been working sometimes down around the City Park.

"And, of course, the festival: I've been doing the Heritage Festival, oh, since about 1970 [1971] *and there's another one comin' up now, starting April 7.*

Kid Thomas Valentine (plus Paul Barnes & Sammy Penn), at: Speck's Moulin Rouge, Marrero, 1958. For many decades Valentine resided in Algiers, across the river. Kid Thomas' Dixieland Band mainly played in that area, dance halls like, for instance, Kohlman's Tavern, a spot where Fess gigged in the early 1950s. Mac Rebennack used to play at Speck's, it's likely that Fess did too. Photo: Walter Eysselinck.

"It's got to be pretty large jobs, though, because I'm increasing the band now and just can't work in small places any more. And the union scale and all has gone up. So that's why you don't get as regular work as you should in New Orleans because you've got to wait for bigger places.

"And the majority of these places have their own selection of bands, such as jazz. Like on Bourbon Street, most of the people just love jazz and Dixieland up there."

"Professor" Byrd's music has, of course much to do with jazz and with blues — though he doesn't care to label it as either — and he has often worked alongside jazz musicians.

"Yes," he said, "I played with Kid Thomas [trumpeter and bandleader Thomas Valentine, 1896-1987] *one time and of course hung out with Jazz people. But really, in the early days I hung around with any people that I thought, like was playing something interesting.*

179

"I didn't pick the music; still don't. I like jazz, I like Dixieland, progressive, ballads, and I like some blues, but I just don't hardly play too many blues myself. I'm more rowdy than that, you know, a little rowdy with my playing. Yes, barrelhouse is right. I like a little pep in what I do."

How 'does the Professor regard" his music-making, since he does not think of it as jazz or blues, strictly speaking, rhythm and blues perhaps?

"I didn't ever give that a thought; either." He laughed almost apologetically. *"Now let's think. If you talk about 'Big Chief,' well, I know that is an instrumental and we'll say rhythm, more rhythm than blues. We couldn't call it blues because it's not a blues theme; no blues, no way.* [...]

"No, I didn't learn Spanish or French in childhood. My grandfather knew some French but my mother never took it up too much. I knew some French things but it wasn't enough to get me through. I mean French and Creole, you know. Very similar."

People speak of boogaloo, rock-and-roll - gumbo and suchlike in summing up the Prof's unusual music. One thing certain is that boogie-woogie is a main ingredient of his style. Just listen to "Gone So Long" on the new album (shades of Jimmy Yancey, no less) or the version of "Stag-O-Lee" for confirmation. But he doesn't call himself a boogie specialist.

"There's a boogie beat to a lot of it, yes. Boogie was out when I was born, I suppose. A whole lot of boogie was played in New Orleans. We had so many boogies; they had as much boogie as they had blues, and everyone play 'em to their own taste, you know."

"But I just got my own version of tunes, the way I feel them, and I mix up a variety of things into what I guess you can call gumbo.

"But you know, if you heard 'Big Chief', that was 22 pieces in there, really. And since then I been carried away with bands. I can feel and hear so much in my mind that I like to do. But I know I'll never be able to hire that many people.

"I like to play new things because it inspires you. Doing the old songs becomes tiresome, playing them over and over, but you have to please the pub-

lic. When you're learnin' something new, it gives you something to work on. And when I get home I have two things that I'm working on to finish. And any time I do that I'm happy until it's completed; then I'll start searching for something else.

"It's not hard for me to create something new. I can just lay down and dream and when I get up the next day it's almost complete. I have the lyrics and all I have to do is fix the melody and beats and background. And when I've finished, then I grab the men and starts teaching them. It keeps me busy.

"I'm a jazzy kind of fellow who has to listen to jazz; it helps me develop in the field that I'm in. But I listen to all type of music and right now I'm interested in Jamaican music, and I enjoy it. It's their own thing, you know, and it's new and has a feeling to it which I like."

Longhair finished by saying that he'd stayed in New Orleans for most of his days and expected to be there for the rest of his life. He had, he said, remained there and had been stepped on, and there hadn't seemed to be much point in going somewhere else where he might be treated worse.

In any case, he added, smiling, he hadn't really been offered anything to inspire him to go no-place. "I feel I'll be there till the end of time.

I had time to ask whether he had written or intended writing, any songs which reflected the race struggle or spoke of the black liberation movements. The head shook slowly but emphatically. "No, I never have," he told me, smiling faintly. "I haven't messed with that in any of my songs. It wouldn't be too good for your health down there in New Orleans." [51]

In Max Jones' review of Fess' Live On The Queen Mary album, Melody Maker, April 15, 1978, Jones mentioned a typing error in the text. Hence, a correction has been made. (A part of Jones' interview got lost in the printing process of the first edition of this book).

* * *

"CAUGHT IN THE ACT: FESS HAS STILL GOT THE FERVOUR"
by Valerie Wilmer, on the March 26, 1978 concert at the New London Theatre, 166 Drury Lane:

Patronage has always played an important role in the lives of musicians from Mozart's day and beyond. That the first time Professor Longhair played here was at a private party hosted by Sir James "Goldenballs" Goldsmith shows that some curious people pay the bills.

This time the legendary New Orleans pianist was here under the auspices of Paul McCartney, but, judged by his compelling, self-possessed performance at the New London Theatre on Easter Sunday, the Professor is in no obvious need of such patronage.

Whether he will continue to be listened to for as long as Mozart has been is open to question. In the specific sense this is doubtful — his talent is a relatively minor one, after all — but in the general sense it is a safe bet that he will still be bending ears a hundred years from now.

This is because his music sums up that blend of African and Spanish rhythms with the blues that is peculiar to New Orleans and which has been cropping up regularly in popular music since the beginning of the century.

Longhair played a total of 16 numbers in concert, accompanied only by Frank Roberts' [Alfred "Uganda" Roberts] conga drums, demonstrating conclusively that none of his rocking fervour has dimmed. This despite the fact that promoter John Stedman seems bent on introducing all his r&b artists in a patronising manner as ancient decrepits who need to be handled with kid gloves.

Longhair played all the expected ones - "Tipitina," Bald Head," "Big Chief," "Rocking Pneumonia," archetypal New Orleans masterpieces with a rolling rhumba bass and constantly changing rhythms. He sang in Creole patois, used his oddly cracked, yodeling voice to scat bebop-style, and turned in a masterly version of the Ray Charles hit, "Mess Around."

He often began hesitantly, appearing to fumble with a melody or rhythm, but it soon became clear that this was a characteristic of his style. Fess within a few bars he would stamp his authority — bam! — on the keyboard in a way that could only provoke a smile. Longhair actually epitomises the tradition of African-American piano music where the piano becomes a dancing drum, virtually a living entity. Just like the New Orleans parade drummers, he manages to invest each piece with a rhythmic quality so persuasive that every listener feels like dancing. There were Yancey-type blues, and the Professor even gave some indication of more sophisticated harmonic ideas that have remained dormant. A true academic of funk, this man.

The concert was not without its bizarre moments. At one point, an oddly-garbed line-up of locally recruited black teenagers appeared on the stage as Longhair sang "Mardi Gras In New Orleans." Their self-conscious attempt at the cakewalk was just one of several ill-conceived notions that promoter Stedman seems to feel the blues is about.

With seats at £ 4. 50 a time in some cases, a less than professional presentation is actually insulting to the artist. And Longhair, only just pushing 60, does not need to be presented as having one foot in the grave. [52]

John Stedman was very upset by the "grave insults" from Valerie Wilmer:

Professor Longhair did not come to the country under the auspices of Paul McCartney. As much as McCartney's staff gave valuable and much-appreciated help on the publicity and P. R. side, the concert was all arranged and contracted before I even knew that the "Queen Mary" record was being released... I would like to know what she means when she says that I introduced them in a patronizing manner and treat them as if they have one foot in the grave. Perhaps she objects to the fact that Fess was helped to walk to the piano.

Let me say that the man has a bad leg and is not in the best of health. If he hadn't been helped, he would probably have fallen over. What price a black artist's dignity if he had fallen down in front of a packed concert hall before he even started playing?

The dancers were not my idea, nor were they paid for by me, but in my opinion, their short appearance worked beautifully [...]

I am sick of these attacks by Valerie Wilmer. In the space of a month, I have brought over, for the first time in public, two special figures in the history of blues/r&b. She should be actively supporting the only person who is doing something positive for blues/r&b in this country. [53]

* * *

Lon Price, a Texas born (1946) saxophonist, put it like this. Fess: *was a piano legend, of course. He influenced everyone from New Orleans — Toussaint, Dr. John, Fats Domino, et al. He was a very sweet man, but very demanding about what he wanted musically. When I was offered the tour with him I had already moved to L.A. [Cal.], and was trying to establish myself there, which was not easy. Also, my wife at the time was expecting a child.*

One of the Fess gigs at the 1978 festival: "Grande Parade du Jazz", Nice, France, was televised (check Youtube). Price still resides in Los Angeles. On his very informative homepage he declared:

New Orleans was a great experience for me musically. I really learned how to play the blues in New Orleans. I did studio work for the great producer/ songwriter/arranger Allen Toussaint, 45 playing on albums by the likes of John Mayall, James Cotton and the vocal group LaBelle (Patti LaBelle, Nona Hendricks and Sarah Dash). That's me playing tenor on the instrumental interlude on "Lady Marmalade", a number one hit for LaBelle. I learned a lot from Toussaint about arranging for horns. He taught me a lot about using space, and that sometimes what you leave out is more important than what you put into a horn arrangement. I also performed with many local legends of R 'n B as a result of my association with Toussaint, including Dr. John, Irma Thomas, Ernie K-Doe [...] [54]

In New Orleans, I had finally made a name for myself. People recognized me on the street and I was somewhat of a star. But I was a medium-sized fish in a little pond, and besides, many of the local musicians didn't accept me, because I wasn't born there and I wasn't black. New Orleans is sort of a self-contained city musically. The local players can be downright snobbish. It's next to impossible for an outsider to become accepted by the locals. The weird thing is that it's not the audiences that have that attitude so much as the players. I always felt accepted by the audiences. I'd never been on the receiving end of any kind of discrimination before living in New Orleans.

In the summer of '78, [...] I went to Europe with New Orleans singer/pianist icon Professor Longhair. We played the summer jazz festival circuit—two weeks at the Grande Parade du Jazz in Nice [July 6-16] and three days at the North Sea Jazz Festival in The Hague in the Netherlands, as well as a few dates in Norway and Sweden. I was amazed at how much more receptive European audiences were than American audiences. There was so much more respect for players and music in general over there than there was in the U.S. I could certainly understand why so many American jazz players had moved over there.

The trip was a great experience for me. Lon Price continued. I fell in love with France, and hoped that someday I'd get a chance to go back there. In Nice I got to hear some of the legends of jazz, including Stan Getz, Dizzy Gillespie (I sat in with him on one of his sets), Eddie "Lockjaw" Davis, the Buddy Rich band, and an all-star band fronted by Lionel Hampton, with too many jazz greats too mention here. Fathead Newman and Hank Crawford were playing sets together. That was a real treat for me. Here

An all red dressed Fess; and Big Will Harvey, mid-July 1978, Nice, France. Courtesy Lars Falk. Used by permission.

Fess, Sundsvall, Sweden, October 10, 1975. Photo: Hans Ivarsson. Used by permission.

were two of my biggest influences, sharing the stage. One day alto sax legend [and singer] *Eddie "Cleanhead" Vinson* [1917-1988] *sat in with them and I swear he cleaned both of their clocks! I got to meet Cleanhead when he came and sat in with Professor Longhair. I knew that Trane* [John Coltrane] *had played with Cleanhead* [in 1947], *so asked him about it. I said, "I understand that Trane used to play in your band". "That's right", Cleanhead replied* [...] [55]

In 2006, pianist singer and actor, Harry Connick Jr., born New Orleans 1967, acknowledged:

When I came along, the purpose of a piano player was not a rhythmic one, at least not in the jazz world. Guys like Professor Longhair, Dr. John, Allen Toussaint, and Art Neville played rhythmically [...] [as opposed to various jazz piano players?]. *Professor Longhair was truly the father of that new wave of New Orleans piano playing. I don't think that anyone could say that he was a great technician in a classical point of view, but rhythmically he was so strong. He played these rumba bass lines, and he put these things on the top. That bass line, for a small person like me, 8, 10 years old, was easy to relate to. Anybody could play that. I couldn't play it as well as Fess, and still can't, but technically that wasn't hard for me to do.* [56]

Finally, pianist and singer Marcia Ball, born Orange, Texas 1949: "on styles, influences, and Professor Longhair":

"The other thing I didn't hear [besides Albert Ammons, Meade Lux Lewis, and Pete Johnson] when I was growing up was Professor Longhair. Because his career, when I was in these formative years, was in a kind of, a little bit of doldrums. Those where the years when he was sweeping out clubs in New Orleans. And that's when Mac Rebennack, who was in New Orleans and following his dad around, loading up jukeboxes at these joints, was getting to talk to him and hear him. But it wasn't until 'Atlantic' reissued these Professor Longhair sides in the 70s [1972], that many of us ever heard what he was and what he did, and that really blew my doors wide open." [57]

HENRY ROELAND BYRD
December 19, 1918 - January 30,1980

A Foundation was established in 1987 to encourage and foster a recognition and appreciation of the music of the late Henry Roeland Byrd, known as "Professor Longhair", and his contribution to the music and cultural traditions of New Orleans.

The Foundation plans to establish and maintain a park and memorial at Tchoupitoulas Street and Napoleon Avenue to be known as "Longhair Square".

For information contact:

THE PROFESSOR LONGHAIR FOUNDATION
1510 Religious Street New Orleans, Louisiana 70130

Fess and his Cadillac. Coco Robicheaux (1947-2011) was the founder of the now inactive Professor Longhair Foundation. Courtesy: The Official Souvenir Program Book, New Orleans Jazz & Heritage Festival: 1990.

6. LAST DAYS

Fess played his very last show on Saturday night, January 26, 1980. The performance took place, as fate would have it, at Tipitina's, 502 Napoleon Avenue. It was a full house concert. Bassist Reggie Scanlan recalled that the band and its leader sounded great that night. To keep Fess in shape, Scanlan fetched Scotch whisky and milk between the sets. According to Allison Miner, Fess, "was burning it up, that night. It was a joyous thing. I'd never seen him so into it, and the set was total perfection." [1] Lots of musicians were spectators, among them, members of the UK "new wave" bands *Police* and *the Specials*. They had performed at the Warehouse, 1820 Tchoupitoulas St. earlier that evening. [2] Bill Payne (born 1949), was one of the US musicians and keyboard player for the Los Angeles, Cal., based blues/rock band: *Little Feat*. A band which at some point incorporated New Orleans musical influences. Here is Payne's recollection of this particular night:

We arrived at Tipitinas [sic], and although it was January and cold outside, inside it was burning hot, a sea of bodies tightly packed in the darkened club. Cat Fish Hodge [blues rocker Bob "Catfish" Hodge], who I knew from the Washington D.C. area, was opening for Fess that evening. He asked me if I would sit in on the second show (I had missed his first set due to our late arrival [...]), and I was pleased to say yes. For one thing, it would give me a chance to play the same piano Professor Long Hair [sic] was playing, an inestimable treat. Phillipe [Philippe Rault, the French record producer etc.] had suggested that half way through Fess's set we should make a break for another club to check out the Meters and make it back in time for me to sit in with Cat Fish and hear the entire second, and last set of the night, with Professor Long Hair [sic]. Everything was running like clockwork [...]

As good as the Meters were, I could hardly wait to get back to Tips. Phillipe [sic] introduced me to Fess on the steps in back of Tipitina's, just before sitting in with Cat Fish. I told the Professor I had inadvertently lifted every lick he had ever played, listening to Dr. John, Allen Toussaint, Fats Domino, and many others. I held that meeting in my mind when I sat in on C.F.'s set, paying homage to the man that would be taking the stage next. It was a night

I'll never forget. When Fess and his band launched into "Mardi Gras in New Orleans" it was if a bomb had gone off in the building, everyone was up on their feet and dancing. Pure magic and joy. That was a Saturday night in 1980. The following Tuesday, January 30, Roy Byrd – Professor Long Hair - died. I was privileged to have met him, and experienced the power of his music in person in New Orleans. His light will shine a very, very longtime. [3]

Alice Walton Byrd recalled:

He came in. I don't know where he'd been, he took a ride. He laid down on the bed, I was in the kitchen. Then, I laid down and automatically I fell to sleep. And the next thing I heard [coughs!], and I raised up, turned on the light. I started screamin', I could see he was dying! The way that he died, I wish I'd die like that, it's a wonderful thing. Ain't nobody in the world that can tell me that a Christian that runs to church often, goes to church often, can die no better than my husband died. He knowed God, loved God. He went by God's rules, he read his bible. He knowed his bible, and everything. It was only one thing missing, he was not in that church. And God asks for the pure heart, and that's what my husband had, a pure heart! [sic] [4]

Henry Roland "Professor Longhair" Byrd was declared dead at six o'clock on the morning of Thursday, January 31, 1980. He resided in his Terpsichore Street house, where he died in a small room next to the kitchen. Pat Byrd became very emotional when she talked about it, in New Orleans, 2014. The house is not very far from Fess' former addresses on South Rampart St. Pat Byrd said. "He'd tell me all the time that if something happened to him, I should take care of my mother, and help her keep the house." [5] According to the M. D. Coroner Frank Minyard (also a trumpeter), the causes of death were pulmonary emphysema, chronic bronchitis and advanced cirrhosis of the liver. [6]

Alice Byrd, said, I "got a turban he used to sleep in, and the night he died, he hung it on a lamp. Yeah, he hung it on a lamp – it was cold, you know. His head would be cold, he'd put a skullcap on, then he put that turban on." [7]

Even the biting cold couldn't keep away friends of the 'Fess. Henry Roland Byrd 1918-1980, professionally known as Professor Longhair, was laid to rest Saturday. Last Wednesday, at the age of 61, Longhair died at his resi-

dence. For years he performed in his own unique, individualistic style. His electric piano and Mardi Gras music were New Orleans traditions. In a matter of hours, it all came to an end at Mount Olivet Cemetery. Forty-degree temperatures didn't deter those who lined up outside the Majestic Funeral Home at 1833 Dryades St. in the Central City to pay their final respects.

Photographers stood atop a nearby business trying to get the best possible shot of Byrd's last ride. Children too young to realize his import watched curiously. They too seemed to sense the loss. It was impossible to count the numbers of people. Many had been there an hour or more before the 10 a.m. service. Others trickled by as the jazz funeral march got under way. For many a performance, the Professor had brought audience to their feet. So did his funeral. Out-of-town license plates—Texas, Ohio, Michigan—made the Dryades Street commercial strip look like a Mardi Gras parade was about to pass. As the pallbearers placed the flag-draped casket into the sky blue hearse, Dejan's Olympia Brass Band [including Milton Batiste, trumpet] struck up a solemn number. For them, it was like witnessing the beginning of the end of something special, something unique, something great. "They're going to kick 'em down," said a photographer who had been to many a jazz funeral. And "kick 'em down" they did. The entourage moved briskly down city streets en route to the Gentilly grave site. Along the way some joined in, others merely watched. A freelance writer who came down just for the Professor's funeral hinted he'd like to be buried amid such revelry, among so many friends. A good friend of 'Fess summed it all up. "You have to be well-liked." As the crowd, and even those who didn't come out either because of the weather or other reasons would attest, the Professor was such a man." [8]
Lovell Beaulieu, *the Times-Picayune.*

Alice Walton Byrd narrated:

It was cold down here the day of the funeral. It was so cold. It must have been zero degrees. But there was so many people come out all the same day, so many people. When they came to pick me up, the limousine man said, 'Mrs. Byrd,' he say, 'I don't know how I'm gonna get you there. This is the biggest funeral we ever had.' They had a jazz funeral, and after they got to Felicity and Rampart my sons had to cut the jazz band loose. There was so many people the cars was just creepin', the limousine wouldn't have never made it to the grave. When we got out there to the cemetery, it was just like carnival – that's how crowded it was out there. Yeah, I'm tellin' you, that was a powerful day. [9]

1738 Terpsichore Street. The Byrd family moved there in January 30, 1979, and according to Pat Byrd: "Fess became a first-time home owner". Photo by the author: November 2010.

"I think about him every day. When a person dies, you know, part of their soul becomes part of those closest to him to him. And part of him is definitely within me (laughs) and I just gotta figure out what to do with it." [10] Allison Miner said.

Earl Palmer, drummer on Fess' wonderful 1953 recording session, recalled:

Well, there used to be clubs in New Orleans like the Elks and so forth. And it was a fad that when you had a club and a member died, that you would honor him by having a funeral procession. They played funeral dirges with the hearse and the cars all the way to the cemetery. The funeral would be over, the body "planted" as they say, and the "second line" would be people who followed the funeral procession and the band. They followed it to the cemetery and danced all way back.

I'll tell you about a planting I remember maybe four years ago when I was in New Orleans with Peggy Lee and playing at the Fairmont Hotel. It was the funeral of Professor Longhair. I was going to see him the night before he died.

BYRD

Henry Roland (Professor Long Hair) Byrd, on Wednesday, January 30, 1980 at 3:00 a.m. Beloved husband of Mrs. Alice Byrd, son of the late James and Ella Mae Byrd; father of Pat, Frances, Barbara, Chinn, Paul, Alexander, and the late Roland Byrd; nephew of William Byrd, of Baton Rouge, La., devoted friend of the Hills family; also survived by 18 grandchildren, and a host of other relatives and friends.

Relatives and friends of the family, also officers and members of Civil Defense No. 714, Magnolia Peace Officers, Brown Patrolman Agency, Daughters of Simon Chapter no 55 O.E.S., Electa Court No. 2, Daughters of Sphinx, Emmortality Chapter No. 10, Daughters of Minerva, Herald of Jericho, Good Luck Lodge No. 1, Ammaron Court, Band members of Isador Tuts Washington, Allen Toussaint, Alford Roberts, Dave Watson, Ronald Johnson, Tony Dagradi, Jim Moore, John Vidocovich, and Tipitina's Club are invited to attend the funeral. Services at Majestice Mortuary Service Inc., 1833 Dryades St., on Friday, February 1, 1980 at 8:00 p.m. Dismissal services at 10.00 a.m. on Saturday. (Jazz Funeral) Reverend Andrew W. Gilmore, officiating. Interment, Mt. Olivet Cemetery. Majestic Service Mortuary, in charge. Parking in rear.

The Times-Picayune obituary, February 1980, through: Hogan Jazz Archive, Tulane University, New Orleans. Note that Alfred "Uganda" Roberts is mentioned as "Alford Roberts".

So when the funeral came up, I took Tom Garvin, who was Peggy's conductor at the time and a good friend of mine. I showed him something he'd never seen before. And Dave Bartholomew, whose orchestra I worked in before I moved to California and who did all those Fats records in New Orleans, came by to go to the funeral. Tom was just flabbergasted. He'd never seen anything like that before in his life. They had three bands and about five hundred or six hundred people in the second line. He couldn't believe it. He said, 'I heard of this Earl, but I just don't believe it.' I said, 'We're not going to stand here all day. We got to leave, 'cause this will go on for the rest of the evening'.

They had three bands – the Olympic [Olympia] Brass Band and two other bands. I don't remember which ones they were, but they were spaced, you know, in between. But so many people wanted to follow the procession. There were motorcycle cops, the whole thing. It was really fantastic. It was one of the biggest funeral parades I've ever seen. I played on some of his early stuff. 'Tipitina,' 'Ball the Wall.' Everybody knew Fess.

His funeral originated uptown, but when I knew him he lived in my neighborhood, the Tremé, so everybody from that part of town knew him. Plus as he became popular, everybody uptown knew him because this was where he began to make a name for himself. So people from all over town turned out for the funeral. It was quite a thing. [sic] [11]

The wake was scheduled at 8:00 p.m. Friday, February 1, 1980. Allan Toussaint and Marshall Sehorn put up with the money for the funeral, which took place on Saturday at 10:00 a.m. Other contributions came from the Musicians Union and some of Professor Longhair's friends. Allison Miner drew together a group of friends to assist the family with burial expenses.

Allen Toussaint and the Turbinton brothers: Wilson ("Willie Tee") and Earl where some of the performers during the wake. The Turbintons: Earl, alto saxophone, and Willie Tee, piano, played a soulful dirge like rendition of the old hymn "Near The Cross." Flower arrangements came from Fats Domino, Irma Thomas, the Neville Brothers and Paul McCartney. Stevenson J. Palfi filmed the wake and the funeral for his documentary on New Orleans piano players. Fess had passed before the documentary was finished. A European tour was scheduled for Fess, in summer the 1980.

Fess' death certificate. Source unknown.

Ernie K-Doe (Ernest Kador Jr., 1936-2001), the fine local singer, was one of the pallbearers. "Cos" Matassa and Quint Davis were there. Bruce Iglauer ("Alligator" label) attended the funeral. Jerry Wexler flew down from NYC, and gave a eulogy. K-Doe sang a gospel song, then pointed at the coffin and said: *I learned a lot from this man, and everybody in New Orleans done learned a lot from Professor Longhair.* He was buried in a borrowed crypt, engraved *Matthew's*, at the Mount Olivet Cemetery, 4000 Norman Mayer Avenue. A Fess benefit concert, February 1980, was held at the Municipal Auditorium.

"The Professor of New Orleans," an obituary (an excerpt), by Tom Stagg, spring 1980:
Professor Longhair came to this country [UK] only twice. Following a European tour Fess returned to this country in 1978 for one concert and to promote his then new Harvest album ['Live on the Queen Mary']. He played piano at a boozy press reception and amidst much ballyhoo went through his

newly recorded numbers although there were no records to promote, EMI failed to deliver on time.

His concert was not exactly a success but enough of this New Orleans genius came through to thrill the people who did attend and Fess seemed happy to be in England again. His appearance coincided with the tail end of a Fats Domino tour and on the night of the Odeon, Hammersmith concert Fess was there backstage, stamping his foot and shouting with enjoyment whilst Fats played GO TO THE MARDI GRAS, and Dave Bartholomew, Lee Allen, and Walter Kimble left the stage to shake the hand of the legend in their midst. Yes, Professor Longhair was a true legend in his lifetime, revered respected by musicians and fans alike; his appearance at the yearly New Orleans Jazzfest ample proof of the following this man had. The Longhair stage was always packed by young and old alike each year and every appearance he made [...] [12]

Fess was inducted into the "W.C. Handy Blues Hall of Fame" on November 16, 1981, and into the "Rock & Roll Hall of Fame" on January 15, 1992. Fess' children do well and they are reported as making more money than Fess did. This is due to attorney Justin Zitler, and royalty accountant Alan Godchaux who, according to Hank Drevich, has done a lot of work for the Fess family over the years. They have helped the family consolidate their holdings through a family corporation, SongByrd, Inc., as heirs to Fess' royalties from sales, publishing and image-related merchandising and commercial usage.

During the "New Orleans Jazz and Heritage Festival" April/May 1989, I suddenly discovered Alice Walton Byrd. She sat alone by a small table under a sign with her name, by the tent of radio station WWOZ. She looked a bit out of place, and forlorn. I took the privilege to shake her hand and thank her for all the joy and pleasure her husband's music has given me through the years.

Since her father's purchase of the Terpsichore St. building, daughter Pat Walton Byrd had resided there with her son. She was there when her Fess died. Pat took permanent care of her ill in bed mother, until her death. Alice Walton Byrd, a victim coronary artery disease (CAD), died at the Touro Infirmary Hospital on October 20, 1989. Alice had turned 68 years old on October 6. For some reason, rather than laying her to rest next to Fess, it was decided to move him from his grave to a double vault, and place him next to her there, at an enormous cost for the family.

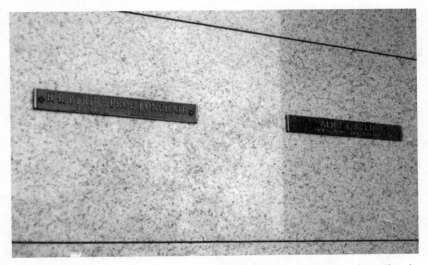

The Byrd vault at Mount Olivet Cemetery, 400 Norman Mayer Avenue, Gentilly, New Orleans. Photo by the late Sven Gustafsson.

7. NOTES ON STUDIOS, MUSICIANS, AND RELATED

I.

There was a place in the neighborhood where we used to play for the fun of it, called the Caledonia. It was a real neighborhood bar on St. Claude and St. Philip, kind of a sawdust-floor place. Those of us who were young veterans just out of the service and hanging in neighborhood would stop in and see Fess. Earl Palmer related:

He'd come in and play for drinks, and he was playing then exactly what he became famous for, because that's all he knew. He couldn't play 'Stardust' or 'I'm In the Mood For Love.' He played New Orleans-type of blues, things like 'Caledonia' with that rolling rumba rhythm he always played on the piano, which set the tone and mood for everything he did. He played old traditional blues and put his own lyrics on them. [1]

Palmer's close friend, "Red" Tyler, characterized the spots' clientele as, raunchy! The Caldonia Inn, in the Treme neighborhood, went under at least three names. Initially called the Japanese Tea Garden (owned by "Lou" Messina, succeeded by "Mike" Tessitore); then the

The Gypsy Tea Room No. 2, August 1942. Photo: "Bill" Russell. Courtesy: Hogan Jazz Archive, Tulane University. Used by permission.

Gypsy Tea Room No. 2. In June 1947, it finally was named as the Caldonia Inn/Club. It was named after the Louis Jordan and his Tympany Five number one chart hit, first cut in 1945. The spot's entertainment consisted of small local jazz and R&B bands; singers; dancers; striptease acts; and female impersonators. In addition, a place where people gathered for wakes. Fess attested:

We were playing at the Caldonia Inn. We had Big Slick on drums, Apeman Black on sax and Walter ["Papoose"] Nelson on guitar. We had long hair in those days and it was almost against the law. By teachin' these fellows Mike [Tessitore] says, 'I'm going to keep this band – we'll call you Professor Longhair and the Four Hairs combo.' [2]

Prof. Short Hair

"This is Professor Short Hair, of the now famed Hair-Combo, which currently appears each week-end (Friday, Saturday and Sunday), at the Caldonia Inn. In reality, Prof. Short Hair is Clarence Fritz, popular musician. The Hair Combo is made up of Professor Short Hair, Long Hair, No Hair and Need Some Hair. They furnish the dance music and rhythmic background for the All-Star Female-Impersonators Show, which features Mattie Campbell each week." Louisiana Weekly, April 24, 1948. Clarence "Big Slick" Fritz died about 1962.

The Caldonia Inn was caught in the 45-minute movie *In Love With The Art Of Drumming*, with Earl Palmer and Matti Oiling (1942-2009). It's a little-known Finnish documentary (directed by one Jarkko Aarniala), that premiered in 1990. The Caldonia sequence is partly a scene where Palmer is dancing with a lady, to Fats Domino's: "Telling Lies", played on a Jukebox (thanks to Jens Lindgren for the video copy). The Caldonia Inn was demolished, most likely in 1980, when the Louis Armstrong Park was built.

In December 1948, singer and pianist Alma Mondy joined Fess and the other performers at the Caldonia Inn. The Louisiana Weekly reported: *Lollipop (Jones) told so many funny stories that the fella in front of me lost his false teeth twice: he was laughing so loud and long... And again, Prof. Roy Byrd, the one and only ballad man... thumped his foot against the piano and brought the house down with 'Bald Head'... And to close the show, Alma (Lollypop) Mundy* [sic] *took the microphone and melted it with three jump-blues numbers.* [3] She recorded for the "Mercury" label in 1949 and 1950.

Caldonia Inn's Prof. Need Some Hair was a headline in the Louisiana Weekly, April 3, 1948. The paragraph came along with a photograph of the left-handed trumpeter Frank "Lefty" Mitchell (1917–1998). The caption read: *Prof. Need Some Hair, of Caldonia Inn's Four Hairs Combo. The professor who toots a mad trumpet is known in some circles by his Christian name, young Louis Armstrong. Other members of the Hairs Combo are Professor No Hair, Short Hair [Clarence Fritz] and [Professor] Long Hair. They furnish the music for dancing and the All Female Impersonators show, which this week features Gloria Jean, sun tan comedian; Mary Ann, singing hot songs; Marion Brown, doing a Hawaiian dance, and Mattie Campbell, the show's producer, doing a new dance from Shanghai.* [4] Frank Mitchell eventually cut with Ray Charles; and Eddie "Guitar Slim" Jones, in 1953. In the late 1950s, early 60s, Mitchell worked and recorded with the Texas blues singer and guitarist Albert Collins (1932-1993).

Frank Mitchell, Louisiana Weekly, April 3, 1948. Courtesy Jens Lindgren (thanks Jens).

I inadvertently ran into Frank Mitchell, a complete unknown for me, late one night in spring 1989. He stood by one of the Preservation Hall windows and watched the band inside. His trumpet-case caught my attention and we began to talk. Many years later, I found out that he tried to get gigs at the distinguished St. Peter Street jazz spot – but, as it seems, never succeeded.

A Caldonia Inn advertisement cites Myrtle Jones (circa 1916-1963) as supported by: "the Hair Combo". Fess was the combo's pianist, with "Big Slick" Fritz ("Short Hair") on drums. Jones' first cut in 1944, for Bill Russell, at the San Jacinto Club, with a pickup band lead by jazz pioneer trumpeter Willie "Bunk" Johnson (1879-1949). She sang with a powerful voice, in the gospel music idiom. Myrtle resided at 918 St. Philip St. in the French Quarter.

Four years later, the *Louisiana Weekly* reported: "Now rising in fame as a recording artist. Myrtle Jones appears to be better than ever." She often performed on the same shows as Roy "Good Rockin'" Brown. On November 9, 1947, Myrtle opened for the influential singer Ethel

At Caldonia Inn

MYRTLE JONES
... Shares top billing with Lloyd Ignicious in Caldonia Inn's Friday, Saturday and Sunday Show.

Myrtle Jones, Louisiana Weekly, September 17, 1949.

Waters (1896-1977) at the original Gypsy Tea Room. Myrtle usually jobbed there supported by Sidney Desvigne's big swing band. She eventually sang with the same orchestra at Club Shadowland, at 1921 Washington Avenue. *In August 1950, Miss Jones made several recordings and toured Louisiana and Texas before returning to New Orleans to join* [emcee Bobby] *Parker's show which is cleverly backed by Lee Allen's combo.* [5] In 1954, she sang at the swanky Club Desire, fronting the Eddie "Spider" [Bo] Bocage orchestra. Myrtle cut with Paul Gayten, 1955 ("Chess"), who considered her as "a coming" singer. Her business card read: *Myrtle 'Miss Blues' Jones and her Atomic Bomb Band.* She died in the early 1960s.

II.

The tenor saxophone, bass player, and singer Leroy "Bat Man" Rankins (1931-1960s?) waxed with Fess for "Atlantic" in 1949. In the same year, the Louisiana Weekly (July 9) reported: *Along with Leroy (Batman) Rankins and Warren O' Cause, he* [Joe "Google Eyes" August] *attempted several excursions into the area of blues and boogie woogie, not as a vocalist but as a drummer.*

"Batman" with his combo. A Louisiana Weekly ad, September 17, 1949.

A couple of months later, the same newspaper stated. *'Bat Man,' who is reputed as being one of the most talented of New Orleans younger crop of musical talents, packed 'em up at Club High Hat, here Sunday evening for a matinee, despite a continuous drizzle. He was featured with his combo that appears at the club during the current autumn season." [...] Joined the outfit this week will be Frank Mitchell, arranging-composer and nationally famous musician. [...] Receiving an excellent hand last week were* [Ike] *'Streamline' Harris and his 'Streamliners' for a second big week at the spot owned and operated by Freeman Riles and Milton Scott. (October, 1949).* [6] "Streamline" Harris, a pianist, was Fess' tap dancing partner in the 1930s.

According to the busy upright bass player Frank Fields: *I started working with a rock group called* [James] *Sugar Boy* [Crawford], *I worked with him about two years* [in the early 50s]. *The personnel we had was Big Boy Myles, trombone, Leroy Rankin* [sic] *on saxophone, we had Chester Jones on drums, Sugar Boy on piano, Billy Tate on guitar and me on bass.* [7] In October 1965, it's reported that: "The Triple Crown is still cooking with the [Irving] Irv Bannister group [a guitarist], featuring LeRoy "Batman" Rankin" [sic]. [8]

Powerful singer Blanche Thomas (1922-1977) made her recording debut in 1954, with the Dave Bartholomew orchestra ("Imperial"). She reached some fame in the 1960 and 70s, through her association with the bands led by Paul Barbarin and Papa French. Thomas toured Europe twice, the last time in the summer of 1975.

The High Hat Club, 1432 St. Ann Street, behind the Municipal Auditorium, opened on Thursday, September 3, 1949: "Featuring Sporty

Johnson: His Show and His Band". The story of this Treme spot goes back to November 1935, when first opened as the *Gypsy Tea Room*. Its owner was Louis "Lou" Messina (1910-1986) – a future successful boxing promoter. The venue soon became a prominent entertainment venue for African Americans. Its seating capacity, in May 1936, was more than 600 customers. There was a four-room apartment upstairs. This dance hall and barroom used to stay packed night after, after night, Pleasant Joseph declared. The High Hat's musical resume includes Louis Armstrong shows in 1941 and '42; a couple of years later, the Smiley Lewis' trio with Tuts Washington. Bill Russell recorded George Lewis' jazz band, in the building in 1943. Fess used to play there with Walter "Papoose" Nelson on guitar. It was the spot for his

very last job with Fess. The *Louisiana Weekly* (Sep. 3, 1949), reported: "The High-Hat will soon have the swankiest kitchen down town". From Dallas, Texas, Jesse Erickson, came into New Orleans in November 1949, seeking talent for his small *Star Talent label.* He put up a temporary recording studio in the High Hat Club, where Fess cut the song: "She Ain't Got No Hair" (Mike Leadbitter, 1970).

Leroy Rankins, bass, with the Dooky Chase Big Band, including drummer Vernell Fournier, circa 1949. Rankins' vocal efforts was brought forward for the band's R&B tunes. Courtesy: Hogan Jazz Archive, Tulane University. Used by permission.

One of the finest sessions this season was that of Sunday evening when 'Bat Man' Rankins, growl sax man, and his combo invaded the club High Hat [...] for a four-hour engagement. Sporty Johnson, master of ceremonies and host, plugged and presented many of the stars who had gathered for the show and jammed with the Rankin's outfit with Lester Alexis being featured on the drums. The Three Harmonics, house aggregation, are heard on Wednesday, Saturday and Sunday nights with Clement Tervalon [bass & vocal, including: Robert Parker, saxophone & vocal]. Each Sunday evening, jam sessions will be featured atop the musical bar of the downtown mecca (Septem-

The "Ebb Tide Nite Club", 1961, former High Hat / Gypsy Tea Room, with weekend entertainments. Fess "played the High Hat all the time", Milton Batiste stated. Photo: Bill Russell. Courtesy, Hogan Jazz Archive, Tulane University. Used by permission.

ber 1949). [9] When Fess jobbed at the spot in the early 1950s, he resided at 1320 St. Philip St., in the Garden District vicinity. "From 1957 until 1959, [cornetist Melvin] Lastie [1930-1972] ran his own night club, 'The High Hat', a block-long affair with three bars that featured entertainment by Lastie's own band and shows which he produced himself."[10] The 1432 St. Ann Street location is a vacant lot in 2018.

III.

"Congratulations to M. G. Stevens [drummer Milton G. Stevens], Henry [Fess] Long Hair, and Joe Mingo, along with his Frog Trio (Kohlman's Tavern) for pulling such fine crowds across the river!!!" "Dr. Daddy-O" Winslow, reported in his newspaper column. [11] Kohlman's Tavern is situated at 414 Homer Street in Algiers (across the river from New Orleans). Its proprietor was Louis Kohlman Jr., father of the late legendary drummer Freddie Kohlman.

The Pepper Pot Club was another 'west bank' venue, mainly known for Fess' association with it. [12]

"Gretna is an old German town", according to the *Gretna Historical Society*, "replete with shotgun houses, camel back houses and Creole cottages". At an early age, Mac Rebennack got involved with the local Black music scene. "It came from two or three accidental things that happened". Rebennack said. "I'd been playing piano since I was maybe five or six years old, playing boogie woogies. My father used to repair radios and televisions and p. a. systems [*Rebennack's TV and Radio Repair*, Metairie] at the local clubs. That's how I came to meet Professor Longhair. When

Dorothy Rebennack (1909-2005), and Malcolm John Rebennack Sr. (1907-1962), 1960 (Mac's parents). Photo and courtesy: Denis Poupart. Used by permission.

'Fess was playing at the Pepper Pot, my father went over there and repaired a p. a. system. I used to love to go wherever he'd go 'cause I'd get to hear the bands. The group was on break because the system was broke and that's when I first saw Professor. So I told him that they wouldn't leave me sit in the club 'cause I was too young. But I noticed, that if I sat on this log outside of the window and looked on in I could see Fess' hands on the piano. That's more or less when I started sneaking out of the house and going to the Pepper Pot every night, so I could watch how old Fess'd place his hands on the keys."[13]

In February 2014, my old musical pals Trevor Richards and Clive Wilson, kindly helped me out with a couple of shots of the light-yellow painted shotgun house. Richards: "We then called [Gerald] Jerry Adams who has always lived in Gretna, and confirmed that that is indeed where the Pepper Pot was and it's still the same building. He used to play there with the Adams family band when Longhair wasn't working. It was Justin [1923-1991] on guitar and vocals, Placide [1929-2003] on drums and vocal and Jerry on bass and they were playing the R&B repertoire." [14] Their mother Dolly Adams (née Douroux (1904-1979) was the pianist in the family quartet, that often jobbed at the West Bank clubs. She was a versatile and well-schooled

The wood building that housed the Pepper Pot Club, 637 Weyer St., corner of Seventh St., Gretna. Photo: Trevor Richards, February 2014 (thanks Trevor). Used by permission

musician, and so were her musical sons: Gerald (1927-2018), bass and piano, who jobbed for Roy Brown in the early 1950s. Placide made his first recordings on drums, for Roosevelt Sykes, and waxed on drums, 1954, for Roy Brown. As a bassist, Placide toured Japan with George Lewis' band, 1964 and 1965. Justin was one of the city's best guitarists. He cut for Fess in 1957 ("Ebb"), and he did countless of recordings, most of them in the R&B genre.

The Adams family band, "was playin' at this place the Million Dollar Room, on Danneel and Sixth [Streets, Uptown], and we stayed quite a while there, people loved it." Placide Adams told.

"Unfortunate the owner was a race horse player and he blow it all [...] We played for him from 1953 to about the middle of 1954. But we used to hang out, the Dew Drop was going strong, and one of us had to take mother home. So, we kind of like vote on this, who could take mother home? I got a chick waitin' [...] But anyway, right back to the Dew Drop, or the Caravan [...] the Pelican, was going, a lot of night clubs. And we'd hang out 'til about five, six, eight o' clock in the morning. Go home. And next night we're on the job. I'm playing drums, sleeping, zzzz; guitar player sleeping [laughter]; bass player, sleeping, zzzz. And we'd sit there. We'd be sleeping. And mother said: *I'll fix that*. She went to a Five & Dime store and bought a water pistol. And we'd sit up there next night, sleeping. And she just turned around, and right in the eyes. And she would keep us up all night, man [laughter]. Oh, she was a beautiful person, beautiful". [15] It's likely that Dolly brought the water pistol to the Pepper Pot as well.

Tenor saxophonist Daniel "Weenie" Farrow was born in Algiers, 1932. He was taught by the legendary local reed player Theodore "Wiggles" Purnell (1909-1974), a brother of Alton. In 1950, Eddie Bo hired Farrow, including Jessie Hill on drums. They worked four-hour sets, from 3 a.m. to 7 a.m. at the "Gunga Den", a Bourbon Street burlesque spot. According to Clive Wilson, Farrow later played many West Bank gigs, usually with a trio. The Pepper Pot Club was one of the spots. Its owner was called "Pepper", but "Farrow does not know his real name". The other band members were, off and on, Reginald "Trees" Johnson (bass, & guitar), Joe Cushenberry (guitar) Edgar Johnson (guitar), and Jessie Hill (drums). Wilson added that, in the late 1950s, early 60s, Farrow played with Bobby Mitchell, and Quezergue's Royal Dukes of Rhythm. Since 1996, Farrow is often employed at the Preservation Hall.

"Robert Parker told me that you got it ["Mardi Gras In New Orleans"] together at the Pepper Pot in Gretna. He remembers playing it for the first time there," Fess stated in 1975. "Well, we was drawin' from 3 to 400 a night in that place. It was on Seventh and Wire… [sic] It's still there but it's been remodeled and all. It don't look the same, all the beauty's gone." [16] Lynn Abbott confirmed the Pepper Pot location. [17]

Reportedly, Fess created the song "Baldhead" aka, "She Ain't Got No Hair", at this club. Fess had a little girlfriend in mind, Rick Coleman stated. According to Parker, they played with trumpeter Al Miller (also a drummer, later with Deacon John Moore), and Louis Joseph, drums (no relation to Waldren). Louis showed Fess some of the unusual Latin Rhythms that Fess began using, Coleman wrote.

"I used to sneak into the Pepper Pot to see Professor Longhair. It was just him and a drummer, but it sounded like a whole band in there." Algiers born Clarence "Frogman" Henry said. "When I played talent shows at school, I played his numbers and dressed just like him with tails and a long Indian wig." [18] Clarence Henry (born 1937) was just a kid when he first heard Fess.

The club was occasionally, and briefly mentioned by Vernon Winslow, late 1940s, and early 50s, in his *Louisiana Weekly* columns: "Boogie-beat jive: By Dr. Daddy-O'". "There'll be a Jax-Party at the Pepper Pot (Gretna) on Thursday... and Prof. Long-Hair will be in charge..." [19] "And out in Gretna at the Pepper Pot, I picked up on that Prof. Longhair Combo... it's tops pops!!!" [20] In December 1950, Winlsow declared in his colorful way: "and have ya seen that slick-looking new green hat that Prof. Longhair is sportin' these days??... it's smooth... and those new sport shirts that Roy Byrd bought in Houston are just like Esquire!!! (I like the tan one!!!)". [21]

The New
Pepper Pot Lounge

GRETNA, LA.

900 SEVENTH STREET

FREE BARBEQUE EVER WED.
NITE - COCKTAIL HOUR 6 P.M.
MON. HIGHBALL 35¢
PROP JOE AND BELL

Courtesy: Inside New Orleans, 1962.

IV.

Mardi Gras Sad Day For Prof. Long Hair, was a headline in the Louisiana Weekly, same date as the advertisement on the following page. In the article, its longtime reporter Earl M. Wright wrote:

"'Come to the Mardi Gras' sang 'Professor Long Hair' during the weeks preceeding [sic] Carnival. His ballad filled the air via radio stations and juke boxes luring many visitors to New Orleans especially to Dumaine and Claiborne where they would see the Zulu King on Mardi Gras Day.

During his grand build-up of 'the day that care forgot,' Roland Byrd or 'Prof. Long Hair,' 40 years old and a musician, was not aware of the fact that he was reputedly tagged for having made a purchase of marijuana from rookie cop, Sylvester St. Cyr during the latter's undercover campaign not long ago.

"Big Carnival Day Dance Mar. 1: San Jacinto Club." Courtesy Louisiana Weekly, February 27, 1960.

1811 S. Rampart St., the Byrd family's residence in 1960. Photo by the author, fall 2014.

"NABBED ON BANDSTAND. Byrd is a traveling piano man and spends a lot of time out of the city. When he arrived two days prior to Mardi Gras a friend tried to tell him that he was wanted by the narcotics men and that he had better see his manager at once so that he might escape going to jail for Mardi Gras. The friend said 'Prof.' argued that he was not the man being hunted but that it was another 'Prof.' about 27 years old. The friend gave up. Came Mardi Gras Day and 'Long Hair' was scheduled to play at The San Jacinto Club on Dumaine Street, two blocks off Claiborne where 'King Zulu' was going to make his appearance. However the narcotics men said they had read an ad in the Weekly where Byrd was going to be playing his piano and singing his songs. Officer St. Cyr and other members of the narcotics squad were waiting for 'Prof.' to escort him off to jail as he mounted the bandstand. They did that and Byrd, who

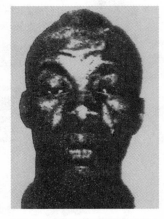

A Fess mugshot, courtesy: Louisiana Weekly, February 27, 1960.

gave his address as 1811 So. Rampart Street was placed under a bond of $2500 which he failed to make at the time. He spent the greater part of Mardi Gras Day in the coop and then some more days.

Byrd's arrest cleared up an erroneous rumor which has been to the effect that Officer Sylvester St. Cyr had been beaten and stabbed by avenging thugs over the wholesale arrests he triggered. Narcotics squadmen said this is far from the truth and if the young officer had been attacked by hoodlums the world would have heard of the repercussions by this time. It would not be a whispering campaign they promised.

Meanwhile Tuesday three of the men bagged in the huge narcotics net copped 'guilty pleas' and received sentences ranging from five to six years in penitentiary." By Earl M. Wright.

Sylvester "Saint" St. Cyr (1931-2002), was a son of the noted New Orleans born, pioneer string player Johnny St. Cyr (1891-1966). He is famous for his work with jazz celebrities like Louis Armstrong, and Jelly Roll Morton. Sylvester's profession provides the background material for the 1972 book, *The Saint and Sinners*. In early 1960:

A New Orleans policeman, Sylvester Armand St. Cyr, 28, who posed as a 'beatnik' for 16 months and caused 100 charges to be filed against 50 narcotic peddlers and addicts, was publicly acclaimed by his superiors in a two-and-half-hour radio and television press conference. Picked for the undercover job by narcotic squad Sgt. Clarence Giarrusso, who decided he had the natural 'cat-like mannerisms,' St. Cyr spent a month learning how to identify narcotics before entering the underworld. He said he feared for his life on one occasion when the word was passed that 'I was wrong.' [22]

Sylvester St. Cyr mentioned various encounters with Fess, and the Caldonia Club/Inn:

The lady of the house put on some soul music and I immediately recognized the sounds of my favorite recording artists.

'Say, landlady, you sure know what to play. That is Professor Longhair's aggregation, isn't it?' "You bet, Slim. You dig on the Prof?' 'He is the man. Ain't nobody can bass like the Professor: Somebody entered the

apartment while the house lady and I were sitting on the sofa. He lit one
of the smokes Bo had rolled and walked into the front room. It was none
other than the professor himself! He gave Bo a drag and brought it into the
front. He passed me the roach and walked into the bedroom. As soon as he
was out of sight I duffed it and hid it in my watch pocket. Professor re-
turned to the living room and asked for the roach. I asked him how long
did he think a roach like he gave me was supposed to last. He laughed and
got another one from the table. The house lady returned from the bedroom
and sat next to me. 'Dammit! What's the matter, Slim?' she questioned.
'I was supposed to cop some milk for the baby and take it home before I came
in town and I completely forgot.' [23]

After the [pool] game I walked over to the Caledonia Club [...] with my pool
partner. We were heading for a club the habitués of which were known for
liking their vice, versa. I wondered about my newfound friend who had sug-
gested going. As far as I could determine, he had no effeminate mannerisms,
but maybe he preferred those who did.

There were a few 'couples' in the club, pimps and prostitutes, queer lovers,
lesbians and those who appreciated the amorous advances of 'turns.' We or-
dered beers and Paul played the jukebox. Just as we pushed the last button,
a photographer walked in and induced us to take a picture. I consented after
being persuaded by Paul. Paul insisted that I keep the photo and I was more
than glad to anticipate a buy with him as a pusher or a connect. Paul said
that he stayed across the street and was going home but would return shortly
[...] [24]

The *Louisiana Weekly*, May 14, 1950, put out one of the earliest reports
of a Fess gig at the San Jacinto Club. The other acts were Dave Bartholomew's big band, augmented by the singer and guitarist Smiley
Lewis. Since 1922, the *San Jacinto Social and Pleasure Club*, had been
host to many African American benevolent aid societies, jazz and
R&B musical events, amateur boxing, Mardi Gras day masquerad-
ers, and other cultural events indigenous to the Black community of
Treme. [25] Around 600 people, could fill the loud big dance hall on a
dance affair. Apartments were for rent upstairs. Edward "Beansie"
Fauria (1893-1975), the proprietor, was a local renowned real estate
man, reportedly, known for various shady business activities, including gambling.

Lil Snooks [Eaglin] & His Band, 5 - 4 Club, late 1961. Courtesy: Louisiana Weekly, December 1961.

The San Jacinto was in a poor condition in 1966, when the last recording session was held there. On the whole, the old, significant Treme neighborhood was in serious decline, at the time. Reportedly, the San Jacinto was abandoned, with broken glass all over the dance floor. This was also obvious in November 1966, when a couple of friends and me suddenly came across it, late at night, on our walk back to the 'Quarter'. The late Mike Hazeldine, a British jazz writer, speculated:"Beansie knew the area was due to be cleared for a housing project and, would you believe, the San Jacinto suddenly caught fire the following year," in January 1967. [26] *Much of the old Treme section, where many of the old* [African American] *musicians […] had lived, was pulled down to make way for an expansion of the city's 'cultural' facilities. The old San Jacinto Hall perished this way, and on its site, was built a new Cultural Center. There could hardly have been a greater irony.* [27] Tom Bethell, a Brit expat and former jazz record company owner.

The 5 - 4, former: San Jacinto Club, 1965. Photo and courtesy: Jan Lindelöf. Used by permission.

"Cosimo "Cos" Matassa was born in New Orleans in 1926, "a single generation after a vigilante mob stormed the parish prison to lynch and shoot eleven Italians prisoners to death. The mob violence was a message to the rising political power of the newly immigrated Italian community; 'get back in line or else.'" [28] During four decades Matassa, was the proprietor of a couple of very important local recording studios. The most celebrated was by far the J. & M., intersection of N. Rampart and Dumaine Streets, operated from 1945 until 1956. "The monopolistic cradle of the New Orleans R&B sound", as John Broven put it. [29] The recordings took place in a small room, circa 16, by 19 feet, with relatively primitive recording equipment. Matassa once waxed Dooky Chase's 14-piece band in this studio. The recordings he made usually came out pretty good. Fess', 1953 recording session, stands as an excellent proof of that. The Matassa produced tracks were, "In The Night"; "Ball The Wall"; "Who's Been Fooling You", and two versions of "Tipitina". Besides Fess, the personnel were: "Red" Tyler, Lee Allen, Frank Fields, "Papoose" Nelson, and Earl Palmer. With Nelson as an exception, they were the core of "studio click". Off and on, it consisted of: Tyler, Allen, Ed Frank, Huey "Piano" Smith, Salvador Doucette, Ernest McLean, Justin Adams, Frank Fields, Earl Palmer, & "Hungry" Williams. In his autobiography, Palmer declared they were chosen because they contributed and weren't just sidemen, they were also assistant producers.

In 1953, the *Flamingos*, led by a teen aged Allen Toussaint, auditioned for Dave Bartholomew at the J&M studio. This seven-piece group included "Snooks" Eaglin, 17 years old. But Bartholomew didn't approve. He didn't think that the band was good enough to record. "For me, to see Bartholomew, and to be in that studio," Toussaint later told, "it didn't get better than that. It took me days to get over the shock." [30]

Fess waxed for "Atlantic" records, 1949; "Federal", 1951; and again "Atlantic", in 1953, all of them at the J. & M., (opposite the Municipal Auditorium). He also cut at Matassas' Governor Nichols studios. For the "Ebb" label, in 1957; "Rip", 1962; and "Watch" records, in 1963 and 1964. "Cos" worked with a wide variety of music genres such as: gospel music, blues, rhythm & blues, rock and roll, pop music, Cajun, country & western, traditional and progressive jazz.

840 N. Rampart, where the J&M Recording Studio was soon to be housed. It was "a record store that had a recording studio in the back," Earl Palmer told. Photo by Walter Cook Keenan, courtesy Southeastern Architectural Archive, Howard-Tilton Memorial Library, Tulane University (with thanks to Lynn Abbott).

"Well, there were two, [studios] actually." Cosimo Matassa clarified for Tad Jones. "The first location I had was 525 Governor Nicholls [a three-story building, purchased in February, 1956]. That's a nice old building down there that has a carriage way through the center. And on either side, on the ground floor was my studio. Now this is a dilapidated old building that's empty, except for my studio, okay? Big building, but empty. It's now [in January 1994] beautiful condominiums. Back then it was just a big old empty building. And facing it, facing the carriage way to the left, was where I had the disk-mastering room and my office; and on the right, was a small studio control room. And the rest of the building was just empty. [...]

Jones: I mean, you bought it; purchased it. Did you think of doing anything with the rest of the building?

Matassa: Oh yeah. I envisioned somewhere down the line restoring that building. Gorgeous! It's got a circular staircase to the third floor, which, a lot of 'em had, like to the first floor were just ordinary. This was a gorgeous thing on either side; matching; gorgeous! Goes up to the third floor; gorgeous!

Jones: Were you ever able to do that?

Matassa: No, no. 'Cause what happened, the building next door became available. 521 Gov. Nicholls. It was a cold storage room for avocados. [...] I got that building and true to my style; I just ripped out the stuff inside and made a studio out of it. You know, it wasn't air-conditioned and it wasn't... [...] I had a small studio and a big studio.

Jones: What year did you buy the 520 building? [...]

Matassa: I'm bad about those dates [...] But it had to be [...] late fifties. And 521 was after, you know, I mean the sequence of time was after; but in that stretch. [...] And the second studio was the first time I had a big room. I really wanted a big room. By then, I had been spending some time self-educating myself about acoustics and things like that. And I could see where separation, just physical separation, could enormously increase the amount of control you had over the sound of something. And I'd been suffering through the other situation where everything was close and you struggled to get separation, and blend, and balance, and all that. And anyway, so I got the big studio and it was really big. Thirty-five feet across; and about sixty-five feet long! [...] You could've stuck the two earlier studios into that, you know, (Laughs) and have room left over. Anyway, so I did some things acoustically in this weird looking control room. [...] Well, it was weird shaped. It was totally unsymmetrical; and highly damped. And the studio itself, the room was live when I started. And I damped it greatly. There wasn't much room tone in that big room. It was more like a sound stage. It was like a motion picture sound stage; pretty dead.

Jones: What type of quality was the space that wasn't dampened? Was it wood, concrete...?

525 Governor Nichols Street, November 2010. Photo by the author.

Matassa: Concrete [...] The floor was the only hard surface in the room [...] And the walls were fiberglass. [...] I built some traps, you know, sound traps. Measured as best I could with the equipment I had the basic resonances and damped those out at the bottom. And that was it. That was it. It was a big dead room.

Jones: Now what was your decision, in other words, what sessions did you do in the big room as opposed to sessions in the small room.

Matassa: For instance, then we started doing strings". [31]

The studios were all named as: *Cosimo Recording Studios*, generally shortened as: *Cosimo's*. Its cork-covered walls were excellent, "great sound in there", Matassa once told. [32]

Cosimo's "seemed always to be in some state of development." According to Harold Battiste Jr. "At one point, the air conditioning consisted of a big fan blowing over blocks of ice, then through a large plastic tube in the studio. But the hits kept coming out of that place! Cosimo was more than a brilliant recording engineer – he loved the music and the people who created it. His contribution was to capture as much of the music's spirit as possible." [33]

"Cosimo built his big recording studio next to the small one on Governor Nichols Street", Clarence "Frogman" Henry said, but Matassa "did not get the same sound in the big one compared to the small one,". [34] The Governor Nicholls studio was operated until May 1968. Despite the Governor Nichols studios important historic musical past, they remain neglected.

V.

Cosimo got into financial troubles and tried to make a comeback. In 1969, he bought a 400-square foot place, in a former storehouse structure uptown, at 748 Camp Street. The new studio was called: *Jazz City Studio*. On Monday, May 14, 1973, the UK rock band *Led Zeppelin* did a show at the Municipal Auditorium. On the same afternoon, the President of "Atlantic" records' Ahmet Ertegun threw a notable party, on the second floor, at the *Jazz City* building. The guests were visiting rock stars: Robert Plant, Jimmy Page, John Bonham and John Paul Jones. Philippe Rault ("Blue Star" label) helped coordinate the party. He put it like this: "They didn't need some ritzy ballroom," Rault narrated. "Just going to a funky, soulful recording studio in a beat down part of New Orleans and to meet the guys they grew up listening to—they were in seventh heaven. [Keyboardist and singer] Willie Tee [Turbinton] was still alive, Ernie K-Doe was there, Professor Longhair—all these guys were former Atlantic artists that Ertegun had a relationship with. To bring them out at Cosimo's party, it gave the band a woody." [35]

A *Led Zeppelin* press release testified that K-Doe performed backed by the Meters, and: "Blind piano legend Professor Longhair also played." Perhaps supported by the Meters? It may have been Fess' black shades that resembled a blind guy? Rault did not mention celebrities like: Allen Toussaint, Lee Dorsey, Earl King, Roosevelt Sykes, Art Neville and the Meters, the Wild Magnolias, Snooks Eaglin, and the Olympia Brass Band. A local music magazine reported that: Soul food comprised the menu that night and all of New Orleans' best R&B and rock legends would perform. [36] It's reported that, Matassa went bust in his Camp Street studio in 1968. One of his creditors came in and, sad to say, literally cleaned the place out and hauled off all the old tapes and discs. The *Jazz City Studio*, closed down in 1977.

Colin Davies, a Canadian radio personality, asked Matassa, if the drums ever sounded too loud in his studio? *No, because a lot of the drums were in the other mics. You know, I only used a little omnidirectional mic over the drums to give it presence and a little balance between the parts. Also the reason the drums sounded that way was because they used animal hides for the drum heads, and there is a difference in that sound from what you hear now with plastic ones. I don't know how else to explain it – a skin head is part of a living thing – and they sound different.* [37]

VI.

If I hear something, immediately I start arranging. Arrangement, to me, has to be part of the song itself, as if the two were made for each other at the moment that the writer wrote the song, and it should fit like a glove, Wardell J. Quezergue declared in a 2010 interview. [38] Quezergue (pronounced Ku-ZAIR) was born to a musical Creole family. His older brothers were: Leo J. Quezergue Sr. (1924-2015), a Dixieland drummer, and the diseased trumpeter Sidney. The surname seems to be of Haitian origin. At age 12, Wardell took up trumpet and piano. He later studied under Clyde Kerr Sr., at the Xavier Preparatory High School. Wardell's musical knowledge improved while in the Army (1951), during the Korean War. Back home in New Orleans in the mid 1950s, he continued his music studies at the important *Grunewald School of Music*, 827 Camp St. It opened around 1945, advertised as the *South's Most Complete Music School*. Saxophonist Alvin "Red" Tyler was one of the students, with Willie Humphrey Jr., teacher on reed instruments. Many musicians of later fame learned there. It was a school for Black and white students, with the education organized as bottom floor for whites and two top floors for blacks. Students were allowed to jam together, despite the persisting segregation laws.

"I played some trumpet and a little piano but I was more interested in the instrumentation," […] Quezergue modestly revealed in 1982.[39] He ultimately formed his first band, the Royal Dukes of Rhythm (including, off and on: Emery Thompson, trumpet; James Rivers, Robert Parker, saxes; Wendell Eugene, "Frog" Joseph, trombones; George Davis, guitar; Ed Frank/Mac Rebennack, piano; George French, bass;

& Smokey Johnson, drums.). This band often supported visiting celebrity acts in the 1960s. Dave Bartholomew introduced Wardell to the recording business. One of the songs that received his prescription was: Earl King's funky, late 1962 item "Trick Bag"("Imperial"). The guys on it were: Dave Bartholomew, Quezergue, trumpets; James Booker, keyboard; "Moe" Bachemin, sax; Carl Blouin, bar. sax; George French, bass, and "Smokey" Johnson, drums. According to Earl King: *Wardell was doin' some of the horn charts on the stuff I did for Imperial, and I did the rhythm charts. But many times, you don't see Wardell's name there [...] I'll give him some of my specifics and he can go on his own from there with what he want to do [...] But I think Wardell and I used to work pretty good, we used to come up with pretty good things [...]* [40]

Wardell Quezergue. A publicity photo. Courtesy Ovation Entertainment, New Orleans, LA. The Author's collection. Used by permission.

The rejoiced "Big Chief" track was cut, in November 1964, at Matassa's big Governor Nichols St. studio. Members of Wardell's Royal Dukes of Rhythm were hired. Fess played right hand piano; Earl King, vocal & whistling; Clyde R. Kerr Sr., Emery Thompson, Eddie Nash, trumpets; Waldren Joseph Sr., Wendell Eugene, Warren Bokes, trombones; Nat Perrilliat, Warren Bell, Clarence Ford, Carl Blouin, saxophones; Mac Rebennack, guitar; Curtis Mitchell, upright bass; "Smokey" Johnson, drums; and Sidney Quezergue, home-made shaker. For John Swenson, Wardell revealed: Smokey "hit that drum so hard, he had blood coming out between his thumb and forefinger." Earl King said that: *Fess gave the drum pattern to Smokey Johnson by playing it on a cardboard box that was lying around and everybody seems to remember the blisters on the drummer's hands at the end of the session [...] That double time rhythm pattern was rough. As far as the whistling goes, I had never done it on record before, so I did the best I could.* [41] In the early 1960s, Quezergue also gigged, on a double bell euphonium, with the Onward and the Eureka Brass Bands.

"Big Chief", Parts 1 and 2, is a true Mardi Gras classic. It's been sampled many times. One of them: "Knock 'Em Out", was included on UK singer Lily Allen's debut album *ALRIGHT, STILL,* UK, 2006. The song is on the repertoires of nearly all local brass bands these days. These are a few of the tracks, some of them chart hits, that benefited from Quezergue's skills: "Chapel Of Love" (1964), & "Iko Iko" (1965), the Dixie Cups; "Teasing' You", Willie Tee (1965); "Barefootin'" (1966), and "Give Me The Country Side Of Life", Robert Parker (1975), a particular favorite of mine (with David Barard, bass, & Herman Ernest III, drums); "Groove Me" (1970), King Floyd; and: "Mr. Big Stuff" (1971), Jean Knight. It's worth mention that Wardell did the arrangements for Rebennack's Grammy-winning CD album: Goin' Back to New Orleans (1992). *I really don't play the piano, I can get on it and play chords. If I can hum something, I can play the chords but not the melodic lines or the fills. When somebody wants me to arrange a song, all I have to know is what key it's in, and I work from there [...]* [42] Quezergue lost his sight in later life, a result of diabetes."

He suffered badly when: *the floods of Hurricane Katrina (2005) swept away his scores along with most of the rest of his possessions. [...] He took part in a concert held in his honor in New York in 2009, at which the performers included many whose careers had benefited from his attention.* [43] Wardell Quezergue, aka "the Creole Beethoven", died in New Orleans on September 6, 2011. His Japan born wife: Yoshi Tamaki, passed earlier in the same year. She gave birth to five sons and eight daughters.

VII.

In 1962, Fess waxed two rare 45 discs for the "Rip Records", owned by Ripoll "Rip" Roberts (1912-1996). In the early 1960s, it was a record company with about fourteen 45s in its catalogue. Reginald "Reggie" Hall's "the Joke", leased by the Chess brothers in Chicago, became Robert's top seller. Rick Coleman told that the year 1948 was the first time that Blacks registered to vote in any numbers. Roberts "led voting drives and held a benefit for the NAACP [...] with singers Roy

Brown, Larry Darnell, Cousin Joe [Pleasant Joseph] and female impersonator Patsy Valadier [Irving Vale]." [44] Vale was one of the Caldonia Inn acts. Ripoll Roberts was Roy Brown's local manager for a while.

Robert - Ripoll Charles 'Rip' Robert, An Entrepreneur, Died Thursday At Mercy and Baptist Medical Center. He Was 84. Mr. Robert Was A Lifelong Resident Of New Orleans. He Owned And Operated Rip's Playhouse, A Restaurant And Bar In The 7th Ward. He Also Worked In The Entertainment World, Bringing Such Talent As Nat King Cole, Count Basie, Lionel Hampton, Fats Domino And Dinah Washington To New Orleans. He Was President Of The 7th Ward Democratic Club. Survivors Include His Wife, Mary Coste Robert; A Son, Ripoll 'Junior Rip' Robert; A Daughter, Elaine Robert Chenier Of Los Angeles; Nine Grandchildren; And 13 Great-Grandchildren. A Mass Will Be Said Tuesday At 11 A.M. At Epiphany Church, 1949 Duels St. Visitation Will Be At 9:30 A.M. Burial Will Be In Mount Olivet Cemetery. Courtesy: *The Times-Picayune,* January 28, 1996.

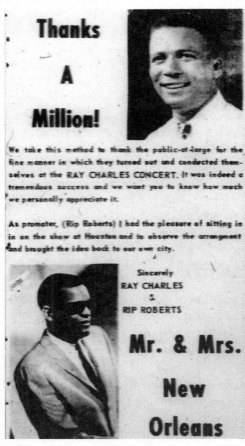

A Rip Roberts advertisement, courtesy: Louisiana Weekly, April 4, 1962. A Club Desire job in August 1951, was Ray Charles' first gig in the Crescent City. He would become a frequent performer in the city.

VIII.

Emery Humphrey Thompson, aka Umar Sharif (1927-1998), was a trumpet virtuoso and a good singer too. His cousin Willie Humphrey Jr., was one his first teachers. Emery joined pianist Valmore Victore's Music Masters, 1941, at the Tick Tock Tavern (in the Astoria building) on South Rampart St. Thompson was inspired by Louis Armstrong, Roy Eldridge and Dizzy Gillespie. The year 1948 saw Thompson as a member of pianist Joe Jones eleven-piece band, among them Alvin "Red" Tyler, tenor; "Hardy", alto (Capt. John Handy?), and Louis Barbarin, drums. Emery's musical resume included bands lead by Luis Russell; the Herbert Leary Society Orchestra; Louis Jordan; Joe Turner; Lionel Hampton; and Lonnie Johnson.

Trumpeter Thomas Jefferson's pick up brass band, with "Big" Emery Thompson, 1951, including Jefferson's older brother Andrew, snare drum; Thomas, trumpet; Rudolph Beaulieu, bass drum; "Kid Sheik"; & Thompson. In 1949, Thomas Jefferson (1920-1986), lead "his Rhythm Ones who put down some 'real gone' be bop", at the Caldonia Club. Photo: Alden Ashforth. Courtesy: Hogan Jazz Archive, Tulane University. Used by permission.

"I think I was the first modern jazz player in New Orleans." Thompson accounted in 1983. "I brought the bebop trumpet here. But being able to get enough work here to keep alive has been the problem. So

I've ended up developing the traditional jazz style, the swing style. But every time I get a chance, I try to play as much bebop as I can." [45] Wardell Quezergue often employed Emery to carry out his brass-drenched arrangements for numerous recordings. Among them, Joe Assunto & Henry Hildebrand, and their "Watch" label sessions. Thompson joined the Nation Of Islam, in the mid 1950s, which helped him get rid of his drug habit. He toured France and Belgium in November 1987, and played with local trad jazz bands. Emery Thompson's last public appearance was in a group led Wynton Marsalis, at the Lincoln Center, NYC, in 1992.

Tenor saxophonist legend Nathaniel "Nat" Perrilliat (1936-1971) was another musician that cut with Fess, in 1964. Harold Battiste said that. "Nat turned Pro when he landed a gig with the legendary Professor Longhair's fabulous hits and funky music. After that grass root beginning, he gigged around town with several musicians during the mid '50's." [46] Perrilliat's row of Fess gigs began in early 1952, and continued for two years. Charles "Honey Boy" Otis, was the drummer. "I made one record with Longhair not so long ago though,

Nat Perrilliat, 1960s. Courtesy: New Orleans Heritage-Jazz 1956-1966.

Big Chief, which was done with Earl King", Perrilliat, said in London, UK, 1967, with Fats Domino. [47] Nat jobbed with the *American Jazz Quintet*, a local progressive jazz constellation, in early 1959. "Featured in the group were Alvin Battiste [sic] on clarinet; Nat Perrilliat, tenor sax; Ellis Marsalis, piano; Otis Duvernay, bass; and Ed Blackwell, drums [...] The clarinet of Alvin Battiste [sic] rode high and wide in unison chariot with the [Sonny] Rollins-like tenor of Nat Perrilliat, while the pace was set in contrapuntal rhythms by drummer Ed Blackwell [...] Perrilliat displayed versatile mastery of the tenor sax, often leaving the powerful softness of [Stan] Getz-tones to soar gossamer wings to the land of never to-the-forgotten Bird [Charlie Parker]." [48]

"To me, Nat Perrilliat was one of the greatest tenor saxophone players I ever heard in my life." Earl Turbinton stated: "John Coltrane and other players were very, very impressed by him. And to know that a mayor talent like that, a mayor mind, could be among us and yet very few people knew about him... [49]

IX.

Joseph F. "Joe" Assunto (1914-1981) and Henry Hildebrand (?-1977) were the owners of the "Watch" record company. Assunto was a younger brother of Jacinto "PaPa Jac" Assunto, a trombonist & banjo player with the successful Dukes of Dixieland. Joe Assunto also had the *One Stop Record Shop*, "back o' town" at 350 South Rampart St., and he was a really beautiful person, according to Rebennack. It was a longtime landmark, opened in 1952. In his 1994 biography Rebennack related: Fess, "after playing cards all night, in the afternoon he'd work the One Stop Record Shop, filling out cards for the jukeboxes, which hilarious because of the way he spelled things. He loved to type, because it reminded him of playing the piano." [...] Assunto "got a kick of it, and let the cards go out the way Fess had typed them".

Joseph "Joe" F. Assunto, around 1960. Courtesy: Kelly McGregor Fournier. Used by permission.

The store became a musician's hangout, with extraordinary vocalist Johnny Adams (1932-1998) as one of them: "In the meantime I was working at the One Stop Record Shop. I was doing a few little gigs on the strength of 'I Won't Cry' and 'Release Me'– yeah, you know, in the country: Houma and Hammond, little places like that – but I would always get up in the morning and go to the One Stop.

We had a light-weight piano in the back of the store, you know – Fess would go to the back of the store and woodshed with himself, Raymond Lewis would come by once in a while, Earl King and myself. This is where all the fun was". [50]

"Where all the fun was": 348-352-South Rampart St., 1952, just before Assunto's record shop moved into the building. Courtesy: The Charles L. Franck Studio Collection, the Historic New Orleans Collection, 1979.352.843. Used by permission.

Hannusch portrayed Assunto's place, in the Black business district: "Earl King walked into the One-Stop Record Shop […] three blocks off from Canal Street in late 1963. […] With 45 rpm records overflowing from boxes and shelves on the walls. In the front a jukebox operator zipped through potential hits-listening to ten-seconds of each record for a grabbing intro, in the back room [Earl] King was astonished to find his New Orleans rhythm & blues cohorts–Professor Longhair, Tommy Ridgley, Eddie Bo and others–sitting around the piano. It was the beginning of Watch Records, one of the classic small New Orleans R&B labels." [51]

In July 1976, Assunto was forced to move his store to 1400 North Broad Street, Hannusch told, "after urban renewal decimated the once-thriving [S.] Rampart Street." From a Black musical history perspective, this seems to be the city's most important street. Nowadays, awfully sad to see with all its empty lots and parking spaces. After her daddy's death in August 1981, Joel Assunto McGregor took over the relocated store – where the retail business continued until January 1983. Joe Assunto was Joseph Ruffino's brother-in-law.

Joseph "Joe"Ruffino (1922-1965), "had a studio on Baronne Street, which I built and designed for him", Eddie Bo declared: "The first record recorded in that studio was Joe Jones 'You Talk Too Much', a million seller right out. I was on piano for 'You Talk Too Much'". [52] Ruffino was the superior for "Ron" and "Ric" records from 1959, until his sudden death at 43. The record labels were named after his sons Ronald and Richard. The recording studio and office was placed on the second floor, with Henry Hildebrand's *All South* [record] *Distributors* on the first floor. This was the heart of the city's record row in the 1950s and early 1960s. Most of Joe's recording sessions went off here. Among them, the very successful 1959 Fess recording session. Mac Rebennack, the arranger and guitarist on the session, described the small studio, situated behind Ruffino's office as, "okay for what it was". At another occasion, in 1973, Mac confessed: "I'm sure that Joe Ruffino never paid me all that I had coming to me on my songs, he was most thuggish in the way he treated his artists, cheating them right down to nickels and dimes. But no matter how rank he was, he had a way of keeping his artists close to him." [53]

Joe Ruffino, "was an immense ego." Cosimo Matassa declared in 1994. "Everything, his clothes, you know, he always dressed up like the little man on the wedding cake… Yeah and everything had to be just so and unfortunately some of his business ethics weren't the greatest. He contributed to that segment of the business that took advantage of the ignorance of the people in the business that they were dealing with. There's been an ongoing legal case that you were aware of, that, […] it had its seed in Joe Ruffino's business practices.

Tad Jones: […] He didn't copyright his songs in his music catalog. He didn't have contracts with musicians.

The remains of Joe Ruffino's former headquarter at 630 1/2 Baronne St. (now demolished). Photo by the author: November 2012.

Matassa: Right, right. He could exist in his sphere without it. [...] And, you know, there's a concept in the law about the four corners [...] of the page upon which it's written. And everything else is just parley, talk. And he understood that it is in his own way so if it wasn't on the paper, it wasn't. And once he got beyond a certain point he wasn't interested he didn't think nationally in the sense that a Berry Gordy might or in multiple releases [...] that kind of thing. He only thought in terms of that particular piece of merchandise and there were a couple of...; he suffered some losses because of that. The Joe Jones thing, with "You Talk Too Much" and things like that [...] [54] A heart attack took Joseph Ruffino's life in March 23, 1965.

X.

French producer Philippe Rault, was responsible for the *Studio In The Country session,* cut in Bogalusa, La., 1974:

"So on a sunny day of April 74, we found ourselves heading to Bogalusa, Louisiana, where Fess was born. Not for sentimental reasons, but simply because one of the better recording studios in the area. Studio in the Country, happened to be located in the middle of a pine forest a couple of miles outside of town.

The Professor had brought with him Alfred "Uganda" Roberts, his regular conga player, and Shiba [Ed Kimbrough], this aging young man whom he had taught drums to some 25 years previously. As it often turns out with true originals, Fess liked to train percussion men himself (from scratch if need be), showing them exactly what to play. Just like James Brown or Captain Beefheart. Who would have known better anyway? Julius Farmer, a promising young player fresh out of Alvin Batiste's music class at Southern University, came in on bass. And on guitar, one of the great blues maestros, Clarence "Gatemouth" Brown, who had just blown into town a few weeks earlier to record a new LP of his own. Fess and he had met again and spent a memorable evening reminiscing about old stories and exchanging licks that had left the rare witnesses crawling on the floor and begging for more. So it was as natural to have "Gate" join forces on this project. The Professor's house had burned down to the ground three days before. No one had been hurt, but in the absence of fire insurance it was a total loss. This event might have been lingering on his mind, but it didn't show when he got behind the Baldwin grand [piano]. For two days and under the expert technical supervision of Stephen Hodge, [...] On the third day we remixed the totality of the tracks and edited. Fess liked what he heard. As a matter of fact, we all liked it and so has most everyone who has heard it subsequently. The album came out in France and various other European countries. A few imports trickled back over into the States, and unfortunately, when the Professor passed away in January 1980, the record still lacked national distribution" [...] [55] Baton Rouge born Julius Farmer (1949-2001) jobbed and recorded with many famous musicians, among them Mac Rebennack and the Wild Magnolias. He died in New Orleans only 52 years old.

"That was a fun album, just playin' [Fess'] stuff". "Gatemouth" Brown declared in 1995: "He's the father of that type of piano player. James Booker [born 1939] came next. Booker used to work for me, for about a year when he was 15 years old [...] He was a great musician—he just had problems.". [56]

XI.

New Orleans born Isidore "Tuts" Washington, nicknamed as "Red", or "Papa Yeller"/"Yellow", is cited as an early influence on Fess. "Tuts", in his turn, acknowledged: "I was glad for Fess when he got those li'l records out and got to be known. Fess always did give me credit. He always had a good word to say about me until the day he died. See it's always good to give the young fellows a break. It don't pay to be selfish." [57]

Washington was essentially a jazz pianist with a couple boogie woogies and blues items on his repertoire. He never learned to read music, yet, he could play songs with advanced chord structures such as: "Stardust." "Tuts" had a long association with Smiley Lewis. He and bassist "Papa" John Joseph (1877-1965), made his first recordings with Smiley in 1947. Fess "makes records; I played with him", Joseph told in 1958. [58] Joseph was a direct like to cornetist and band leader Buddy Bolden (1877-1931), first jazz man. The Washington and Lewis cooperation begun in the 1930s in Thomas Jefferson's small band, and ceased in the early 1950s."He played the whole piano..."Allen Toussaint said: "'Tuts' played half stride and half Junker". [59] Allen used to catch "Tuts" at the Lucky Pierre, 735 Bourbon. In the 1970s, "Tuts" sometimes played with Blue Lu and Danny Barker.

"Played on the Delta Queen boat in 68 – Play with Papa Celestine [sic], Kid Rena, Clyde Kerr [Sr.]. Recorded for Smiley Lewis in 1949 [between 1947, and 1952]. Played in St. Louis Missouri with [alto saxophonist] Tab Smith [1909-1971] Orchestra in 1945 – Play in Santa Rosa California at the Buck Horn night (club). Played at the Court of Two Sisters from '68 to '73. Started when I 10 years old speak easys and fish frys [sic]. Born in New Orleans La. 1907–24 of January at Eight and Rampart Street. Yours truly, Isidore Tuts Washington [1974]." [60]

Washington perished under dramatic circumstances, August 5, 1984, while performing at the 1984 *New Orleans World's Fair.* "After his first number and his usual response to the applause, ('Thank you, music lovers.') He said, 'I'm really happy to be with you here today. I don't know how much longer I'll be able to do this. I'm getting pretty old, you know...' He then played a little riff and stopped for a moment. He started playing another bit of a song and paused again before playing a couple of bars of a different song and then he died. Right there at the piano!" [...] [61]

"Tuts" Washington, Jazz Fest, Fair Grounds, New Orleans 1972. Photo: Hans Lychou. Used by permission (thanks Hans).

XII.

Bruce Iglauer (born 1947) is the founder and head of "Alligator" records, in Chicago Ill. Iglauer, Andy Kaslow and Allison Miner produced Fess' very last recordings, released as the *Crawfish Fiesta* album. It was waxed at Toussaint's and Marshall Sehorn's, now defunct, *Sea-Saint Studio*, 3809 Clematis Avenue, Gentilly, a New Orleans suburb.

"I had loved Professor Longhair's music ever since I first heard the [1972] Atlantic reissue of his early sides." Iglauer stated in 2011.

"It was one of those records I listened to over and over […] I gave Fess lots control in the studio and he worked very hard to make sure it was a special record. He was a tough taskmaster, calling for additional takes when we all thought we had a great performance, and proving that he himself could do the song slightly better. […] He did the final vocals live. It was Mac who suggested the instrumentation for the title track, with tuba bass and snare drum with cardboard taped on it.

I didn't spend a lot of time with him, but one day in the studio he and I arrived first and played some games of bumper pool together. We talked about a lot of things and he told me that he hated leading a band on the road because he didn't like to order other musicians around. He preferred being one of the guys and not the big boss man. I which I could have known him better." [62]

In 1997, Mac Rebennack recounted Fess' last recording session: "I played guitar because Snooks Eaglin couldn't make it. That was where I was trying to make [Fess] remember the Caribbean tunes. At least I got him to cut "Rum And Coca Cola." He couldn't hardly play that anymore. He used to do this one thing he always called "Swanee River," but it wasn't. It was parts of a lot of famous Spanish songs all rolled into one of his things. We came with the name for the album because Fess always started gigs saying, 'We're gonna have a little crawfish fiesta tonight. Want y'all to bring your owns along.'" […] [63]

The "Alligator" album was reissued in October 2012. A couple of months earlier, Iglauer put it like this:

"We are only rereleasing the album on vinyl with what is essentially the original packaging. We added a rehearsal rundown (not really a take) of "River's Invitation" [by Percy Mayfield]. That's the only additional song. In the process, I listened to the two-track that we ran while recording was going on. It had roughs of all the takes. There were only one or two takes of the songs, maybe three of one. We had definitely chosen the best takes, and I didn't think that anyone's reputation would be enhanced by releasing the takes with weaker solos (the big issues were more among the tenor saxes than anywhere else. There were also a couple takes with some very forgettable baritone solos.

I had dreamed of recording Fess but he was managed by Quint Davis. Every time I contacted Quint, he told me they were waiting for that elusive big label deal. Finally, I was helping a friend book a festival for November or December of 1979 in South Bend, Indiana. He wanted Fess. I called Quint, who told me that his old girlfriend Allison [Miner] Kaslow was now managing Fess. So I called her, and we negotiated the festival appearance. At the end of the conversation, I said "I know you're looking for a major deal, but if you ever want to deal with an honest independent who loves Fess' music and would treat him right, call me.

A few days later (maybe the next day), Allison called back and asked me to come to New Orleans that same weekend (it might have been August) to hear the band. I flew down and heard them for two nights at Tip's [Tipitina's] and wrote down all the songs they played. We then began to negotiate a deal and came to one fairly quickly. I have a letter from Fess' lawyer from October 21 confirming the deal. As you can imagine, I was hugely excited to have my dream come true, and heartbroken when Fess died." [64]

Iglauer gave the recording dates as (Friday) November 16, 17, and 18, 1979. Iglauer: "Fess was using a few different guitar players for his live gigs. None was great. Snooks was discussed, but Tad Jones was tight with Mac and he suggested Mac come and play. Tad may have told Mac that Snooks was considered, but I don't remember anything about Snooks not being available. Mac was a huge help in the studio. The Oct. 21 letter mentions Mac being involved, so it wasn't the very last minute before the sessions.

Bruce Iglauer, March, 2016. Photo and courtesy Tommy Löfgren. Used by permission (thanks Tommy).

We didn't see Toussaint at all. Fess told us to take the master tapes to the hotel every night or Marshall Sehorn would secretly copy them, so we did what he said." [65]

Toussaint and Sehorn, mid 1970s. Unknown photographer. Courtesy: Hogan Jazz Archive, Tulane University. Used by permission.

Bass and Sousaphone player Walter Payton Jr. (1942-2010), was also involved, but his Sousa is only heard on the title track, "Crawfish Fiesta". He was left out in the original liner notes by Mindy Giles; and the late Tad Jones. Payton's name is added on the new printing. In the 1960s, he cut with guys like: Lee Dorsey, Aaron Neville, and Robert Parker. Payton was also known for his jobs with the New Orleans Ragtime Orchestra, and the Preservation Hall Jazz Band. "Tad and I worked together on those notes. Fess was so amazing... he never SAW the cover of the album. I described it to him in detail on the phone....no computer, cell phone etc. back then..." Mindy Giles, February 2018. [66]

Did you notice any sign of Fess' illness during the 1979 recordings? The causes of his death were "chronic bronchitis, pulmonary emphysema" and "advanced cirrhosis of the liver".

Iglauer: "He smoked a lot but I didn't see any evidence of emphysema or cirrhosis. I don't recall him drinking". [67]

"At the end [of the 1979 recordings] Fess declared that it was his favorite of all recordings he had done. He approved of the final mixes and I think the cover. Then, on the day we released it, January 30th, 1980, I received a message on my answering machine from Tad [Jones]. He was crying so hard he couldn't talk. Even though Fess hadn't been sick, I knew immediately that he had died. 'Crawfish Fiesta' is one of my proudest achievements. I feel blessed to have made it, and to have known Fess and made the record possible." Bruce Iglauer, 2011. [68]

The Crawfish Fiesta LP album. The record was found in the collection of the iconic, Swedish born actress: Greta Garbo (1905-1990). Photo: Hans Schweitz.

For John Wirt, writer for *the Advocate* newspaper, Iglauer revealed that, "the 1980 Longhair release "Crawfish Fiesta" has a special resonance for him. It's one that I come back to over and over again. Of course, record company guys don't have the best reputations, Fess probably was trying to decide whether I was a straight-up guy or somebody else who would make a deal with him that would never be honored. That had happened to him often in his past." [69]

The *Crawfish Fiesta* musicians etc., were: Tony Dagradi, Andrew "Andy" Kaslow, tenor saxophones: James "Jim" Moore, baritone saxophone; Mac Rebennack, guitar; Alfred "Uganda" Roberts, conga drums; David Lee Watson, el. bass; John Vidacovich, drums; and Walter Payton, Sousaphone. The sessions were engineered by Freddie Breitberg, and Skip Goodwin.

XIII.

Documentary filmmaker Stevenson J. Palfi died of self-inflicted gunshot wound on December 14, 2005, in New Orleans. "He was 53. Palfi was, reportedly, deeply depressed over loss of much of his property and possessions from Hurricane Katrina. Palfi was best known for his 1982 documentary *Piano Players Rarely Ever Play Together*, about New Orleans pianists Isidore "Tuts" Washington, Henry "Professor Longhair" Roeland Byrd [sic], and Allen Toussaint. He also produced several short films for television's The Learning Channel, and was completing production on Songwriter, Unknown, a documentary feature on Toussaint." [70] Palfi worked for 15 years on the Toussaint feature. In 1977, the filmmaker did a documentary on New Orleans string player Emanuel Sayles.

XIV.

Hurricane Katrina hit New Orleans on Monday, August 29, 2005. "The day before [...] I checked in at a hotel on the corner of Canal St, and Bourbon – and thought I'd just go home next day". Allen Toussaint recounted for a Swedish African American music radio show:

"But as we know now, as the water begun to rise and all that, it didn't work out. But I stayed until four days after the storm, thinking that things may improve sooner than they did. Of course, it didn't turn out that way. When Marshall Sehorn and I parted ways, friendly dissolved our studio connection. The masters of my own, my son did get those and took them to another place. But all of the other masters that were in the studio, that wasn't myself personally, was still there.

When Katrina came those were heavily damaged and I think, set outside on a heap on a pile. In fact, the studio was no longer a studio. And when I did go back and take a look it, yes, everything in it was a big grey mess. And on the piano, you couldn't see one key from the next, you couldn't see where keys were divided, it was just a big grey mess. So, the water was higher than the piano of course. And, also the outside was damaged, as if, I guess the winds were much harder over there. Even the front looked like a bomb had hit it. The studio didn't make it at all, sorry to say.

Mats Nileskär: That was a part of your legacy.

Toussaint: Yes, but I accepted it right away. This is life." [71]

Sea-Saint Recording Studio Inc., 3809 Clematis Avenue; set up in 1973. It was flooded by eight feet of water during Hurricane Katrina, August 2005. Photo: Paul Harris, May 3, 1979. Used with kind permission.

8. FESS – NEW ORLEANS MUSIC – AND ME

I.

It was in the summer of 1973, that Professor Longhair's music really got hold of me. And it is very much related to one specific track. From New Orleans, a friend of mine brought back a stack of local R&B 45 rpm discs. These were recordings impossible to purchase in Sweden; because the small independent New Orleans labels usually lacked European distribution. Anyhow, one of the discs was: Professor Longhair, "RON 326", with "If I Only Knew," and "Cuttin' Out" (by: "Byrd" & Theresa? "Terry"). The latter song, hit me in my stomach and made me very excited. It was simply some of the best music I had heard. Much of it lies in Fess' very personal vocal, piano playing, the *irresistible* groove plus the arrangement. Fess always sang and played with a wonderful sense of time, his singing is very underrated.

"RON 326". Courtesy: Hogan Jazz Archive, Tulane University. Used by permission.

John Boudreaux's complex, ingenious drumming contributed greatly to the track. His drumming had deep roots in the fundamental New Orleans parade beat pattern. On this particular recording, mixed with a Caribbean flavored beat. "Mac" Rebennack, only 19 years old at the time, was the arranger and rhythm guitarist. He once stated that: "I first worked with Fess back in the late fifties at Cosimo Matassa's

Studio" [Governor Nichols St.]. Yet Fess' "Ron" recordings were cut at Joe Ruffino's Baronne St. studio. *A bunch of us,* Rebennack told, *John Boudreaux on drums, Eddie Hynes on trombone, Morris Bachamin* [Bachemin] *on trumpet* [tenor saxophone], *myself on guitar, and Otis Deverney* [Duvernay] *on bass – fell into a session with him, during which he gave us a taste of his fonky genius. We began recording his song "Hey Now Baby, Hey Now Honey Child". For starters, Fess sat down on John's drums and played what he wanted John to play. Fess was very specific about what he was looking for in the drums; John played it to death and Fess was content.* [1] Reportedly, Fess lowered Boudreaux's high-pitched snare

John Boudreaux, mid 1970s. A publicity photo.

drum head to get the preferred sound. "Hey Now Baby, Hey Now Honey Child" is the original title of "Cuttin' Out", a tune Fess waxed several times. "Mardi Gras In New Orleans", from the same 1959 session, has the extra bars written in to the arrangement. Rebennack "had done a couple of gigs with Fess and knew what he was going to do, and the whole band knew how to go with him." [2]

Morris "Moe" J. Bachemin Jr. (born 1935), attended Joseph S. Clark Senior High School (1301 N. Derbigny St.), where he studied music under the legendary Yvonne Busch (1929-2014). The Hawketts was his first band, its members were suggested by Busch, among them: Art Neville, and John Boudreaux. The Hawketts' remake of "Mardi Gras Mambo" (a 17 bar item) became local hit in the next year. Bachemin played the simple, melodic tenor saxophone solo. "Moe" resided at 5000 N. Miro, Lower Ninth Ward, when the "Ron" session took place. He recorded for Earl King from 1960 until 1963. [3] Morris' last session for Earl took place in Detroit, 1963, for the "Motown" label. [4] Bachemin moved to California in the 1960s, where he waxed with

"Moe" Bachemin, April 21, at the New Orleans Contemporary Arts Center. Courtesy: New Orleans Jazz Fest: A Pictorial History by Michael P. Smith, © 1991 used by permission of its publisher: Pelican Publishing Company, Inc. www.pelicanpub.com.

Mac Rebennack's *Gris Gris Band* (1972). Some of the cuts came out in 1972, as the celebrated album, Dr. John's Gumbo. In addition, Morris worked with Mac's Los Angeles, Cal., located *NOMA Band*. This was mainly a group of New Orleans musicians that usually came together for recording sessions. Bachemin's musical resume includes gigs with Joe "Mr. Google Eyes"; he toured Jamaica, 1961, with Ernie K-Doe; a 45 rpm disc, 1968, with a group named as the "Cal-Full Allstars". Morris Bachemin retired in 1998 for failing health. He died of a heart attack, September 10, 1999, in his hometown New Orleans. [5]

The year 1947 saw Otis Duvernay Sr. (1921-2007) at the Beachwater Club in Biloxi, Miss. (Lester Alexis' hometown). During spring 1948, the bass player was engaged five nights a week at the classy Club Desire (Upper 9th Ward, corner, Law and Desire St.) with the Five Sharps. The five-piece band consisted of Frank Mitchell, trumpet; Russell Fernandez, saxophone; Ike "Streamline" Harris, piano; Kingston Alexis, drums (Lester's brother); with added singer Erline Harris (1914-2004). She was married to "Streamline" Harris, usually mentioned as a dancer. John Broven pointed out that Harris tap danced with Fess in the French Quarter, in the early 1930s. [6] Duvernay played with the Lloyd Price band for a while in 1953; and jobbed with the American Jazz Quintet in late 1950s. In the year after, Duvernay received attention in a Louisiana Weekly review of the band: *The second set allowed bassist Otis Duvernay to exercise his nimble fingers on "Willow Weep For Me", only to be encored by a crescendo of applause to do another ballad: "Lover Man". Duvernay is a truly one of greatest bass players to emerge from New Orleans in a month of Sundays. The*

The Beachwater Restaurant And Club, Central Beach, Biloxi, Miss., 1947. L- R: Otis Duvernay, bass; Walter Lewis, piano; Waldren "Frog" Joseph, missing; Jack Willis, cornet; Lester Alexis, drums; and Teddy Johnson, alto sax & leader. A couple of years later, a youngish Elvis Presley sat in, sang and played guitar with the band. Photo, courtesy Barry Martyn.

fullness of tone produced by fingers that galloped up and down with drive of a precisioned [Oscar] *Pettiford pulsated each composition with heartfelt warmth.* [7] In the Membership Directory, Local 496, February 1, 1960, Duvernay is listed at 1405 St. Anthony St., New Orleans.

Got a call from a slow talking, fast thinking swinger named Mac Rebennack, Algiers, La., born trombonist Edward "Eddie" Hynes (1933-2005) narrated. *Did this guy have ideas, ones that were ahead of our time, about what he wanted to do. I really liked Mac, but he surrounded himself with some strange sidemen. He was really good to me, and we got along better than anyone I ever worked for. Mac put me on Record Sessions with the likes of Jimmy Clanton, Ike Clanton, Johnny Adams, Jerry Byrnes* [Byrne], *Fess Longhair and a few other artists I can't recall. It was a fun packed few years standing between Lee Allen and Red Tyler, you'd better be having fun or else. These guys are real*

"Eddie" Hynes, 1964. Courtesy: The Big Easy Street Sounds website.

241

princes in every meaning of the word. As you know Mac went on to be Dr. John, and I'm still Eddie Hynes.

Just a small insight about my relationship with Mac. White musicians and Black musicians on the same stage was a no-no. This caused Mac, he was the record agent, to book the studio at 1:00 or 2:00 AM. It worked out really well. Usually the sessions would start after a gig, so most of us were all set to play. Mac and I got hired to blow a Rock Show at Lincoln Beach, with a twelve-piece group headed up by Wardell [Quezergue's Royal Dukes of Rhythm]. *Can you picture twelve Black musicians, two white musicians and 10,000 Afro-Americans all jumping and grooving together? We looked at each other just once the whole night! I was even invited to go up to the Carver House* [Carver Theatre, 2101 Orleans Ave, Treme] *and sit in with the House Band. I think it was Roy Brown, they featured me and my favorite tune: 'Body and Soul'. You couldn't speak to me for weeks.* [8]

Mac Rebennack and the Skyliners, circa 1960. Ronnie Barron, vocal and piano; Earl Stanley, bass & guitar; Paul Staehle, drums; Tony Monjure, tenor sax; Rebennack guitar & piano. A publicity photo.

II.

My fondness for New Orleans jazz, blues and early Rock & Roll began around 1960. A Little Richard LP album, a "Sonet" label reissue, with his immortal "Specialty" chart hits, was the first New Orleans R&B disc

I purchased. The song: "All Around the World"(Rock'n Roll Is On Its Way) became a certain favorite. It's an upbeat tempo track, propelled by a bouncy New Orleans parade beat pattern, sometimes referred to as the "Second Line Beat". Penniman's raw, gospel music influenced vocals, and the infectious groove the band achieved, knocked my socks off. The musicians involved were: Alvin "Red" Tyler, bar. saxophone.; Lee Allen, ten. saxophone; Huey "Piano" Smith, or Edwin "Ed" Frank, piano; Frank Fields, bass; and Earl Palmer, drums. "Red" Tyler told: *The things I was playing with Little Richard were basically a rhythm sort of thing, almost like the old tubas in Dixieland.* [9]

According to Dave Bartholomew: *The marching bands, the street bands and the bass drum is where I got the beat from, but what I did, I eliminated the Dixieland with everybody soloing at one time. I stuck more or less to the rhythm section.* [10]

Fess' definition was: "the parade street beat". Albeit, in the 1960s, I was totally unaware of the New Orleans origin of some of Penniman's 1950s "Specialty" recordings – as well as the term "New Orleans parade beat". Palmer put it this way: *There's a little bit different approach to the feel of the music and the rhythm, particularly for the rhythm players, in New Orleans. There's always something somewhere in their playing that has that old New Orleans parade meter feeling. You could always tell a New Orleans drummer the minute he sat down to play. First thing you could tell is how he played the bass drum. He was influenced by the parade drummer.*

The parade drummers were pretty much the beat and pulse and influence of the parade bands because they set the pace. For example, going to a funeral, they would set it off with three or four beats on the bass drum. On the way back, after what we used to call the "planting," the band would set the meter for the second line. The people would form a 'second line' behind the band and dance back to town or wherever they went. [11]

For the US. musicologist and writer: Robert Palmer (1945–1997), Fess testified in 1974: *They don't have the second line like they used to. In those days it was a second band in back of the first band. Cats would have buckets, pans, bottles, sticks, pieces of iron, bells. If they could include the sound, they were welcome to join the second line. And they'd actually be getting a better sound with those things than the band would be getting in front, because the band could only play two or three numbers, mostly hymns. And meanwhile those cats behind would be really ballin' with that junk they had. You can get a good version of that from what the Mardi Gras Indians are singing and playing now. That's mostly the way we did back then.* [12]

Fess must have had some of the rough, non-union brass bands in mind when he did the statement. Because organized units with union musicians, for instance the Eureka Brass Band, indeed had a pretty wide repertoire. Fess considered "Second line music" as "strictly soul".

III.

The New Orleans traditional jazz genre, including the brass bands, plus the music of the Mardi Gras Indians, are partly the foundation for the city's R&B music. "Everything in New Orleans is interrelated, wrapped around itself in ways that aren't always obvious", Mac Rebennack declared.

I first caught a New Orleans jazz band, live, in Stockholm, in the fall of 1964. It was Albert "Papa" French's Original Tuxedo Jazz Band (once lead by Oscar "Papa Celestin). The lineup was, Joshua "Jack" Willis, cornet; Joseph "Cornbread" Thomas, clarinet & vocal; Waldren "Frog" Joseph Sr., trombone; Jeanette Kimball, piano; French, banjo & vocal; Frank Fields, bass, and Louis Barbarin, drums. Musicians comfortable with a wide range of music, including the R&B/Rock & Roll genre. Two years before the 1964 tour, Albert French's band recorded the Bartholomew/Domino song, "It's You I Love", "Imperial" LP-9119. The only track with Dave Bartholomew fronting the "Papa" French band.

"Jack" Willis (1920-1989) toured and recorded with Lee Allen's band ("Savoy", 1954). In 1955, Willis cut and arranged for Ray Charles, "Atlantic". Willis and Joseph were a long-time team, ever since their late 1930s, and early 1940s engagement in pianist Joe Robichaux's big band.

"Frog" Joseph's (1918-1984, also a pianist & bassist), travelled with Ida Cox, Queen of the blues, in the mid 1930s. He toured Cuba with Robichaux's big band in September 1938. Besides his Dixieland and big band experiences, he cut and played with, amongst others: Dave

Papa French's Band, Stockholm, October 3, 1964 (they played in Paris Oct. 2): Albert French, Louis Barbarin, Frank Fields, Joseph "Cornbread" Thomas, Joshua "Jack" Willis, Jeanette Kimball, and Waldren "Frog" Joseph. The band also backed the wonderful: Sister Rosetta Tharpe. Photo: Nils Edström? Courtesy, Orkesterjournalen, and The Swedish Jazz Archive, with thanks to Roger Bergner. Used by permission.

Bartholomew, Fats Domino and Earl King. Joseph's horn is audible on King's: 1961 recordings for "Imperial" (he plays a fine solo on "We Are Just Friends"). When back in New Orleans, a couple of weeks after his 1964 European-sojourn, Waldren recorded with Fess, Earl King, and Wardell Quezergue. It's the legendary "Big Chief" track. Joseph's "bone" is also audible on 1960s recordings produced by Allen Toussaint.

Plaquemine, La. born Frank Fields (1914-2005) was on bass on the majority of Little Richard's 1950s successful "Specialty" tracks. Fields cut for Fess in 1953 ("Atlantic"); and 1957 ("Ebb"), plus hundreds of sessions from the same era. Fields played with Dave Bartholomew's great small band unit for many years. George French, Albert's son, seems to be the bass player on Fess' 1962, "Rip" recordings.

Pass Christian, Miss. born: Jeanette Kimball (1908-2001) had a wide musical experience. From circa 1946 to 1949, she was employed in the band lead by guitarist Erving "Buddy" Charles Sr. (? -1988). The band worked at the Dew Drop Inn. It's said to be the first featured band at "the Drop". Charles' group occasionally supported celebrated acts such as Big Joe Turner, Wynonie Harris, and sometimes Dave Bartholomew.

New Orleans parade beat expert: Louis "Bob" Barbarin (1902-1997), was Earl Palmer's teacher at the *Grunewald School of Music*. According to writer Al Kennedy, Barbarin was one of the guys at the school's *Educational Gateways* faculty. His career spanned seven decades. It's likely that Louis Barbarin and the early jazz drummers of New Orleans invented the snare drum backbeat. In the 1950s, it was accentuated by R&B/Rock and Roll drummers like Earl Palmer.

IV.

At the ripe old age of 20, I made my premier sojourn to the Crescent City in the fall of 1966. It was very strange to find African Americans always in the back of busses and streetcars. Sad to say, I didn't catch any live R&B acts. I asked a friend where to find Snooks Eaglin, whom had a steady gig with a combo, at the *Playboy Club* in the French Quarter (often with Bill Huntington, bass). But I spent nearly every night at the Preservation and Dixieland Halls, they let me in free. Some of the musicians at the latter place had recorded with several R&B acts. They were Jack Willis, Dave "Fat Man"Williams, the bass playing brothers Gerald ("Jerry") and Placide Adams. Both had toured etc., with Roy Brown. Papa French's group was a steady weekend act at this 516 Bourbon Street spot. I tried to catch parades and funerals, with various brass bands. I once caught a Eureka Brass Band parade with Eddie Bo's uncle, Peter Bocage (1887-1967) in trumpet section. On another occasion, Barbarin's Onward Brass Band was one of the parade bands, November 10, 1966, at a Canal St. parade.

Buster Holmes's soul food restaurant ("Buster's"), corner of Burgundy and Orleans Street in the French Quarter, was my favorite supper restaurant. A delicious plate of red beans and rice was just 26 cents! I also made frequent visits to: "William's", a dark, hole-in-the-wall restaurant on the Burgundy too, closer to Canal St. Its patrons were strictly African Americans. I really dug Eddie Bo's "Tell It Like It Is" ("Ric", 1960) on the jukebox at 'William's'. [13] It's a lovely ditty, propelled a by tambourine (Mardi Gras Indian type) and a foot-tapping parade beat rhythm. The singer, pianist & composer Eddie Bo was completely unknown to me. Many decades later, I found out that Placide Adams was the bass player on "Tell It Like It Is" (not to be confused with Aaron Neville's ballad chart hit). [14]

I dug the local R&B and Soul music on the jukebox at "Buster's". Lee Dorsey's "Working in the Coal Mine" (by Allen Toussaint) was a huge international hit that year, and another tune with a parade beat pattern. Each time someone put a dime in the Jukebox, trumpet player Kid Sheik Cola begun a fake shoveling coal on the floor and chuckling in his inimitable way. Buster's Restaurant and Bar (corner of Orleans and Burgundy) was a prominent African American musician's hangout. Fess must have been one of its occasional patrons. Tommy Ridgley recounted: "Coz was one of the boys. We were all a closely-knit bunch of guys. When we had a break [at the J&M Studio], we'd go over to Buster Holmes' Restaurant because it was just behind the studio, and it was the cheapest place in town to eat. You'd always see plenty of musicians hangin' around Buster's; there was always a chance they'd need another trumpet or guitar player, and there would surely be somebody over there to fill in". [15] Burgundy St. was still the French Quarter's Black neighborhood.

When I returned to New Orleans in late 1969,"Buster's" had turned into a place for hippies, and the African-Americans begun to move out of this area in "the Quarter".

V.

Ask 90 per cent of New Orleans jazz and blues enthusiasts who Professor Longhair is and you will probably get one of two answers. Either 'never heard of him!' or 'he plays rock and roll, doesn't he? Tom Stagg, UK, in 1973. [16]

It was in 1975 that I first heard him in the flesh, in Stockholm, where Fess was rather unknown too. This was his very first Scandinavian tour and Fess' third visit to the old world. He was signed for series of concerts at *Mosebacke etablissement*. But his very first performance took place at the *Atlantic*, a restaurant, nightclub and hotel (where Louis Armstrong had stayed in 1933). The pianist was, strangely enough, recognized by a young, alert, music interested cab driver. He offered the artist a free ride to the *Atlantic*, in the city's central parts. The free-lancing cab driver was Svante Grundberg, an actor, deejay, and an old friend of Jonas Bernholm. Consequently, Fess' manager thought that the pianist was a noted artist in Sweden. Quite a few spectators attended the *Atlantic* concert on Monday night, September 29. Telge

Blues, a local, Chicago blues type band, was engaged as a support
band. A blues fan complained on the sparse audience! Yet, Fess replied, "I was having a good time."

Robert Harvey; David Berger; Fess; "Ed" Kimbrough; and "Big" Will Harvey. Mosebacke Etablissement,
early October, 1975. Photo: Hans Ekestang, used by permission.

On Tuesday, September 30, Fess did his first show at the music
venue and restaurant: Mosebacke (named as "Moose Back" by
another Crescent City colleague). It's situated at a height with a
wonderful view of the Stockholm harbor and the ancient part of
the city. The initial shows were poorly attended, but luckily, the
spectators increased by the end of the week. US music writer, Sam
Charters (1929-2015) dug Fess and retailed the album: *Professor
Longhair: New Orleans Piano*, "Atlantic" (1972). He may have done
so as a friendly turn to the pianist? Sam did research in New Orleans in the 1950s, and the early 1960s. Albeit, in due to the segregation laws, never caught Fess live. Charters relocated to Stockholm
in January 1971.

The next day: Wednesday, October 1, the five-piece combo, plus
Quint Davis, were off for a sole performance in Helsinki, Finland (a
55-minute flight from Stockholm's airport). The band was contracted

for a show at the *Tavastia club*. It's one of Europe's oldest rock clubs, situated in central Helsinki – and still operated. This well attended gig proved to be Fess' one and only in (Suomi) Finland.

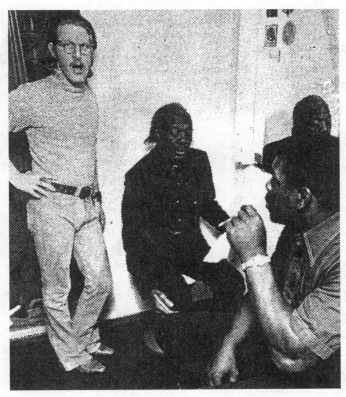

Quint Davis, Fess, and Big Will Harvey, at the Tavastia club, Helsinki, Finland. Photo: Jarmo Santavuori, courtesy: Blues News Magazine & The Finnish Blues Society, with thanks to Pete Hoppula. Used by permission.

Fess returned to Stockholm for five nights, starting: October 2. The weather was nice, relatively warm, and a clear blue sky. I had a little chat with Fess at the *Mosebacke* and found him sympathetic and low-key. He mentioned the personnel on the aforementioned "Cuttin' Out" track. My fondness for the band's music increased every night. It was bit shocking to witness his bad physical condition. He stood up, and walked very carefully, as one knee was liable to just give away. Prior this tour, David Berger (1951-1999), a white harp player from California, had only did two gigs with Fess. Berger was hired for the tour by Quint Davis. Guitar-

A 1975 flyer. Notice that Alfred "Uganda" Roberts, and Walter Lastie (1938-1980), a former Fats Domino drummer, were scheduled to do the tour (Lastie drummed on Eddie Bo's "Tell It Like It Is"). Courtesy: Jan Ytterberg. Used by permission.

ist Big Will Harvey had fixed a job for his son Robert L. Harvey, on bass. Both of them are largely unknown musicians. Will Harvey, passed away in New Orleans, November 1982; and Edward "Ed" Kimbrough, in October 2006. Robert ("Bob") is still a working musician in New Orleans.

During his Swedish sojourn, Fess smoked marijuana almost every day – although his doctor forbade him to do so. Fess' last Stockholm gig, this time, was an extra show, Wednesday, October 8, at the *Mosebacke*. In total, the band stayed for 12 days in my country. It was then off to *Club 7* in Oslo, Norway, October 12. Eventually down to Copenhagen, Denmark, and its legendary Montmartre Jazz club. Nevertheless, Fess returned to Sweden again on October 14, for two unscheduled concerts, 7 and 9:30 pm, at *Lund's Stadshall*. Lund is a small university town way down south in Sweden. The shows there were sparsely advertised with some tiny ads in local newspapers. Lennart Persson (1951-2009), a celebrated music writer, and music freak, reviewed the performances:

An Audience Fiasco!
"Is the blues-interest in the southern part of Sweden really that bad? Professor Longhair – legend, trendsetter and brilliant artist from New Orleans – played a concert [sic] Tuesday evening at a barely half full City hall in Lund. And it was the first of two shows. At the second performance, the concert organizers apparently expected so few people that they generously gave out free tickets to anyone who attended the first show!

You can only blame yourself if you were not there – the professor and his band offered a swinging party without equal. He had a solid blues band behind him. No remarkable solo performances, but a straight and steady rhythm throughout. [sic] The young harmonica player [Berger] was the only down point. He threw himself eagerly into solos without any feeling. [sic] for the nuances and pauses that make a great harmonica solo. Also, his contribution often, and quite unnecessarily, messed up the ensemble playing.

But despite that, a fine concert experience. The professor gave ample proof of his unique piano style that set the standard for so many New Orleans musicians. He embroiders the most amazing patterns on, under, over and around the beats and still swings, in such a genuine and enjoyable fashion. He had a good support from an experienced drummer [Kimbrough], who really knew about the "second line". This very special beat that characterizes the music of New Orleans, since way back. [17]

The concert was at its best when he sang, whistled and played his own songs, leaving room for long piano solos. The traditional blues songs like 'How Long' and 'Everyday I Have the Blues', could easily have been left out of the program. But his piano playing on Ray Charles' 'Mess around' was a gem! [sic] And rarely has it felt stronger: the concert environment with its inactive 'digging' of the music and polite applause was completely out of place. This was music that preferably should be enjoyed in a more intimate setting, with room for greater movements than an armchair in a concert hall would permit. [18]

Longhair came back, with a new group in 1978. Big Will Harvey was the only guy Fess had kept. I had no chance to catch the band. [19]

The last time I experienced Fess live in Sweden was in the city of Malmö, by the Oresund channel, Thursday, March 22, 1979. Fess' six-piece outfit were booked for a Swedish tour from March 3, until April 1. With the exception of six days in Stockholm, they did one nighters. I bought a ticket for the show at the main stage of *Malmö Stadsteater* (erected, 1944), notorious for its bad acoustics. Around 200 people attended the venue of 1500 to 1600-seats. Fess entered the gigantic stage, assisted by a walking stick in his right hand, immaculately dressed in red. But I felt the performance uninspired and I simply didn't like the band, overall a disappointment. [20] The show lasted for nearly two hours. Fess ran through his regular repertoire: "Everyday I Have The Blues", "How Long Has That Train Been Gone", "Got My Mojo Working", "Mess Around", "Rockin' Pneumonia", "Stack-O-Lee", etc., and of course "Go To The Mardi Gras".

The bland Malmö show was a reason that I, regrettably, didn't care to catch the Fess show, May 6, during my New Orleans visit in April-May 1979. I only heard him distantly (John Vidacovich was the new drummer, a huge improvement), on the last day of this brilliant festival. There were simply so many other good music acts to enjoy (Huey "Piano" Smith; Irma Thomas & Barbara Lynn etc.). This performance on Sunday, May 6, 6.30 pm, at "Stage 4", was Fess' last ever "Jazz Fest" appearance.

VI.

Andrew "Andy" J. Kaslow (born NYC, 1950), was Fess' bandleader from 1977 until 1980. Yet, according to "Hank" Drevich the final say on who's to join the band was Fess': *I'm the one that's got the sound judgement on things and sometimes it bugs me. It really worries them be-*

cause they don't know how to bypass things, y'know. The first thing is that the players have to learn not to annoy one another so you can get the best out of what you're doing. You gotta stop drowning one another and turn as low as you can and come up where you can be heard — it's so much work. [21]

VII.

Tipitina's, at 501 Napoleon Avenue, corner of Tchoupitolas, affectionately known as "Tip's", opened on January 14, 1977, on a very low budget. The first show was "the Meters" playing a *Get a Piano Benefit*. Fess appeared the next weekend and performed on the new piano. "Hank" Drevich was the one who found the location. Earlier, "the 501 Club" was situated in the building, and reportedly, once a week hired by the local Ku Klux Klan. Fess used to perform at "Tipitina's" once a month or so, until he died. Drevich and Steve Armbruster did the bookings.

Steve Armbruster, present at the creation, and someone who has lovingly watched Tip's grow by start and fits, states baldly "It wasn't started as a business. It was a place to hear New Orleans musicians who just didn't get regular bookings. Armbuster credits Hank Drevich as the original impetus behind such a club. As he tells it, "Hank and several others had attended a gig of Professor Longhair's and had been knocked out by his piano playing. Hank later approached 'PL to ask him where his next date would be. 'PL smiled and told him probably the Jazz Festival —which was six months away." So like Charles Foster Kane thinking wouldn't it be fun to run a newspaper, Drevich and a handful of others thought it would be fun to run a club. Unlike Charles Foster Kane, they didn't have millions to lavish on their whim. And the years spent getting the hang of it have been costly. [22]

Tipitina's is still (2018) operated at the same address. It was closed down for a couple of years in the mid 1980s, after some serious tax troubles. There's a moving sequence in the Jools Holland 1985 TV show *Walking To New Orleans*, where Allan Toussaint plays his own Fess tribute: "The Old Professor". Toussaint was captured in the empty and closed down Tipitina's. He played the same piece in the wake for Fess. Earl King, James Booker, Huey "Piano" Smith, and Jessie Hill, were all stockholders in Tipitina's.

THE BEST OF FESS: 1949 - 1979

Hey Little Girl (Paul Gayten), "Atlantic", 1949.

The New Orleans Sessions 1950, "Mercury", "Bear Family Records" (1989).

In The Night (Big Bill Broonzy/Billy Wright), "Atlantic", 1953.

Tipitina, two takes, "Atlantic", 1953.

Ball the Wall, "Atlantic", 1953.

Who's Been Fooling You, "Atlantic" 1953.

Misery, "Ebb", 1957.

Baby Let Me Hold Your Hand, "Ebb", 1957.

Cuttin' Out, "Ron", 1959.

Go to The Mardi Gras, "Ron Records", 1959.

I Believe I'm Gonna' Leave, "Rip", 1962.

Whole Lotta Twistin', "Rip", 1962.

There's Something on Your Mind (Cecil "Big Jay" McNeely), "Watch", 1963.

Bald Head, (R. Byrd & T. Terry), "Watch", 1963.

[Oh, When The] "Saints", 1972, Bo Dollis & The Wild Magnolias (Fess, piano, with Willie Tee & The Gaturs), AIM 5012 CD, 2008.

Sick and Tired (Chris Kenner), 1972, Mardi Gras In Baton Rouge. Rhino/Bearsville, 1991.

House Party New Orleans Style: The Lost Sessions 1972-1973. A "Rounder" album, 1987.

Cry to Me (Bert Berns), TV show, Montreux, Switzerland, 1973.

Junco Partner, Rock 'N' Roll Gumbo, "Blues Star" 1974.

The London Concert, 1978. A "JSP Records" album, 1981.

Crawfish Fiesta, 1979. An "Alligator" album, 1980.

In 1954, the fabled African American poet, novelist and playwright: Langston Hughes (1902-1967) created a list of 100: "favorite recordings of Jazz, Blues, Folk Songs, and Jazz-influenced Performances". *Professor Longhairs' Mardi Gras In New Orleans*, "Atlantic", 1949, was one of the tracks.

9. NOTES

1. FESSOLOGY – PARTS I & II

1. Jack Dupree, interview, Allison Miner, May 5, 1991, Musical Heritage Stage, New Orleans Jazz & Heritage Festival. Champion Jack Dupree - Freedom ǀ WWOZ New Orleans 90.7 FM. https://www.wwoz.org/.../182906-champion-jack-dupree-freedom. For Paul Oliver, Dupree stated: "In these and other [S. Rampart] joints other pianists also worked, amongst them Willie Hall, "Red" Toots ["Tuts" Washington], Bill Fugus and a 'great girl pianist, Margaret Bush who played real barrelhouse music at the Cotton Club on [S.] Rampart Street'". *Jazz Monthly*, January 1960.

2. Jeff Hannusch, *I Hear You Knockin': The Sound of New Orleans Rhythm and Blues*, Swallow Publications, Inc. US, 1985.

3. Bart Bull, "the Absent Professor", *Spin magazine*, Vol. 3, No. 2, May, 1987.

4. Bunny Matthews, "Barefootin' With Robert Parker", *Wavelength: New Orleans Music Magazine*, Issue NO. 31. May 1983. The Music Maker (UK), Vol. 1, No. 2, October 1966, reported: *Robert Parkers's name wasn't exactly a household word in even the most pop-conscious homes until last month he came "Barefootin'" into the charts. And notched up a sizeable hit for the independent Island label. [sic] Now he is due for his first look at British fans on a 14-day tour starting on September on September 30. He's 24 and yet another Negro star from New Orleans. The success of "Barefootin'" spotlights the way in which the small independent companies are gaining an ever-increasing slice of the pop cake.*

5. Mick Burns, *The Great Olympia Band*, JAZZology Press, New Orleans, 2001.

6. Robert Palmer, "Ed Blackwell: Crescent City Thumper", *Down Beat*, June 16, 1977.

7. Eddy Determeyer, Big Easy Big Bands: Dawn and Rise of the Jazz Orchestra, Rhythm Business Publishing, the Netherlands, 2012.

8. Interviews, conducted by Tad Jones, New Orleans, March, 22, and April 23, 1986. http://musicrising.tulane.edu/listen/detail/574/T.-Ridgley-Interview-1986-04-23

9. Rick Coleman, "Charles Connors: Upsetters", Wavelength, Issue 66, April 1986, New Orleans.

10. Seamus McGarvey, "Charles Connor That New Orleans Rhythm Man! Part One", *Now Dig This*, No. 70, January 1989.

11. Charles Connor, with Ziv Biton, Keep A Knockin': The Story of a Legendary Drummer, Waldorf Publishing, 2015, US.

12. Tad Jones, "Charles 'Hungry' Willams", *Wavelength*, Issue 37, November 1983. The drummer Clayton Fillyau, *heard a group called Huey Smith & the Clowns, out of New Orleans. Now this is where funk was really created! That's where funk originated […] I couldn't understand how to do it, so this drummer from Huey Smith's band* ["Hungry" Williams] *showed me how to play.* Clayton Fillyau (1934-2001), interviewed by Jim Payne, on the origins of the 'James Brown Beat', *the Great Drummers of R&B, Funk & Soul*, home of the groove.blogspot.

13. John Wirt, Huey "Piano" Smith and the Rocking Pneumonia Blues, Louisiana University Press, Baton Rouge, 2014.

14. *Rock and Roll, Renegades; Interview with Lloyd Price* (circa 1992). *Part of Rock and Roll* [part 2 of 3]. Open Vault from WGBH. http://openvault.wgbh.org/catalog/V_526618E785CF478C-B0497C99EA6DA35777. Price cut a phenomenal, heavily Fess influenced track, "Tell Me Pretty Baby", "Specialty". Perhaps with the lineup, Dave Bartholomew, t; Joe Harris, s; Herb Hardesty, s; Edward Frank, p; Ernest McLean, g; Frank Fields, b; & Earl Palmer, d., June 26, 1952, the J&M studio.

15. Cosimo Matassa, *Let The Good Times Roll*, August 1991?, a BBC radio series on New Orleans R&B.

16. Steve Armbruster, "Part II: The J&M Studio Story: Alumni of the J&M school of Rock 'n' Roll", *Wavelength*, Issue 73. November 1986.

17. Todd Mouton, "Cosimo Matassa: backtalk", *Offbeat*, August 1997.

18. Jerry Wexler & David Ritz, *Rhythm and the Blues: A Life in American Music*. Jonathan Cape. London. Wexler also stated: "If Professor Longhair was the George Washington of New Orleans, then Champion Jack Dupree was its Thomas Jefferson". "In the Night"/"In The

Dark"(January 5, 1950), was attributed to Billy Wright; with Big Bill Broonzy's "Wee Wee Hours"(July 17, 1941), as a potential predecessor.

19. "Max Jones talks to Jerry Wexler", *Melody Maker*, February 15, 1975.

20. Tony Sherman, *Backbeat: Earl Palmer's Story*, Smithsonian Institution Press, 1999.

21. Domino's first chart hit: "The Fat Man" reached position six on *Billboard's* R&B charts, April 1950.

22. Jewel King was married to guitarist Jack Scott, who recorded with Fess for "Mercury". "Stagger Lee", became a Lloyd Price chart hit, 1958.

23. Robyn Flans, "Earl Palmer", *Modern Drummer*, May 1983. Dave Bartholomew's band, plus Fess and Fats Domino did the tour. Lee Allen, the sax player on the tour, told: *We stayed pretty busy around that studio* [the J&M], *but like I said I never was too much on travelling because I was raising a family and had a house on Mandeville Street over by the Falstaff Brewery. The only time we really went on the road was a mid-west tour with Fats and Professor Longhair and that was some trip. None of the club owners wanted Professor Longhair to play their piano because he would kick holes in the bottom keeping time. That was his thing.* Jeff Hannusch, "Cooking with Mr. Lee", *Wavelength*, Issue 33, July, 1983.

24. Bill Millar, Clarence Henry interview, *Soul Music Monthly*, January 1, 1967. Pianist, singer, & big band leader: Walter "Fats Pichon (1905-1967) was, as far as known, never mentioned as an influence on Fess.

25. Peter Guralnick, *The Listener's Guide to The Blues*, Blandford Press, UK. 1982.

26. Debra De Salvo, Alvin "Red" Tyler, interview, *Blues Revue*, No. 16, March / April 1995.

27. Alvin "Red" Tyler, interview, by Tad Jones, New Orleans, June 19, 1996. http://musicrising. tulane.edu/listen/detail/44/Alvin-Red-Tyler-1996-06-19#

28. *Louisiana Weekly*, August 20, 1949, reported: *Nearing completion, the High Hat bar and grille, at the spot where the old Gypsy Tea Room once stood; will soon be ready for its gala grand opening, according to Freeman Riles and Milton Scott, owners. Riles said here Monday that a band and show will introduce the spot's regular policy in entertainment and that stars of stage, radio and screen will be imported to the city's newest downtown nitery. The musical bar and hotel accommodations and all features will be exploited in this paper.* [sic]

29. Mick Burns, *The Great Olympia Band*, New Orleans: JAZZology Press, 2001. Used by permission by Mick Burns (1942-2007). Milton Batiste once stated: *The first band I had the pleasure of working with was Professor Longhair, (1950), "along with Charles (Honeyboy) Otis, drums; Edwin "Guitar Red" Maire, guitar; and Norman "Bill" Sinegal, bass.* From 1977, until 1994, the Olympia B. B. put down 12 versions of "Mardi Gras in New Orleans" on wax, with vocals by Milton Batiste. There is also a 1985 track entitled, "Ghost of Longhair".

30. Music Rising at Tulane: The Musical Cultures of the Gulf Coast: M. Batiste Interview, February 5, 1997, Hogan Jazz Archive, Tulane University. Batiste's back side of his skull was removed after accident when he was 11 years old, therefore the nick name 'Half a head'. Milton's very first recording was for Champion Jack Dupree. Batiste told, I played bass, "on the G string all the way", "King" records, Cincinnati, 1953).

31. Jeff Hannusch, "C. P. Love: You Call The Shots", *The Soul of New Orleans: a legacy of the blues*, Ville Platte, La., Swallow Publication, Inc. 2001.

32. Marv Hohman, "Roots Conquer All; Dr. John", *Down Beat*, Vol. 42, No. 10. May 22, 1975.

33. Debra DeSalvo & Andrew M. Robble, "No Jive... Just a Good Vibe, Telling it like it is!! Dr. John" [sic], *Blues Revue*, No. 16. March/April 1995. LINCOLN BEACH (for Negroes) on the Lakefront. *A recreation center with sand beach, bathhouse, amusement park, picnic and playgrounds,* the Transit Guide and Street Map of New Orleans, June 1964.

34. Bart Bull, "the Absent Professor", *Spin magazine*, Vol. 3, No. 2, May, 1987.

35. Bill Milkowski, "Fi Interview: Dr. John", *FI: The Magazine of Music & Sound*, Volume 2, Issue 4, May 1997. In 'Professor Longhair a Remembrance' by Vincent Fumar: Lagniappe section, *New Orleans' States-Item*, February 2, 1980, Fess said, *After the last session I did with Mac in 1965, we didn't see each other again until he had me out in L.A., in '68, but we didn't play together then.* It seems as Rebennack (leader of NOLA musicians in exile in Cal.), had booked Fess in a Los Angeles go-go joint. Mac led the house band, and the go-go girls often complained about their medium-tempo blues tendencies. He narrated: *You know, L.A. go-go girls work their butts off. But Fess worked them too hard. When he started playing they couldn't keep up with him. They*

couldn't believe he was actually playing that fast.

36. Mac "Dr. John" Rebennack, *Let the Good Times Roll*, an August 1991? BBC radio series, on New Orleans R&B.
37. Mac Rebennack with Jack Rummel, Dr. John: Under a Hoodoo Moon: The life of Dr. John the Night Tripper, St. Martin's Press, New York, 1994.
38. Max Jones, notes for, *"Chris Barber and Dr. John: Take Me Back To New Orleans"*, "Black Lion Records", Stereo BLM 61001, 2 (1981). For more Fessology, read the interesting book,
39. Jeff Hannusch, "Talkin' 'bout New Orleans: John Boudreaux", *Offbeat*, March 2002. The *Lafitte Projects* was a black Housing Project, located in the 6th Ward, Treme. It was one of the city's oldest housing developments – severely flooded during Hurricane Katrina, 2005 – erased in 2008.
40. Bart Bull, John Boudreaux, The Absent Professor, *Spin magazine*, Vol. 3, No. 2, May, 1987.
41. Daniel Glass & John Boudreaux, The Roots of Rock Drumming: Interviews with the Drummers Who Shaped Rock 'n' Roll Music: Additional editing by Steve Smith. Hal Leonard. *Hudson Music*, 2013.
42. Rick Coleman, "Carnival Music", *Wavelength*, Issue 76, February 1987. Vernon Winslow was the first black R&B deejay in New Orleans. He did for the first radio airplay of the original 1949 version of "Mardi Gras In New Orleans". Winslow later became a legend in gospel radio.
43. Rick Coleman, excerpted from: *The Mercury New Orleans Sessions 1950*, "Bear Family" BFD 15308.
44. Cary Baker, "Ronnie Barron: The Man Who Was Almost Dr. John", *Goldmine*, June 1982. Barron stated that Fess was "his idol." Barron waxed "Hey Now Baby", plus another a Fess tribute, on the album: My New Orleans Soul, "AIM" 1038.
45. Rick Coleman, "Carnival Music", *Wavelength*, Issue 76, February 1987.
46. Sheppard A. Samuels, "It's Spelled Q-U-E-Z-E-R-Q-U-E", *Wavelength*, Issue 21. July 1982.
47. John Swenson, "Wardell Quezergue Architect of the Sound", *Offbeat*, May 2000.
48. Hans Andréasson, Tommy Löfgren, & Hans Schweitz, *Jefferson* blues magazine (Sweden) no. 30, autumn 1975. Earl King interview, New Orleans, October 1974. Also in *Crazy Music*, Australia, January 1976.
49. Tad Jones, "Living Blues Interview: Earl King", *Living Blues*, part 1: No. 38 May-June; part 2: No. 39 July-August, 1978. Interviews conducted: June & August 1973; October 1974, and June 1976.
50. Herlin Riley & Johnny Vidacovich, "Professor Longhair", *New Orleans Jazz and Second Line Drumming*: interviews by Dan Thress, *Manhattan Music Publications*, Warner Bros., Publications INC. (1995).
51. From an interview conducted by Tad Jones, New Orleans, April 2nd, 1996. http://musicrising.tulane.edu/listen/detail/118/Curtis-Mitchell-1996-04-02
52. Michael Swindle, "Half-Frettin' With George Porter", *Wavelength*, Issue 115, May 1990.
53. John Swenson, "The Bass-ic George Porter", the *Offbeat* website, 1999.
54. Mary Ellison, "the Blues Don't Have No Short Cuts, Snooks Eaglin, the Human Jukebox talks to Mary Ellison", Blues & Rhythm, Issue Number 55, September 1990.
55. Ben Sandmel, Fird Eaglin interview, New Orleans Special, *Living Blues*, # 128, July/August, 1996.
56. Don Snowden (notes for), *Fess: The Professor Longhair Anthology*, "Rhino" R2, 71502, (1993).
57. Bill Millar, "Meter Man", *Let It Rock*, April 1974.
58. Jerry Karp, "Cyril Neville: Out to change the way the world perceives New Orleans music", *Wavelength*, Issue 67, May 1986. The Neville Brothers made their very first tour, September 1977, to California.
59. Alvin Batiste, *WRFG Program Guide and Music Newspaper*, Atlanta, GA., July - August 1987. Batiste also wrote a piece entitled "Picou"(first name, Alphonse, a clarinet pioneer), based on a Fess song.
60. Jeff Hannusch, *I Hear You Knockin': The Sound of Rhythm and Blues*. The one-story building, formerly Blue Eagle, 1824/2026 Felicity St. (ran by Dave Brown, "The Mayor of Rampart St."), is still there. "I was born on Saratoga Street between Euterpe and Terpsichore… and at the end of that street, Saratoga, as it ran into Felicity, was a place called the Blue Eagle." Reed

player Earl Turbinton (1941-2007) told. His family lived there until 1948, and for Earl the place was like a magnet. "Whenever my mama would send us to the store to get something, they would have people like Guitar Slim, Gatemouth Brown, B. B. King, Bobby Bland, and those female impersonators, groups like Mattie Campbell and the All-Star Review, faggots in drag, snake dancers and stuff, and the shake dancers, that whole thing." "Earl Turbinton At Home Again", Jason Berry, Wavelength mag., Oct. 1981.Jessie Hill played drums with Fess from 1953 until 1955. He's visible, drumming with Fess, in the late Les Blank's documentary, *Always for Pleasure*, playing: "Big Chief." In the 1980s, Hill wrote and waxed: "Dedicated to Professor Longhair", New Orleans Will Rise Again, "Night Train" NTI 7152.

61. Larry Appelbaum, interviewee Henry Butler, Library of Congress, November 7, 2007.
62. Roger Hahn, "Henry Butler: Unlocking the Keys", *Offbeat*, May 1998.
63. Peter Goldsmith, "Dave Bartholomew: Er dominiert in Dominoes Band", Blues Forum (Germany), Nr. 2 – March/April/May 1981. Thanks to Tom Nässbjer for the German-English translation.
64. Philippe Grancher, "Interview: Dave Bartholomew", Soul Bag, NO. 120, France 1989. Thanks to Alan Balfour for translation.
65. http://openvault.wgbh.org/catalog/V_C62E90C1D5B74587AD6FBFF0A83A7107 . Open Vault from WGBH: Rock and Roll; Renegades; Interview with Dave Bartholomew (early 1990s) [Part 1 of 2].
66. Ernest McLean, excerpts from an interview conducted by Nina Falk Aronsen, 2004, Los Angeles, Cal., 2004.
67. Francis "Frankie Ford" Guzzo, "Let the Good Times Roll", a BBC radio series on New Orleans R&B, August 1991. In Wavelength, Issue 76, February 1987, Guzzo recalled: *My first memory of Mardi Gras music was Dixieland. And then the Indians, I used to love listening to them. But every little hole in the wall in Quarter used to have a band. As a young audult I remember 'Fess and Fats. "The Saints"and "Bourbon St. Parade" and Fess, that's why I redid "Mardi Gras in New Orleans." No way did I think I could ever come near it, but in a different vein we did that, and, of course, it's gotten a lot of airplay in a lot places [...] I think the high school bands in this area were the first ones to start doing contemporary music, because before that it was always marches. And so here in town for Mardi Gras balls when the bands from out of town would come in, they'd say, 'Wow, these bands from New Orleans are doing different stuff.' A very memorable moment is hearing one of the high school bands doing "Going to the Mardi Gras." The kids from out of town said, "Man! What's that music ya' ll playing?*
68. Mike Stephenson, Tony Watson, and Phil Wight, the Curtailed Eddie Bo Interview, Blues & Rhythm the Gospel Truth, #221, August 2007.
69. Jason Berry, Jonathan Foose, & Tad Jones, "Chapter Fourteen: Piano Players", *Up From the Cradle Of Jazz: New Orleans Music Since WWII*, the University of Georgia Press, Athens and London, 1986.
70. Eddie Bo, *Offbeat* website, November 1999, e-mail question to Eddie Bo: "Can you recall the first time that you met Fess?": *I posed your question to Eddie. While he didn't give me a year, he remembers it was here in New Orleans where he first met Professor Longhair. It was on [South] Rampart Street. Fess was looking at a lot / property to purchase. Eddie said he went up to him and said,"You look like Professor Longhair". In his gravel type voice, Fess replied," That's me." Again, thanks for your patience ~~~ and for writing. Veronica, Personal AsSIStant to Eddie Bo.* [sic]
71. John Sinclair, "Breaking Bread With R&B Legends: Deacon John, Eddie Bo & Chuck Carbo", *Offbeat*, May 1996.
72. Allen Toussaint, "Piano Styles", interviews by Jim Gabour, a 1988 BBC TV documentary. Sincere thanks to Gerd Wieben (Germany), for the video-copy.
73. Joel Dufour and Jacques Périn, "Allen Toussaint: the southern knight", interview, Paris, June 1989, *Soul Bag*, NO. 120, France, 1989. Sincere thanks to Alan Balfour for the translation. Toussaint wrote a Fess tribute entitled: *The Old Professor*. In the *Living Blues*, July/August 1996, Toussaint recalled the "Minit" years, in the early 1960s, as: "some of the best moments in my life, and I loved it". The recordings display Toussaint's Fess influenced piano style.
74. Larry Appelbaum & Allen Toussaint, excerpt, "music conversation", Library of Congress, November 1, 2007, www. Fess first cut "In the Night" in 1953, "Atlantic". The song seems to be a remake of Big Bill Broonzy's "Wee Wee Hours", 1941; eventually cut by Billy Wright as

"After Dark Blues", 1950.

75. Ric "Rico" Olivier, "Bruce Raeburn," *Wavelength*, Issue 34, August 1983. Ed Volker was the keyboardist for the local rock band the Radiators.

76. Bart Bull, "The Absent Professor", *Spin magazine*, Vol. 3, No. 2, May, 1987. Scanlan was the bass player in the NO.LA rock band the Radiators. Ed Volker composed: "Long Hard Journey Home", a song about Fess, released on their: *New Dark Ages* CD.

77. Laura Camille Tuley, excerpt, "An Interview with Reggie Scanlan", New Orleans Review, Vol. 33, No. 1, June 2007, www. Allison Miner, fired Fess' support band. It's last date with Fess, including the great David Lastie (tenor), was January 28, 1978. "It was low-rent move on Allison Miner's part, but that's the politics of music," Scanlan narrated for John Wirt, Offbeat, August 29, 2016.

78. http://www.npr.org/2013/01/05/168638183/preserving-the-home-and-history-of-new-orleans-piano-professor

79. John Sinclair & Bill Taylor "Wild Indians Down in New Orleans: Bo Dollis and Monk Boudreaux", *Blues Access*, Issue 43, fall 2000. Bo Dollis interview conducted by John Sinclair & Bill Taylor: May 2000.

80. Dick Gordon, excerpt, transcription from the interview, "Alfred 'Uganda' Roberts And His Drums", the radio show, *The Story*, APM (American Public Media), New Orleans, November 15, 2012. In the early 1960s, Roberts went by the nicknames "Bongo Al" and "Jamaica Joe". Alfred, "caught a dance troupe from Uganda that came to one of the universities [in New Orleans] and I went to the performance. And they had one guy play three congas, I think he called them talking drums".

81. Pete Welding & Toby Byron, "Deep South Piano and the Barrelhouse Blues", *Bluesland: Portraits of Twelve Major American Blues Masters*, A Dutton Book, 1991. "Kid Stormy Weather" (Edmond Joseph: 1913-early1960s) from New Orleans, was an influence on Fess. Joseph used to play the song: "Stormy Weather". Karl Gert zurHeide, Blues Unlimited No. 79, January 1979). Joseph was still around in the late 1950s, when he sometimes showed up and played piano at Associated Artists Studio (later the "Preservation Hall"), 726 St. Peter St.

82. Johnnie Allan (Lafayette, La.), E-mail, via John Broven, February 28, 2000. Allan also added: *I don't recall Fess playing in Louisiana around my area of the state.*

83. Henry "Hank" Drevich, Florida US, E-mail to the author, June 16, 1999. Drevich was one of the founders of *Tipitina's* and, of course, "an ardent Fess fan".

84. Steve Armbruster, Road Food – Advice From Pros, *Wavelength magazine*, July 1991.

85. Bart Bull, "The Absent Professor", *Spin magazine*, Vol. 3, No. 2, May, 1987.

86. Bunny Matthews, "Johnny Vidacovich", March 1, 2002, through: http://www.bestofneworleans.com/gambit/a-place-for-fess/Content?oid=1249052

87. Robert Santelli, "the Drummers of New Orleans: Johnny Vidacovich", Modern Drummer, October 1990.

88. Yorke Corbin, "Fess's Drummer Is a Jazz Master", *Wavelength*, December 1980.

89. Jason Berry, "Drumvoices: The Roots of New Orleans Rhythm", Wavelength # 9, July 1981. Vidacovich demonstrates his drumming on the Crawfish Fiesta recordings session, in the video, "New Orleans Drumming: Street Beats: Modern Application" DCI VHO 168, 1979.

90. Gerri Hall, interview by Rick Coleman, the September 2010 Ponderosa Festival Conference, Louisiana State Museum, New Orleans. "Gerri Hall is famed as the female member of Huey Smith & the Clowns, the piercing foil to Bobby Marchan on 'Don't You Just Know It' and the lead singer on 'Popeye.' But Gerri also recorded a handful of collector-prized 45s, including a version of 'I Cried a Tear' […] leased for Atlantic Records. A native of the Lower Ninth Ward, she was actually nicknamed "Gerri" because of her crazy antics similar to the most popular clown of the time, Jerry Lewis. She is the sister-in-law of Rosemary (Hall) Domino and Reggie Hall. As a longtime habitué and waitress at the Dew Drop Inn, she experienced incredible New Orleans music history firsthand and knew virtually all of the local musicians. Always known as a wild lady, Gerri is a vivacious septuagenarian who is still speaking her mind. She is a New Orleans rock 'n' roll legend." Ponderosa Stomp Home Page.

2. WALTER NELSON SR. AND FAMILY

1. Walter Nelson Sr., interviewed by Bill Russell, October 6, 1960 (Hogan Jazz Archive, Tulane University). Other nicknames for Nelson, Sr. reportedly included "Captain Midnight" and "Rawhead."
2. Edna Nelson obituary, *New Orleans Times-Picayune*, April 7, 1982.
3. Bill Greensmith & Bez Turner, "'Fess'," *Blues Unlimited*, no. 130 (May / August 1978),
4. Nelson Sr., interviewed by Russell.
5. Ibid.
6. Karl Gert zur Heide, "Kid Ernest, the Nehi Boy from New Orleans," *Blues Unlimited*, no. 145, Winter 1983/1984.
7. Jeff Hannusch, I Hear You Knockin': *The Sound of New Orleans Rhythm and Blues*, Ville Platte: Swallow Publications, 1985.
8. Nelson, Sr. interviewed by Russell. Nelson referred to "Walter's Special", as his signature blues composition.
9. Mick Burns, *Keeping the Beat on the Street: The New Orleans Brass Band Renaissance* (Baton Rouge: Louisiana State University Press, 2006).
10. Pete Deuchar, "Passing of Picou", *Jazz News* (UK), Saturday, February 18, 1961.
11. Mike Pointon & Ray Smith, *Goin' Home: The Uncompromising Life and Music of Ken Colyer* (UK: Ken Colyer Trust, 2010).
12. Ibid.
13. "Mother, Son Die in N.O. Fire," *New Orleans States-Item*, January 30, 1960 (Vertical File, Subjects: Bars, Buildings, Etc., Where Jazz Was/Is Played: Local, Luthjens, Hogan Jazz Archive, Tulane University); Nelson Sr. interviewed by Russell.
14. Walter Nelson, Sr. is visible in film footage used in *Sing On – A Film of New Orleans Brass Bands*, American Music AMVD-Two.
15. "Laid to Rest 'Dixieland Style,'" *Sepia*, April 1961 (Alphonse Picou vertical file, Hogan Jazz Archive, Tulane University).
16. *Stevens Point* (Wisconsin) *Daily Journal*, February 11, 1961.
17. "New Orleans Bids Goodbye to Alphonse Picou," *Ebony*, May 1961
18. Jason Berry, "Uncle Lionel Batiste: A player in time," *New Orleans Magazine*, vol. 14, no. 6, March 2009.
19. Nelson Sr. obituary, *New Orleans Times-Picayune*, March 2, 1984; "Walter C. Nelson funeral today," New Orleans Times-Picayune, March 2, 1984. Via Hogan Jazz Archive, Tulane University.
20. Jennifer Quale, "Rockin' along with Professor Longhair," *Dixie* Magazine, *New Orleans Times-Picayune*, February 6, 1972.
21. Charlie Gillett, "The Dr. John Story," *Let It Rock*, June 1973.
22. Burns, *Keeping the Beat on the Street*. Drummer James Black, composed and played on the recording of a song titled: "Monkey Puzzle."
23. Herb Hardesty, "The Chicken Twist" / "Why Did We Have To Part". Federal 12460, 1962. Nelson Jr.'s also sings on "It Must Be Wonderful". Rereleased on: Herb Hardesty & his Band: The Domino Effect, "Wing and Federal Recordings 1958-61", "ACE" CDTOP 1333, (UK), 2012.
24. Rick Coleman, *Blue Monday: Fats Domino and the Lost Dawn of Rock 'n' Roll* (Cambridge: Da Capo Press, 2006).
25. Walter (Papoose) Charles Nelson obituary, clipped from unidentified newspaper and attached to an eyewitness account of the funeral attributed to Marjorie T. Zander (Vertical File, Persons: Harold Dejan, Hogan Jazz Archive, Tulane University).
26. Richard Knowles, "Preface" to Mick Burns', *The Great Olympia Band*, New Orleans: JAZZology Press, 2001.
27. Mick Burns, *Keeping the Beat on the Street* (Baton Rouge: Louisiana State University Press, 2006).
28. Walter (Papoose) Charles Nelson obituary.
29. This according to Fats Houston, who also marched in the funeral, and who is quoted in the eyewitness account in the Harold Dejan vertical file, Hogan Jazz Archive, Tulane University.
30. Bill Dahl, "Fats Domino –The King of Blue Berry Hill," *Goldmine*, June 29, 2001.
31. Prince La La, "You Put the Hurt on Me" / "Don't You Know Little Girl (I'm in Love)," A.F.O.

45-301. On some pressings, the title is alternately given as "She Put the Hurt on Me."

32. Harold Battiste Jr., *Unfinished Blues: Memories of a New Orleans Music Man* (New Orleans: The Historic New Orleans Collection, 2010). The Spencer Davis Group, UK, cut a (slightly corny) remake in 1967.

33. Andy Kaslow, interviewee Fess, November 1979, included on, *Fess' Gumbo*, "Stony Plain", SPCD 1214, Canada, 1214.

34. John Sinclair, "Breaking Bread with R&B Legends Deacon John, Eddie Bo & Chuck Carbo," *Offbeat*, vol. 9, no. 5 (May 1996).

35. Jeff Hannusch, "Talkin' 'bout New Orleans," *Offbeat*, vol. 10, no. 8, August 1997.

36. "Need You," an originally unissued track, was finally released on the 1993 CD compilation "Gumbo Stew: Original AFO New Orleans R&B," Ace CDCHD 462 (UK). Jessie Hill created the song.

37. Gillett, "The Dr. John Story".

38. "'Prince La La' Found Dead," *Louisiana Weekly*, November 9, 1963. Hannusch, "Talkin' 'bout New Orleans."

3. TWO PROFESSOR LONGHAIR INTERVIEWS

1. Hans Schweitz, e-mail to Per Oldaeus, July 9, 2012.

2. The 1936 New Orleans City Directory record Roland Byrd and his mother Ella Mae Byrd, residing on 936 Julia Street, New Orleans.

3. One *"Sullivan Rock"*, a "rounder and roustabout on the docks of New Orleans, furnished the words for Stagger Lee", recorded by John A. Lomax, New Orleans, July / August 1933, *American Ballads and Folk Songs*, page 93; and, *Blues & Gospel Records*, 1963 edition, page 754. It's not known if this was the same "Sullivan Rock" as mentioned by Fess. He also named him alternately as "Rocky Sullivan" or "Rock Sullivan." Hudson Marquez 1969, Hogan Jazz Archive (Tulane Univ.) interview, according to Fess, Sullivan said: *Come on boy, let me show you how to play a fine gut boogie-woogie, so you have something to begin. Sullivan Rock could play "Pine Tops Boogie Woogie" better than his friend* [Little] *"Brother" Montgomery.* Fess declared Montgomery as the originator of "Pine Tops Boogie Woogie".

4. A 45 rpm disc was released with "Mardi Gras in New Orleans" and "Rum and Coca Cola", "Blue Star" records.

5. For more about Kid Stormy Weather, real name: Edmund Joseph (b. around 1913; d. New Orleans late 1950s.) check a Karl Gert zur Heide piece, *Blues Unlimited*, No. 79, January 1979. Edmond "Kid Stormy Weather" Joseph recorded in Jackson, Miss., October 1935. One of the track was "Short Hair Blues". String player: Harrison Verrett worked with Stormy Weather in the French Quarter, he used to play the "Junkers Blues". (interview: Hogan Jazz Archive, Tulane University, August 1961).

4. "ROCK JAMAICA ROCK" – From New Orleans To Jamaica.

1. Danny Barker, quote by pianist, composer, James P. Johnson (1891-1955), *Buddy Bolden and the Last Days of Storyville*, Continuum, 2001.

2. Max Jones, "Professor Longhair talks to Max Jones", *Melody Maker*, April 1, 1978.

3. "My Josephine" reached number six on the Jamaican Hit Parade in November 1960. "Let The Four Winds Blow", reached number one in October 1961.

4. Derrick Morgan, Mike Connolly, *Reggae – The Story of Jamaican Music – Program One – Forward March*: A BBC TV-documentary, 2002.

5. Leigh Urfer, "Laurel Aitken: http://www.working-class.com/laurelaitken/mtska.htm

6. Chris Blackwell, New Orleans, March 2005. Courtesy: http://www.artistshousemusic.org/videos/chris+blackwell+on+the+connection+between+new+orleans+music+and+reggae. Blackwell is also reported as a "shrewd businessman".

7. Steve Barrow, interviewee: Prince Buster (Cecil B. Campbell): 1995, courtesy: http://www.

reggae-vibes.com/concert/princebuster/princebuster.htm

8. Max Jones, interviewee Cap. John Handy, London, UK, 1966, notes to "Handyman Vol. 1: Capt. John Handy's Quintet featuring Barry Martyn". 77 Records, 77 Leu 12/16.
9. Justin Hines in: http://www.nghthwk.com/Artists/4/4.html. Thomas Wong (of Chinese descent), committed suicide in 1971.
10. Jonas Bernholm, "Huey "Piano" Smith", *Shout* magazine, no. 70, October 1971.
11. *The Daily Gleaner*, Wednesday, July 15, 1959.
12. *The Daily Gleaner*, Thursday July 30, 1959. For more about the Jamaican election 1959, see: http://www.eoj.com.jm/content-73-191.htm.
13. John Wirt, Huey "Piano" Smith and the Rocking Pneumonia Blues, LSU Press, US, 2014.
14. Geraldine Wyckoff, "Jimmy Cliff talks back", Offbeat, October 2014. James "Jimmy Cliff" Chambers performed at the House of Blues, New Orleans, October 6, 2014.
15. Allen Toussaint, "Following the Ebb and Flow", *Washington Post*, June 9, 2006.
16. Grace Lichtenstein, *A Musical Gumbo: The Music of New Orleans* (1993).
17. Tad Jones, "Living Blues Interview: Earl King", *Living Blues*, No. 38, 1978. Courtesy: http://www.skaville.de/sites/rnb.htm

5. PROFESSOR LONGHAIR IS BACK

1. Peter Haby, letter, January 17, 2002, plus various e-mails. On April 22, 1974, at 8 am, a "Fire Relief Benefit for Professor Longhair" took place at the Warehouse (1820 Tchoupitoulas), the participating acts were Dr. John; Allen Toussaint; The Meters; Willie Tee; the Olympia Brass Band; Snooks Eaglin; Benny Spellman; Earl Turbinton Jr. and the Nucleus; Tommy Ridley, and the Wild Magnolia Mardi Gras Indians (tickets $ 5). The Social Security Death Index, the Census (1920, 1930) and the *U.S. WWII Enlistment Records*: all records Leon Gross's birth date as the year 1916. Courtesy Eric LeBlanc.
2. Alton Purnell, interview by Sinclair Traill, "In My Opinion" Jazz Journal Vol. 18, No. 10, October 1965. The Santiago solo tracks, released on: *The John Reid Collection from the Arkansas Arts Center*, "American Music" AMCD-44 (1992). Palmer, in: Tony Sherman, *Backbeat: Earl Palmer's Story*, Smithsonian Institution Press, 1999. Burnell Santiago was mentioned, as "Bumel Santiago" in: *JAZZMEN*, Ramsey Jr. & Smith, 1939, one of the earliest books on Jazz.
3. John Broven & Mike Leadbitter, "Behind the Sun", *Blues: Unlimited*, No 76, October 1970.
4. John Broven, e-mail to the author, October 14, 2000.
5. Bruce Raeburn, "What the 'Professor' taught us," *Louisiana Cultural Vistas*, spring 2005.
6. Michael P. Smith & Allison Miner, *Jazz Fest Memories, Pelican Publishing*, 1997. Fess and Alice met in 1958, and married in 1975. Chris Strachwitz ("Arhoolie" records etc.) claimed that, "Allison was the heart and soul of the festival in its early years."
7. Parker Dinkins, *Blues Unlimited*, UK, No. 83, July 1971.
8. Lars Edegran, "New Orleans Jazz and Heritage Festival 1971", *Jefferson* (Sweden), no. 15, 1971.
9. Paul Lentz, "Festival Focus: New Orleans '71", Down Beat, July 22, 1971.
10. Nick Buck, *Blue Flame* magazine, (Chicago, Ill.): November - December 1971. An edited version of Buck's piece was published in *Blues Unlimited*, NO. 90, April 1972.
11. Ray Charles first New Orleans session took place in August 1953, for: "Atlantic".
12. Jennifer Quale, "Rockin' Along with the Professor", *Times-Picayune, Dixie*; February 6, 1972.
13. Timothy Crouse, "Resurrecting New Orleans – The Gulf Coast Originals Never Left Home", *Rolling Stone magazine*, issue 108, May 11, 1972.
14. Bill Wyman, *Bill Wyman's Blues Odyssey: A Journey to Music's Heart & Soul*, DK Publishing, (New York), 2001.
15. Jon Newlin, "Rock: Prof. Longhair in Concert, And Foghat," *The Figaro* (NO.LA.), Saturday, October 21, 1972.
16. Valerie Wilmer, "As serious as your life: John Coltrane and beyond", Allison & Busby Limited (UK), 1977.
17. The late Sir James "Goldenballs" Goldsmith was a wealthy financier, and according to Brian Wood, UK: "of a particularly arrogant disposition. He was involved with an extreme right

wing party, which put up a few candidates at the last but one General Election in the UK, but they were soundly rejected by the electorate." The satirical magazine *Private Eye* was involved in a number of lawsuits with him. It was *the Eye* which dubbed him "Goldenballs". Sir James died in 1997 in Spain, he was 64. Goldsmith started his career as a hotel cook, and became one of the world's wealthiest guys.

18. Mike A. Leadbitter?, "London Surprise", *Blues Unlimited*, No. 99, February-March 1973.
19. Tom Stagg, "The Professor of New Orleans", *Footnote*, Vol. 11, No 4, April/May 1980.
20. Tom Stagg, "Puttin' on the Ritz: Tom Stagg reports on an historic jazz jam." *The Melody Maker*, UK, January 20, 1973. The Iconic New Orleans jazz researcher etc., Bill Russell, arrived in London on the same flight, January 7, 1973. "Puttin' On the Ritz" by Irving Berlin, 1929. Its title was derived from a slang expression, meaning to dress very fashionably, inspired by the Ritz Hotel, *Wikipedia*.
21. Ibid.
22. Ibid.
23. Richard Milward, *Facebook* message to the author, October 4, 2013.
24. Nina Prommer and Rosalyn Singer, *London Hotels of character, distinction & charm*, A Prion Guide, 1992.
25. Geoffrey Wansell, *Tycoon: the life of James Goldsmith*, Grafton, London, UK, 1987.
26. Tom Stagg, "Professor Rock", *Melody Maker*, April 14, 1973.
27. Ibid.
28. Ibid.
29. Vance duRivage, *the 2nd Annual Grease Ball*, "The Warehouse Concerts List: 1970-1982", http://www.blackstrat.net/
30. Terry Pattison, "New Orleans Jazz & Heritage Festival", *Living Blues*, No. 13, summer, 1973.
31. Norbert Hess, "Montreux '73", *Living Blues*, No. 14, autumn, 1973.
32. Michalis Limnios, "New Orleans"premier bassman George Porter Jr. talks about Meters, Earl King, Snooks Eaglin, & Saints City's Music: Posted by Michalis Limnios BLUES @ GREECE on April 23, 2012". www.
33. Hans Andréasson, "Montreux 1973", *Jefferson* (Sweden), no 22, 1973. Author's translation.
34. John Broven, "New Orleans Supersession", *Melody Maker*, June 9, 1973.
35. Robert Partridge, "Professor of rock", *Melody Maker*, September 8, 1973.
36. Ibid.
37. Nick Gravenites, "Bad Talkin' Bluesman", *Blues Revue*, Issue No. 23, June/July 1996.
38. Anton J. Mikofsky, "Professor Longhair in New York – 'Byrd's The Word'", *Living Blues*, winter 1973–1974.
39. Perez Prado (1916-1989), born, Cuba. Pianist, bandleader, composer etc. Moved to the US, late 1940s, developed the mambo, an early 1950s fad.
40. John Broven, e-mail to the author, November 3, 2000. There's no support for Jessie Hill as the vocalist, in Rick Coleman, *Blue Monday: Fats Domino and the Lost Dawn of Rock 'n' Roll*.
41. Robert Palmer, "Professor Longhair's Rock And Roll Gumbo", *Down Beat*, March 28, 1974
42. Tad Jones, "New Orleans Jazz & Heritage Festival", *Living Blues*, summer 1974.
43. Tad Jones, "Letters", *Living Blues*, No. 24, November-December 1975.
44. Rick Coleman, "Benny Spellman", *Wavelength* magazine, New Orleans, issue 86, December 1987. Wings, the McCartney's couple band, had partly recorded at the Sea-Saint Studios, for the album *Venus and Mars*, released May 27, 1975.
45. Goldmine, June 1982. The session was released by the UK, Harvest label.
46. Tad Jones, "New Orleans News", *Crazy Music*, Australia, May 1975.
47. Bunny Matthews, "Professor Longhair: The Man Who Taught New Orleans Music", *the Figaro* (New Orleans), June 29, 1977.
48. Tom Mazzolini, "San Francisco", *Living Blues*, No. 35, November-December 1977.
49. Jimmy Lyons with Ira Kamin, *Dizzy, Duke, The Count and Me: The Story of the Monterey Jazz Festival*, 1978.
50. One of Dupree's many songs is named "Tee-Na-Neena-Na", with the same chords as "Tip-itina", cut in 1962, for "Storyville". (There's also a September 28, 1960 version, included on: "Magpie", CD 4453).
51. Max Jones, "Professor Longhair talks to Max Jones", *Melody Maker*, April 1, 1978.

52. Valerie Wilmer, "Caught in the Act: Fess Has Still Got the Fervour" (London concert, Sunday, March 26, 1978), *Melody Maker*, April 1, 1978.
53. John Stedman, letter, *Melody Maker*, April 15, 1978.
54. Lon Price, e-mail to the author, 2001: *Toussaint's band did a short tour with Little Feat—Boston, NY, Philly, D.C., and the New Orleans Jazz and Heritage Festival* [1975]. *Gary Brown played all of the sax solos, though* [...] *Allen also wrote a film score that year. The movie was "Black Samson", one of those '70s black exploitation movies. I played on that too. I know that it has played in Europe, because I still get a small payment for it every year.*
55. Lon Price, webpage: http://www.txstnr.com/
56. Michael Bourne, "Booker, Fess and beyond: Harry Connick Jr. sits at a piano to riff on his home city's piano legacy", *Down Beat*, September 2006.
57. Marcia Ball, http://www.youtube.com/watch?v=V3AVYqXFhdE&feature=related

6. LAST DAYS

1. Allison Miner Kaslow, *Wavelength* magazine, unknown title and issue date.
2. The Warehouse was "a bare-bones, 30,000-square-foot" music venue. It was demolished in April 1989. Fess had played there October 21, 1972, and January 26, 1973, as well.
3. Bill Payne, extracts from: New Orleans: April 17, 2010: http://www.billpaynecreative.com/index.php?page=writing&b_id=459565.
4. Alice W. Byrd, "Piano Players Rarely Ever Play Together", the late Stevenson J. Palfi's film documentary, 1982.
5. Keith Spera, "New Orleans piano legend Professor Longhair's final home is brought back to life", http://www.nola.com/music/index.ssf/2014/02/professor_longhairs_final_home.html
6. Frank Minyard, a long time serving Coroner of Orleans Parish. He was a friend of Milton Batiste, and Minyard recorded with the Olympia Brass Band.
7. Bart Bull, "the Absent Professor", *Spin magazine*, Vol. 3, No. 2, May, 1987.
8. Lovell Beaulieu, "Professor Longhair Mourners Are Undeterred by Biting Cold", *The Times-Picayune*, Sunday, February 3, 1980.
9. Alice W. Byrd, *Piano Players Rarely Ever Play Together*, Stevenson J. Palfi.
10. Bart Bull, "the Absent Professor", *Spin magazine*, Vol. 3, No. 2, May, 1987.
11. Max Weinberg, with Robert Santelli, *The Big Beat: Conversations with Rock's Great Drummers*, Billboard Books, US., 1991.
12. Tom Stagg, "The Professor of New Orleans", *Footnote*, Vol. 11, No 4, April/May 1980.

7. NOTES ON STUDIOS, MUSICIANS, AND RELATED

1. Don Snowden, notes for: *Fess: The Professor Longhair Anthology*, "Rhino" R2, 71502, (1993).
2. Tad Jones, "Living Blues Interview: Professor Longhair", conducted, November 13, 1975, *Living Blues*, March-April No. 26, 1976, US.
3. *Louisiana Weekly*, via Rick Coleman, notes for *The Mercury New Orleans Sessions 1950*, BFD 15308, "Bear Family Records", Germany (1989). A vinyl double album.
4. *Louisiana Weekly*, "Caldonia Inn's Prof. Need Some Hair", April 3, 1948.
5. *Louisiana Weekly*, August 5, 1950. The Caldonia Inn was mentioned in lyrics for "Burgundy St. Blues" ("Jazz Man", 1953), cut by the George Lewis Ragtime Band, rap & sing vocal by: Monette Moore.
6. *Louisiana Weekly*, October 8, 1949.
7. John Broven, *Behind the Sun Again*: "An Interview with Frank Fields," *Blues Unlimited*, (UK), No 107, April/May 1974.
8. *Inside New Orleans*, October 23, 1965. The February 1960, Membership Directory, Local 496, lists Leroy Rankins as a saxophonist, residing at 1632 Tricou St. (Lower Ninth Ward). He was missing in the July 1965 directory.
9. *Louisiana Weekly*, September 24, 1949.

10. Harold Battiste, booklet for the vinyl box: New Orleans Heritage: Jazz: 1956-1966, (US), 1976.

11. Vernon Winslov, "Boogie-beat jive: By Dr. Daddy-O'", *Louisiana Weekly*, August 20, 1949. Perhaps pianist Clarence Henry, 13 years old, included in *the Frog Trio*?

12. "The ultimate story of [Ahmet Ertegun and Herb Abramson, and] their time together, which both men loved to tell, concerned the night in New Orleans [in 1949?] when they went to find an unknown genius named Professor Longhair who was playing in a joint [the Pepper Pot] across the river, where no taxi driver would take them. Their cabbie dropped them off in the middle of a field. After walking a mile in darkness, they saw a brightly lit house in the middle of town so full of people that they seemed to be falling out of the windows as music blared. Talking their way past the guy at the door, who assumed they were cops, the pair made their way inside. Out came Professor Longhair, who played a piano with an attached drumhead that he would hit with his right foot. As people danced, Ahmet and Jerry could barely contain themselves. An utterly primitive, completely original artist was making a kind of music they had never heard before. Rushing up to Longhair after his set was over, they told him just how much they wanted to sign him to Atlantic. 'I'm terribly sorry,' said Longhair. 'I signed with Mercury last week.' In Ahmet's version of the story, the pianist then added, 'But I signed with them as Roeland Byrd. With you, I can be Professor Longhair.' Robert Greenfield, "The Greatest Record Man of All Time", *Rolling Stone*, issue 1018, January 25, 2007.

13. Marv Hohman, "Roots Conquer All; Dr. John", *Down Beat*, Vol. 42, No. 10. May 22, 1975.

14. Trevor Richards (a British born jazz drummer, writer & researcher.), e-mail, February 16, 2014.

15. Placide Adams, interviewers: Tad Jones and John Foose, March 20, 1981, Hogan Jazz Archive, Tulane University.

16. Tad Jones, "Living Blues Interview: Professor Longhair" conducted November 13, 1975, *Living Blues*, March-April No. 26, 1976.

17. Lynn Abbott, e-mails, November, 2013: "To me, it seems very likely that you are indeed looking at the Pepper Pot, since the corner location checks with Fess' recollection, with "Wire" being Tad's phonetic spelling of "Weyer," based on Fess's pronunciation of it. Further: "The 1936 Sanborn Insurance Map describes this building [the Pepper Pot] as a store with a residence in back; and the two high windows [...] further suggest that it was originally intended for commercial use. The 1936 Insurance Map also shows an awning across the entire front of the building, possibly of the same sort of construction as what you can see over the door [...] You can see a beam across the front of the building where the old awning used to be."

18. Jeff Hannusch, "The Soul of New Orleans: A Legacy of Rhythm and Blues," Swallow Publications, Inc. (US), 2001.

19. Vernon Winslow, *Louisiana Weekly*, Saturday, August 27, 1949.

20. Winslow, *Louisiana Weekly*, Saturday, September 3, 1949.

21. Winslow, *Louisiana Weekly*, Saturday, December 16, 1950.

22. *Jet Magazine*, (US), February 18, 1960.

23. Sylvester Armand St.Cyr, *The Saint and Sinners*, Vantage Press, US, 1972, (158 pages).

24. Ibid.

25. "Ebony Sketches Of Louisiana": Calendar for 1990 (New Orleans Forget-Me-Knots, Inc. 1990), through: Hogan Jazz Archive, Tulane University.

26. Mike Hazeldine, review of, "Kid Thomas: The Last Session At San Jacinto" (GHB BCD-409), *Jazzbeat*, Vol. 15, No. 3 & 4, Winter/Spring 2004.

27. 27. Tom Bethel, "George Lewis: A Jazzman from New Orleans", University of California Press, US, 1977.

28. Jamie Dell'Apa, "Cosimo Matassa Within New Orleans' History", https://www.wwoz.org/blog/3815, September, 2014.

29. John Broven, Record Makers and Breakers: Voices of the Independent Rock 'n' Roll Pioneers, University of Illinois Press, 2009.

30. Keith Spera, "Cosimo Matassa" New Orleans recording studio owner, engineer and rock 'n' roll pioneer, has died", the Times-Picayune website: http://www.nola.com/music/index.ssf/2014/09/cosimo_matassa_new_orleans_rec.html

31. Tad Jones, interview with Cosimo Matassa, January 15, 1994, Reel III, Hogan Jazz Archive,

Tulane University.
32. Cosimo Matassa, *Gambit*, 2006, through the website: KnowLa: Encyclopedia of Louisiana.
33. Harold Battiste Jr, Unfinished Blues: Memories of a New Orleans Music Man, Historical New Orleans Collection, 2010.
34. Paul Harris, "Clarence 'Frogman' Henry remembers his New Orleans colleagues", *Jefferson*, no. 73, summer 1986.
35. Randy Savoie, Philippe Rault, *Offbeat* website, "Stairway To Bourbon Street: Led Zeppelin In New Orleans", May 1, 2011.
36. Ibid.
37. Colin Davies, *the Sound of New Orleans: Colin Davies talks to legendary Crescent City recording engineer Cosimo Matassa*, New Orleans, November, 2002. (The polyester plastic drumhead was invented around 1956) http://theprofessorrocks.com/2012/06/18/cosimo-matassa/
38. William Grimes, "Wardell Quezergue, R&B Hitmaker, Dies at 81", *the New York Times*, September , 2011, via the NPR" series: American Roots, 2010.
39. Sheppard A. Samuels, "It's Spelled Q-U-E-Z-E-R-Q-U-E", *Wavelength*, Issue NO 21, July 1982.
40. Tad Jones, "Living Blues Interview: Earl King", *Living Blues*, part 2: No. 39 July-August 1978. Interviews conducted: June & August 1973; and October 1974, & June 1976.
41. Jeff Hannusch, Earl King, *Mardi Gras in New Orleans*, "Mardi Gras Records", MG 1001, (US), 1976.
42. Vincent Fumar, "Fest Focus: Wardell Quezergue", *Offbeat*, (US), May 1996.
43. Richard Williams, *the Guardian*, (UK), September 14, 2011.
44. Rick Coleman, *Blue Monday: Fats Domino and the Lost Dawn of Rock 'n' Roll*.
45. Vincent Fumar, "Blue Room trumpeter longs for bebop", *Times-Picayune, Lagniappe section*, September 16, 1983. Courtesy Hogan Jazz Archive, Tulane University.
46. Harold Battiste, booklet for the vinyl box: New Orleans Heritage: Jazz: 1956-1966, (US), 1976.
47. Mike Vernon, "Domino Men: Nat Perrilliat & Wallace Davenport". *Jazz Monthly*, (UK), August 1967.
48. Maurice Martinez Jr., American Jazz Quintet Swings At Xavier [University] Gig, *Louisiana Weekly*, January 31, 1959.
49. Earl Turbinton, interview, Tad Jones, September 1, 1990, Hogan Jazz Archive, Tulane University. http://musicrising.tulane.edu/listen/detail/230/E.-Turbinton-Interview-1990-09-01
50. John Sinclair, "Offbeat Interview with Johnny Adams", *Offbeat*, US, Oct 1, 1993.
51. Jeff Hannusch, notes for: "New Orleans Soul '60's: Watch Records", "Mardi Gras Records", MG1047, US.
52. Rick Coleman, "Eddie Bo", *Wavelength*, March 1986, Issue NO. 65.
53. Charlie Gillett, "the Dr. John Story: Part One: New Orleans," *Let It Rock*, UK, June 1973.
54. Cosimo Matassa, interview, Tad Jones, January 15, 1994, reel one. Hogan Jazz Archive, Tulane University.
55. Philippe Rault, notes for: "Rock 'n' roll Gumbo", "Dancing Cat Records", DC 3006, (remixed, US., 1985). The original album, released on: "Blue Star/Barclay", (France), 1974.
56. Scott Jordan, interviewee: "Gatemouth" Brown, "Swinging Gate", Offbeat, February 1, 1995. http://www.offbeat.com/articles/swinging-gate/
57. Jeff Hannusch, notes for, "Tuts Washington: New Orleans Piano Professor," "Rounder Records" 2041, US, 1983.
58. John Joseph, interview, Bill Russell & Dick Allen, November 26, 1958, Hogan Jazz Archive, Tulane University.
59. Kathy Sebastian, "I just take life the way I find it: a reflection on Isidore "Tuts" Washington", *New Orleans Music*, Vol. 3 No. 6, December 1992.
60. "Tuts" Washington, *Official Souvenir Program*, Jazz and Heritage Festival, 1974.
61. Unknown source www. Check out the album: *Isidore 'Tuts' Washington; New Orleans Piano*, "504"CD 32, UK: Duo jam sessions, privately recorded in New Orleans, around 1960.
62. Bruce Iglauer, e-mails to the author, September, 2012.
63. Bill Milkowski, "Fi Interview: Dr. John", FI: *The Magazine of Music & Sound*, Volume 2, Issue 4, 2012.
64. Bruce Iglauer, e-mails to the author, September, 2012.
65. Ibid.
66. Mindy Giles, e-mail, February 24, 2018.

67. Iglauer, e-mails to the author, September, 2012.
68. Hans Andréasson & Hans Schweitz,"Genuine Houserockin´ Music", The Alligator Story pt., 3., *Blues & Rhythm*, # 264, November 2011.
69. John Wirt, "33 years later, Professor Longhair is still the soundtrack of Carnival": http://theadvocate.com/csp/mediapool/sites/Advocate/assets/templates/FullStoryPrint. csp?cid=4762397&preview=y
70. Stevenson J. Palfi obituary, *Los Angeles Times*, US, December 29, 2005.
71. Allen Toussaint, interview, Mats Nileskär, *P3 Soul*, Swedish Radio Broadcasting Corporation.

8. FESS – NEW ORLEANS MUSIC – AND ME

1. Mac Rebennack with Jack Rummel, *Dr. John: Under A Hoodoo Moon: The Life of the Night Tripper*, St. Martin's Press, New York. 1994.
2. Bill Milkowski, "Fi Interview: Dr. John", *FI: The Magazine of Music & Sound*, Volume 2, Issue 4, May 1997.
3. Earl King cut for "Imperial", 1961, with: Dave Bartholomew & Wardell Quezergue, tp:s; Waldren "Frog" Joseph, tb; "Moe" Bachemin; James Booker, p; George French, b; & Bob French; alternately Joe "Smokey" Johnson, dr. Only two songs were released. Source: Earl King & Tad Jones: *Earl King Discography, Living Blues* # 41, 1979.
4. The "Motown" personnel was: Johnny Adams, Chris Kenner, Eskew "Esquerita" Reeder vocals; Earl King; Teddy Riley, trumpet; "Moe" Bachemin; Edward "Kidd" Jordan, bar. sax; Wardell Quezergue, trumpet & arr., Reggie Hall & Joe Jones, piano: Leo Nocentelli, guitar; George French, bass; "Smokey" Johnson, drums. Detroit, August 18, & September 8, 1993. In 1996, three Earl King tracks (produced by Joe Jones) came out: *Motown's Blue Evolution: Various Artists*, "Motown" 530 613-2.
5. "Morris Bachemin Jr., jazz R&B saxophonist", *the Times-Picayune*, September 16, 1999, through Hogan Jazz Archive, Tulane University. The survivors included his wife: Theis Bachemin, plus five daughters. Morris Bachemin was a Baptist.
6. John Broven, with Dale Comminey, "Erline Harris: Rock & Roll Lady: and the Genesis of New Orleans R&B", Juke Blues, Issue NO. 69. Fess named Harris as "Streamline Isaac" (Tad Jones' Fess interview, November 13, 1975, *Living Blues*, No. 26, March-April, 1976)
7. Maurice Mendez Jr., "American Jazz Quintet Swings at Xavier Gig", *Louisiana Weekly*, January 31, 1959.
8. Eddie Hynes, "BigEasyStreetSounds": http://bigeasystreetsounds.tripod.com/id185.html
9. John Broven, liner notes for, *Alvin 'Red' Tyler and the gyros: Rockin' & Rollin'*, "ACE" CH 182.
10. Rick Coleman, "The New Orleans Sound of Fats Domino And Dave Bartholomew", booklet notes: *Fats Domino: Out of New Orleans*, a "Bear Family" 8 CDs box set, 1993. Bartholomew was never involved in Lil' Richard Penniman's recordings.
11. Robyn Flans, "Earl Palmer", *Modern Drummer*, no. 5, May 1983.
12. Robert Palmer, "Professor Longhair's Rock And Roll Gumbo," *Down Beat*, March 28, 1974.
13. Walter Lastie was the drummer. Eddie Bo later cut a couple of great Funk 45' discs.
14. Placide Adams, interview conducted by John Foose and Tad Jones, March 20, 1981, Hogan Jazz Archive, Tulane University. Adams also stated that: "Over the river anything goes". "As long as I was with adults I could go anyplace and play music. But I couldn't go without an instrument." He was 15-16 years old then (circa 1945).
15. Jeff Hannusch, "Tommy Ridgley: The New Orleans King of the Stroll", *I Hear You Knockin': The Sound of New Orleans Rhythm and Blues*, Swallow Publications, Inc. US, 1985.
16. Tom Stagg, "Professor Rock," *Melody Maker*, April 14, 1973.
17. Lennart Persson, "An Audience Fiasco" (Publikfiasko), *Arbetet*, Malmö, October 16, 1975.
18. Ibid.
19. Besides Fess, the summer 1978 lineup was: Lon Price, soprano and tenor saxophone; Andy Kaslow, tenor saxophone; George Porter, bass; and Earl Gordon, drums.
20. The 1979 Euro tour comprised: Andrew Kaslow, Anthony Dagradi, tenor saxophones; Ron Johnson, guitar; David Lee 'Watson, bass; Alfred "Uganda" Roberts, conga drums; and Earl Gordon, drums.

21. Robert Palmer, "Blues 'Professor' Gives a Lesson", *New York Times*, December 2, 1977.
22. Bunny Matthews, "Professor Longhair: The Man Who Taught New Orleans Music", *The Figaro*, June 29, 1977. "Professor Longhair had all these apocryphal stories about where the name 'Tipitina' came from. One was that his neighborhood pot dealer was Tipitina. She had no feet, just two stumps. And she would hobble out to the car to bring the weed out, tipping over. Her name was Tina, so she was Tippy Tina." https://www.bestofneworleans.com/gambit/a-place-for-fess/Content?oid=1249052

10. INDEX

Boldface numerals indicate images.

11. APPENDIX

I.

Unknown source. The authors collection.

II.
Gary Edwards, New Orleans, April 25, 2001, a letter to Per Oldaeus.

"Per Fessly
When John Broven came to N. O. he hooked up with Tommy Ridgley, who gave him worlds of contacts that made it possible for him to advance so quickly with his book(s)[.] Tommy is gone, and so are almost all of the old guys who were around. Just a lot of us newcomers available.

I was interviewed by someone 2-3 years ago about a Longhair book, and he showed me some old TV news footage of the first NO Jazz festival. My SONO signs were visible on the front of the stages. He promised to make me a copy of the video, but I never saw him again.

My wife and I spent a good deal of money resurrecting fess before any of the other do gooders came around, then when I got him walking again, they accused me of all kinds of shit, really a bad scene, and of course, Allison was the worst. Quint and I are still on good terms, and he actually knows what went down. Tommy is dead, but someone did a little video of him explaining how I traded tommy a bass speaker cabinet if he would find fess and bring him to meet with me, which he did. That was in 1967-8, I am just not sure any more. My exwife would probably be able to pinpoint the date, she was much better on that stuff than I am. [sic]

In any case, I had some great tapes that burned in my holocaust Jan 27, 1987. Real tragedy for me, I had guarded them for years, and no one had a copy. Too bad. Fess was a strange 'Byrd' to make a pun, really was not much of a musician, but just had a stylized, limited way of playing. Black musicians of good quality avoided him like the plaque. Great stories about that, the good players wanted double scale to play a gig with him, so I hooked up with two white guys who could play well (they are both still professional musicians to this day)[.] Quint insisted that it was a terrible error to have fess play with white people. As you know, later fess's best recordings were done with white players. I knew that all along that the black guys just did not like fess's limitations. I have a couple of personal stories that we can not publish, just out of respect for the other guys, one of whom is now deceased also. [sic]

Ellis Marsalis critiqued the tape that I had made and was perfectly satisfied with the white guys, except that fess confused them a bit with his right hand always breaking time, pleasantly, but always breaking away from the time, in a strange syncopation, copieable of course, lots of people can make it sound exactly like fess, some even better than fess. [sic] There was someone in CA recording before, during and after fess who also played the same style, if you don't know about that, it would be fun research to do. [sic] I don't know the name, but DJ collectors around here must know about the guy. Ask around, late 1940s, early 50s. Lots of good stories, and you can still talk to some of the real guys. Placide Adams and Jerry Adams, Chuck Badie, the real musicians who actually played the sessions, they are older, but still have good brains. You should talk to them before you apse off and write some shit that is not exactly the whole truth [...] Keep in touch."

Gary Edwards, owner and producer, the Sound of New Orleans label: "SONO". He described himself as: "an early supporter of the career of Professor Longhair and I am a friend of his daughter, Pat Byrd."

III.
Henry Butler on Fess and related, an excerpt from: "An Interview with Henry Butler", pianist, vocalist, composer and arranger. Interviewer: Larry Appelbaum, Library of Congress, Washington DC, November 1, 2007.

Butler: "Every language, every code, every piece of music can have nuances. If you're playing, say in the Professor Longhair style. You know it has just a ting if swing to it, which is kind of one of the nuances [plays a couple of bars on: "Tipitina"]. So, you have a little bit of Caribbean rhythm there, some people call it mambo beat.
Appelbaum: Sometimes it's a calypso, also.

Butler: Well, some people call it that.
Appelbaum: Or a carnival sound.

Butler: I would say that it's all based on the Bamboula [claps the rhythm, the same beat as the Meters recording of: "Hey Pocky A-Way", 1974.] You can play it slower or faster. Any rhythm has its dialects. So that when somebody in Georgia, say like Bo Diddley, use that and it sounds a little bit different. One of the prime rhythms of Bo Diddley [Ellas Otha Bates, 1928-2007] was: [plays the rhythm pattern on piano]. And people in New Orleans used the same rhythm. But when you put everything together, with the drums and all that, it starts to sound a little bit different. And that's based on the New Orleans subculture.

Appelbaum: You've mentioned Professor Longhair a couple of times [...] When did you first encounter his music?

Butler: The first recordings I know from Mr. Byrd were from 1947, 48 or the 49 period. I used to hear his stuff when I was very young, four or five, back in the mid 50s. But I was too young to really be able to play anything. I used to hear "Tipitinas"[sic]. Later on, when we used to go to the Mardi Gras parades, we'd always hear "Mardi Gras In New Orleans". There are several names for that song, but that's the one that apparently was copyrighted under his name ["Mardi Gras In New Orleans" (Roy Byrd), "Atlantic" 897, 1949].

Appelbaum: So these are standards?
Butler: These are New Orleans standards, yeah, for that culture, definitely. And then we used to hear "Big Chief", but that was written by Earl King, probably in the early 60s or so? Big Chief sounds like this [plays Fess's piano lick]. And it goes on. *That* particular piece, particular song, demonstrates a very unique style of piano. Just as Professor Longhair had demonstrated all of his life. What Professor Longhair did for piano, is brought more rhythm, more syncopation into piano playing. Before that, there were many great piano players [...] who used some boogie woogie, and some shuffle, and just normal blues playing like Johnnie Johnson [1924-2005; of Chuck Berry fame]. But Professor Longhair had the Caribbean rhythms, had some blues on top of that. And when he was singing he also used a little country flavor, 'cause he could yodel a little bit as well.

Appelbaum: Do you hear any kind of link or connection between Professor Longhair or someone like James Booker and Jelly Roll Morton?
Butler: Well, yeah. I mean Professor Longhair occasionally would use this: [plays "The Mess Around", cut by Ray Charles, 1957. Ahmet Ertegun, composer.] And that's actually where Ray Charles got that from. [Editor's note: not very likely!] If you go back to Jelly Roll. Jelly Roll used that, can't remember the name of the piece that's in, but it's definitely one of his prime licks in that piece: [plays a couple of choruses of "New Orleans (Blues) Joys", first cut in 1923]. So Professor Longhair, Ray Charles, and everybody else that used it in the 50s – that's exactly where they got it."

The 1929 recording: "Texas Shout", by Charles "Cow Cow" Davenport (1894-1955), sounds very much as a forerunner to "The Mess Around". Editor, with thanks to Peter Lundberg.

"Don't you ever forget – in America you have to learn to be black. You're constantly learning wherever you are. You've always had to be smart as a goddam fox – smarter. You still have to play those roles today, still have to be wily and crafty and cunning to be black in America. You got to be sharp, have your antennae up all the time, to feel where it's coming from. Things change, sure – but don't you ever forget those grains of sand. That's the way it's been, and that's the way it still is." **Danny Barker** (1909-1994), in 1978.

The source for the quote is the album liner notes for, Don't Give The Name A Bad Place: Types & Stereotypes In American Musical Theatre 1870-1900, "New World Records" NW 265, Stereo (1978).